French Erotic Fiction
Women's Desiring Writing, 1880–1990

Edited by
Alex Hughes and Kate Ince

BERG
Oxford • Washington, D.C.

First published in 1996 by
Berg
Editorial offices:
150 Cowley Road, Oxford, OX4 1JJ, UK
13950 Park Center Road, Herndon, VA 22071, USA

Berg is the imprint of Oxford International Publishers Ltd.

Library of Congress Cataloging-in-Publication Data

A catalogue record for this book is available from the Library of Congress.

British Library Cataloguing-in-Publication Data

A catalogue record for this book is available from the British Library.

Cover photograph: Lady Milbanke as *Queen of the Amazons* (Penthesilea) from the
'Goddesses' series 1935 by Mme Yevonde. Reproduced by kind permission of
The Royal Photographic Society. © The Royal Photographic Society.

ISBN 1 85973 019 1 (Cloth)
1 85973 049 3 (Paper)

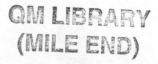
Printed in the United Kingdom by WBC Bookbinders, Bridgend, Mid-Glamorgan.

French Erotic Fiction

Berg French Studies

General Editor: John E. Flower

ISSN: 1354-3636

John E. Flower and Bernard C. Swift (eds), *François Mauriac: Visions and Reappraisals*

Michael Tilby (ed.), *Beyond the Nouveau Roman: Essays on the Contemporary French Novel*

Richard Griffiths, *The Use of Abuse: The Polemics of the Dreyfus Affair and its Aftermath*

Alec G. Hargreaves, *Voices from the North African Immigrant Community in France: Immigration and Identity in Beur Fiction*

Colin Nettlebeck, *Forever French: The French Exiles in the United States of America during the Second World War*

Bill Marshall, *Victor Serge: The Uses of Dissent*

Allan Morris, *Collaboration and Resistance Reviewed: Writers and the Mode Rétro in Post-Gaullist France*

Malcolm Cook, *Fictional France: Social Reality in the French Novel 1775–1800*

W.D. Halls, *Politics, Society and Christianity in Vichy France*

David H. Walker, *Outrage and Insight: Modern French Writers and the 'Fait Divers'*

H.R. Kedward and Nancy Wood, *The Liberation of France: Image and Event*

David L. Looseley, *The Politics of Fun: Cultural Policy and Debate in Contemporary France*

Contents

Notes on Contributors

Diana Holmes is Professor of French at the University of Keele. She has written a book on Colette (Macmillan *Women Writers* series) and articles on several French women writers. Her book on *Women's Writing in France 1848–1994* will appear shortly in the Athlone series *Women in Context*. She is currently working on a study of the films of François Truffaut.

Margaret Callander's field of research is twentieth-century poetry and prose writing. A particular focus is the poetry of Pierre Jean Jouve, of whom she has published a study. In the area of prose narrative she has published articles on Gide and Proust, and her work on Duras and Colette fits into undergraduate and postgraduate teaching strands concerned with women's writing. Colette is of special interest to her and she has published a study of two of Colette's novels.

Alex Hughes is a Lecturer in French at the University of Birmingham. Her research interests lie in the field of women's writing, autobiography, and feminist and gender theory. She has published books on Violette Leduc and Simone de Beauvoir, and articles on Leduc, Beauvoir, Serge Doubrovsky and gender issues in post-war France. She is currently editing an *Encyclopedia of French Culture* (with Keith Reader), to be published by Routledge.

Jennifer Birkett is Professor of French Studies at the University of Birmingham. She has published on twentieth-century women's writing in French and English (ed. with Elizabeth Harvey *Determined Women: Constructions of the Feminine Subject 1900–1990*) and on the nineteenth-century Decadence (*The Sins of the Fathers: Decadence in France 1870–1914*, 1986) as well as articles on eighteenth-century fiction. She is currently completing work on *The Macmillan Guide to French Literature* (with James Kearns) and writing a book on *Sexuality and Fiction in the French Revolution* for Quartet Books.

Notes on Contributors

Emma Wilson is an Assistant Lecturer in the Department of French, University of Cambridge, and a Fellow of Corpus Christi College. She has written a book, *Sexuality and the Reading Encounter*, which is forthcoming from OUP, and she has published various articles on contemporary French fiction.

Kate Ince is Lecturer in French at the University of Birmingham. Her teaching and research interests are in the writing of Marguerite Duras, Samuel Beckett, and in aspects of critical and feminist theory. She has published articles on Duras, Luce Irigaray and the teaching of critical theory.

Introduction: Reading the Erotic

Alex Hughes and Kate Ince

This is a book about desire and its representation. It will explore, specifically within the context of modern French women's writing, the pleasures – and the torments – of love and sexuality, as they are depicted in the work of six twentieth-century authors: Rachilde, Colette, Leduc, Wittig, Cixous and Duras. These writers speak of love in a multiplicity of ways, and from a variety of perspectives. Taken together, as the individual author-based chapters of this study reveal, their desiring texts constitute a rich and startling palette of sexual/ textual invention.

The subtitle of this book, *Desiring Writing*, both echoes and translates the title of one of the few full-length critical works on women's erotic writing to exist in French, Claudine Brécourt-Villars's *Ecrire d'amour: Anthologie des textes érotiques féminins 1799–1984* (Editions Ramsay, 1985). It seems important to signal to the reader, as Brécourt-Villars does at the beginning of her introduction, the possible unexpectedness of this choice of subject area, and to explain in detail the parameters of the analysis of it offered here. This study sets out to chart the developing history of erotic literature written by French women from the late nineteenth century up to the late 1980s, from Rachilde's *Monsieur Vénus* (1884) to Marguerite Duras's *Les yeux bleus cheveux noirs* (1986). In this introduction to the six essays which constitute the main part of the book, we will attempt to address, one by one, the areas of enquiry that undertaking such a study raises – considering, firstly, the critical attention that has been paid to women's erotic writing hitherto, and the questions such criticism has raised; secondly, the diverse areas of enquiry raised by our contributors in their respective chapters; thirdly, the cultural and political background against which women's erotic writing has developed in France over the twentieth century; and fourthly, the impact that issues raised in the first three sections have had and continue to have upon the development and current state of women's erotic writing in France.

The task of bringing attention to erotic texts written by French women is one which seems only to have begun in earnest in about 1970, with the publication of the first of the two volumes of *Littérature érotique féminine*, by Denise Miège. After the appearance of the second volume three years later, 1982 saw the publication of Françoise Ducout's *Plaisirs d'amour: L'Almanach érotique des femmes* (Lieu commun, 1982), and 1985 of Brécourt-Villars' *Ecrire d'amour*. The common feature of these books, and that which distinguishes them from this one, is that they are largely composed of selected extracts of women's erotica, rather than being intended principally as works of criticism. This 'encyclopaedic' approach to erotic writing has, as Brécourt-Villars points out (p. 16), existed for as long as the genre has, and has been gaining in popularity recently, even in the case of erotic texts by women. As an approach, it is perhaps to be expected. Erotic fiction aims, after all, to stimulate what might be called the sexual (or erotic) imagination, and the compilation of a variety of erotic extracts maximizes their potential to arouse. However, the anthologizing of erotica militates also, obviously, against any real analysis of the texts collected, reinforcing the longstanding and still prevalent assumption that erotic writing belongs to 'low' culture and is not worthy of critical attention.[1] In so far as it contains both a fascinating selection of French women's erotic writing from 1799 onwards and a lengthy critical introduction, Brécourt-Villars' *Ecrire d'amour* already begins to open up the space into which it is our intention here to move, and, if possible, to expand. This volume of essays by women writing in English reflects a continuing trend in feminist scholarship whereby texts by women are uncovered/recovered so that their significance *vis-à-vis* the female tradition might be assessed. Regrettably, in French studies, this project has been pursued with greater vigour in the United States and Britain than it has in France, despite the wealth of literary and theoretical writing by women still being published there.[2]

As Claudine Brécourt-Villars points out in the introduction to *Ecrire d'amour*, other types of approach to French erotic texts do not so far appear to have given women's writing the coverage she (and we) feel it is due. The three volumes of Jean-Jacques Pauvert's *Anthologie historique des lectures érotiques*,[3] like most of the 'incursions de l'Université' Brécourt-Villars identifies, are mainly concerned with erotica written by and for men.[4] Feminist studies of erotic writing by women tend to regard that writing as 'a simple metaphor for relations of domination and coercion . . . and condemn it out of hand';[5] this persistent tension between the subject-matter of eroticism and feminist critical analysis is one which will recur throughout the chapters of this book. We shall devote further discussion to how positively the recent history and current status of French women's erotic literature can be evaluated in the final part of this introduction.

However, no evaluation of that history and status can be made before an attempt is made to question what its specificities might be. Can modern French women's sexual discourse as exemplified by the authors constituting our corpus be viewed as qualitatively different from that produced by male authors of erotica? This question immediately divides itself into two of the main issues we wish to address in this introduction: the issue of gender, and the issue of genre, or the possible distinction between erotic writing (whatever the register in which it is cast) and pornography. The excellent overview of the field of French women's erotic writing provided by Lucienne Frappier-Mazur for the 1988 issue of *Yale French Studies* entitled *The Politics of Tradition: Placing Women in French Literature*[6] shows that these two issues are in fact closely linked, since the distinguishing feature of all those erotic stories whose female authorship is documented is that they do not fit into a neatly definable generic category, but present instead a blend of 'eroticism' and 'pornography'. Frappier-Mazur's definitions of these two terms are a succinct summary of the entries to be found in most dictionaries:

> The sole goal of pornography is to be sexually stimulating and, whatever its form, its primary generic identity is as pornography. *Eroticism*, on the other hand, denotes a quality, and erotic texts may belong to a variety of generic categories.[7]

The chief distinction that can be made between pornographic and erotic texts is, in other words, one of quality, and this distinction appears to be inseparable from the question of the gender of the author. Texts which can be reliably identified as having been written by women mix pornographic and erotic elements, thereby blurring the tidy generic boundaries enclosing male-authored 'erotic' texts, whose concerns and motifs all too often exactly coincide with those of commercial pornography. Frappier-Mazur chooses to define the collective term 'erotica' and the adjective 'erotic' by saying that 'whilst retaining the basic motifs of commercial *pornography* and illustrating its formulaic model, they also go beyond its limits' (p. 113). This excess or transgression of the pornographic by the erotic appears to be a recurring feature in the female-authored texts on which this book exclusively focuses.

A different but related dimension of the issue of genre is raised by the selection of authors included in this book, and by the construction that selection puts upon twentieth-century French women's erotic writing. What all the authors have in common, apart from their gender, is that they can be classified relatively unproblematically as writers of 'high' literature. As Frappier-Mazur notes, the relation of 'low' to 'high' literature or culture 'partially overlaps that of pornographic to erotic'.[8] Classifying Rachilde, Colette, Leduc, Wittig, Cixous and Duras together as writers of 'high' and 'erotic' literature is not in any way an attempt to elide the considerable differences between their styles and reputations. An author such as Violette Leduc, whose writing encountered the abrupt refusal of censorship and the opprobrium of public opinion, clearly presents a different case from Colette, the first woman writer to whom France accorded the honour of a State funeral, or from Cixous and Duras, widely recognized as among the leading literary figures in France today. These distinctions between individuals are vital. However, it should be evident that in selecting just six women authors of erotic fiction from among hundreds, our intentions are different from those inspiring collections which set out primarily to make lost or forgotten texts available to a reading public.[9] The authors under scrutiny are women one would expect to find represented in an anthology of female-authored *erotic* fiction being compiled in the 1990s.[10] They are also – unlike many other authors who might be included in such an anthology – women writers recognized for the totality of their *oeuvre*. They have been selected for this volume by virtue of the particularly telling insights their texts offer into female erotic experience and feminine sexuality, insights which are particularly pronounced in the texts selected. But, since their status as authors does not rely on their classification exclusively as writers of eroticism, considering them under this heading itself has implications for the status of women's erotic writing as a genre.

Another key issue raised by women's erotic writing is the way in which female-authored erotic texts may be considered to link up and interconnect, both within a particular historical period and across the twentieth century as a whole. As Claudine Brécourt-Villars points out at the very beginning of *Ecrire d'amour*, it would be absurd to imagine women's erotic writing as constituting 'an unbroken thread being unwound throughout the centuries'.[11] The relatively short traceable history of the genre, if such it is, can only be dated to 1799 (the date at which Brécourt-Villars's anthology commences), with the publication of *Illyrine, ou l'Ecueil de l'inexpérience*, by G. . . de Morency (Suzanne Giroux). In the nineteenth century the picture is complicated by the widespread use of pseudonyms, but in summary, a brief post-Revolutionary flourish seems to have given way to a long lull scarcely relieved until the onset of the Decadent period in which Rachilde is such an important figure.[12]

The context or sociohistorical background against which women's erotic fiction has developed in the twentieth century, which for our purposes begins with the work of Rachilde, is the subject of the third section of this introduction. However, before that background can be addressed, the conclusions reached about individual authors by our contributors, and the interconnections and divergences between the 'desiring writing' of each of them, require summary.

The Erotic Inscribed

Rachilde

In 'Monstrous Women: Rachilde's Erotic Fiction', Diana Holmes shows the eroticism of Rachilde's texts to be marked indelibly by the patriarchal sexual ideology of *fin-de-siècle* society, but to operate specific reversals within the power relations characteristic of Decadent literary representations. Although Rachilde's politics and ideological stance were complicit with those of her male contemporaries, *Monsieur Vénus*, *La Marquise de Sade* and *La Jongleuse* show the tables to be turned on male protagonists both economically and sexually, with all influence and control passing to the novels' 'heroines'. Female desire is the narrative's driving force, although the perversity of its forms distinguishes it from the goal-centred, linear libidinal model familiar from male-authored fiction. The status of male lovers is reduced to that of an object, often a pitiful and helpless one, with female protagonists displaying a concomitantly increased interest in autonomous pleasure and lack of interest in penetrative sex. But despite the disturbance and transgression of social conventions and structures by feminine eroticism in Rachilde's fiction, its perturbing influence is ultimately limited. Men remain 'kings' and 'castrators' of female sexual power in a society where any femininity not corresponding to that of the 'monstrous' woman constructed by Decadent misogyny is suppressed or negated. There is a total absence of love or desire between women, and eroticism is only expressed in relation to male authority. Despite the potent anger of Rachilde's women characters, the eroticism articulated in her novels does not ultimately offer an alternative to the ingrained patriarchal power structures of *fin-de-siècle* society.

Colette

Margaret Callander's chapter explores the central thematic and stylistic role played by reticence, silence and ellipsis in the desiring writing of Colette. This account of the centrality of silence may surprise the reader familiar only with the 'Claudine' texts; texts which, written under the direction and influence of Colette's journalist husband Willy, are characterized by a certain provocative salaciousness. Margaret Callander's discussion reveals Colette to have been a writer who pursued, in her evocations of feminine sexuality, the creation of an erotic discourse that was multifaceted but above all 'chaste'; a discourse in which much was intimated about female – and more particularly lesbian – desire and pleasure, but little was stated overtly. This account of Colette's erotic writing foregrounds the revelatory power exerted within it through what Sherry Dranch terms the 'clearly stated unsaid'.[13]

Violette Leduc

Alex Hughes's chapter focuses on the account Violette Leduc offers, in her autobiographical text *La Bâtarde*, of the impossibility of love. Leduc sought, in her personal evocations of the sexual, to be daring, to go further than her 'foremothers' (specifically Colette) in her transcriptions of feminine desire. The reception of her autobiography by certain French critics of the 1960s suggests the extent to which *La Bâtarde* was in fact deemed by Leduc's contemporaries to be disconcerting (and shocking) in its explicitness. However, today's reader, particularly if s/he is a feminist, is more likely to be disconcerted by the pessimistic elucidation of love (particularly lesbian love) contained in Leduc's text. Leduc is undoubtedly a radical and pioneering writer; she was the first woman author in France to articulate, overtly and in the first person, the experience of desiring as a lesbian. However, unlike Wittig and Cixous, she eschews a political or celebratory treatment of feminine homoeroticism, preferring rather to document her experience of lesbian – and heterosexual – desire as, ultimately, an oppressive one.

Monique Wittig

Rooting the erotic writing of Monique Wittig firmly in its historical context, Jennifer Birkett reads three of Wittig's fictions as having been made possible by women's reappropriation, from the 1960s onwards, of the right to represent their own sexual pleasure. The female sexuality and desire in question are sited securely in the lesbian body, whose marginality in relation to phallocentric structures permits a radical and transformative view of heterosexual pleasures and bodies. Herbert Marcuse's Utopian vision of a world in which the death drive would be reconfigured to lessen social repressiveness and liberate hitherto unutilized erotic impulses informs Birkett's reading of Wittig. The privileged role given to the aesthetic and thus to literature in the primarily sociopolitical transformations Marcuse envisages enables Birkett to make connections between Marcuse's theories and Wittig's inspiring fictions of lesbian subjectivity. Birkett shows that by means of the highly intertextual and poetic character of her writing, her reworking of myths and her employment of particular graphic conventions, Wittig succeeds in reconstructing a newly energized form of lesbian and female sexuality.

Hélène Cixous

A crucial element of the argument Emma Wilson puts forward in 'Hélène Cixous: An Erotics of the Feminine' is that *Le Livre de Promethea* marks the beginning of a period in Cixous's work devoted exclusively to women and to their social and erotic relationships. This focus still leaves, within the space of Cixous's 'entre-femmes', possible distinctions between homosexual and heterosexual forms of feminine desire, and between 'closetted' and 'outed' (or secret and displayed) forms of feminine homosexuality. However, *Le Livre de Promethea* is shown to trouble these borderlines. Emma Wilson draws out the unasserted and unnamed possibility of lesbian identity in *Le Livre de Promethea* and *La Bataille d'Arcachon* with reference to the argument – offered in Judith Butler's *Gender Trouble* (1990) – that identity, instead of preceding gender performance, is actually constructed by and within that performance. She suggests that in *Le Livre de Promethea*, Cixous pursues elusiveness and ellipsis not because she wishes to deny the specificity of feminine homosexual experience, but because she seeks to avoid the fixed, reifying identity category of 'lesbianism'. So when the politically charged difference between private and public sexuality that is staged in Cixous's work is read against Eve Kosofsky Sedgwick's distinction (cf. *Epistemology of the Closet*, 1990) between universalizing and minoritizing definitions of homosexuality, the conclusion reached by Wilson is that *Le Livre de Promethea* 'emphatically exceeds any minoritizing classification'. The overall effect of the lush, sensual imagery of Cixous's eroticism is revealed, further, as constantly blurring and breaking down borders whose fixity was and continues to be the cause of hierarchical and often violent relations of power.

Marguerite Duras

In the last chapter of this collection Kate Ince uncovers a style or mode of eroticism which could hardly be more of a contrast to that of Cixous, and which seems to cast shadows over the lavish and lyrical positivity of erotic relationships between women explored in *Le Livre de Promethea*. In *L'homme assis dans le couloir*, *La Maladie de la mort* and *Les yeux bleus cheveux noirs*, which were amongst the most significant writings published by Marguerite Duras during the 1980s, the dominant emotional atmosphere is one of violence, melancholia and near-despair. Whilst *L'homme assis dans le couloir* places the issue of sexual violence and the problematic distinction between erotica and pornography centre-stage for both female and male readers, *La Maladie de la mort* and *Les yeux bleus cheveux noirs* reveal sexualities that are so complex and unstable as to refuse the establishment of any lasting relationship. It is difficult to present such texts as pleasurable or easily acceptable reading, or to account for them within any familiar feminist framework. Their appearance in the 1980s perhaps undermines any attempt to identify a predominantly positive emergent tradition of women's erotic writing.

The chapters of this book and the summaries of their contents are presented chronologically, by publication date. This is not, however, meant to imply any easy progression in the development of the 'genre' of women's erotic writing. Any claim to 'comprehensive coverage' would also be misplaced. The authors discussed have very different erotic 'voices', and no clear or certain linkages between these voices are implied. However, it will be evident from individual essays that there are numerous thematic, conceptual and textual overlaps between authors, foremost amongst which must be the flexibility of gender positions their novels reveal and explore. This flexibility is perhaps most striking in the texts of Rachilde, Leduc, Cixous and Duras, but also plays a significant role in the work of Colette, whose emphasis on the naturalness of sexuality is so strong as to offer considerable resistance to the theory that gender identity is thoroughly (if not entirely) cultural, which has recently come to dominate feminist and queer theory and criticism.[14]

Amongst the four authors in whose writing unstable and uncertain sexual identity is so important, Cixous is the only one for whom the masculine term as signifier of authority appears to have been relinquished altogether. Her lyrical evocations of love between women remind us that lesbian love is another theme central to the writings of four authors in this book, and for three of these silence and obfuscation characterize, in a variety of ways, the transcription of feminine homoeroticism. Wittig is obviously the exception here. Leduc avoids naming lesbian desire in its specificity in *La Bâtarde* because, for her, all desire, whether homosexual or heterosexual, is equally prone to prove damaging, especially where she herself is concerned. Colette's 'silencing' of lesbianism derives from a need to detach herself from a mode of erotic discourse which was not her own and which exploited explicitness in order to titillate. Cixous's silencings are qualitatively different. Her refusal to employ the signifier 'lesbian' is an intrinsic part of a politics of representation and is driven by a desire to avoid the categorizations of sexual identity produced by the heterosexual symbolic.[15] Cixous's 'political ellipsis' and the direct evocations of the lesbian body politic produced by Wittig stand in clear contrast to the lesbian discourses of Leduc and Colette. This is not to say, however, that the representations of feminine homosexuality produced by these latter writers must be dismissed as insipid or as lacking in revolutionary impact. As Elaine Marks suggests in her essay 'Lesbian Intertextuality',[16] Colette and Leduc are key contributors to that 'sexual and textual revolution' whereby, in twentieth-century French literature, 'the lesbian . . . has undergone a radical transformation from impertinent young woman, fragile couple, solitary writer . . . to aggressive lover and namer'. Wittig's *Le Corps lesbien*, and arguably Cixous's *Le Livre de Promethea*, may constitute the 'omega texts' of that revolution; Colette and Leduc give it its impetus. That this is so is evidenced by Wittig's acknowledgement of Leduc in the preface to the English translation of *Le Corps lesbien*.

The reticences about the overt thematization of lesbian eroticism which are particularly evident in the work of Colette and Cixous are markers of the more general phenomenon of silencing which is an important element of the predominantly male erotic tradition, and of which pseudonymous and anonymous authorship are significant indicators.[17] There is sometimes a close relationship between the concealment of identity and the concealment of desire, and it is in Emma Wilson's reading of Cixous's *Le Livre de Promethea* that the silences affecting them are revealed to operate most similarly. However, other patterns of sexuality and erotic relationships drawn out in other chapters cast the concealment or suppression of erotic desire rather differently. In particular, connections may be traced between such silencings and the aggressivity or violence of the desire(s) in question. Although in Wittig's fiction lesbian eroticism is confidently and openly asserted, it sites and states itself within the context of the most oppressive sociocultural and linguistic forces. It is in the rich intertextual poeticity of her language that Wittig turns the energies released by such clashes of interested desire to advantage. By confronting the question of whether violence is necessary for political transformation, Jennifer Birkett's reading of Wittig broaches the taboo association of violence with female desire and feminist politics, and reveals such unpopular considerations to be important concerns of Wittig's charged and powerful fictions.

Wittig's texts dramatize the clashes between the forces of women's desire and the rigid social structures of patriarchy with a particular aim in view – the free expression of lesbian eroticism. It is for want of such a horizon of possibility, the envisioning of which was impeded by Decadent ideology, that Rachilde's female characters are shown as trapped in violent relationships with men and women. They either exercise erotic mastery over their male lovers or demonstrate their independence from them. However, since the violence immanent in the hierarchical power relationships of a patriarchal society subtends their erotic relationships, their rebellious desire and assertive behaviour are represented as characteristics of 'monstrous' femininity rather than as emerging varieties of autonomy.[18]

Rachilde is not, however, the only author in this book to whose constructions of femininity the description 'monstrous' might be applied. At nearly a century's distance from the Decadence, the shadowy and anonymous women of Duras's erotic narratives retain, or echo, some of the startling perversity of its forms. Rachilde and Duras are the two authors for whom, at least as far as the texts discussed here are concerned, erotic relationships between women are not a significant issue. A further and more striking parallel between the two authors revealed by this concentration on male-female relations is the inadequacy of heterosexuality, or a single heterosexual relationship, to fulfil the imaginary expectations of heterosexual erotic love. They offer, therefore, an illustration of Lacan's dictum 'There is no sexual relation'.[19] The lack of interest or pleasure in sexual intercourse displayed by Rachilde's and Duras's women is a stark reminder of subjectivity's entrapment in symbolic structures which allow no unmediated relation between the sexes, except in (erotic) fantasies of wholeness which the subject imagines the loved other can bestow. This 'impossibility' of satisfying or stable sexual relationships is, of course, equally to the fore in Leduc's *La Bâtarde*, although, interestingly, it is primarily lesbian relationships which are the focus there. The writings of Leduc, Rachilde and Duras might all, therefore, be said to share an openness to impossible and/or 'monstrous' desire which reveals the insufficiency of (hetero)sexual relationships as a form for containing or expressing ill-matched configurations of desire. This in itself could be interpreted as a quiet comment by women writers of eroticism on the dominance of heterosexuality in the erotic writing of the Western literary tradition.

The dissatisfaction and difficulty of erotic relationships occupies a prominent place in a number of the texts discussed in this book. However, this is only one perspective on a heterogeneous range of depictions of desire, the writing of which is often shot through with pleasure. Although the instability of gendered subjectivity is a source of disquiet in a number of the texts discussed, it also frequently adds a flexibility and unpredictability to representations of sexuality which is itself erotically charged. Sensuality pervades the perverse sexualities of Rachilde's female characters, the practices of pleasure of Wittig's warrior-women, and all of the erotic relationships depicted by Colette and Cixous. The relaxedly lush imagery of the natural world lends a particular lyricism to Colette's erotic discourse, whilst the apparently effortless flow of Cixous's writing mimes the lightest and most mobile forms of pleasure, and imparts a sense of wonder at their ceaseless novelty. Consequently, it is the desiring writing of these particular authors (rather than to the darkly solipsistic erotic narratives of Duras and Rachilde, or Wittig's erotico-political productions) which is likely to stimulate, most immediately, the reader's own sensuality.

Our discussion of 'connections' returns us to the issue of whether it is possible, and useful, to talk of a female-authored erotic tradition or distinct genre of women's sexual/textual practice. It raises the related questions of what the (sociopolitical) consequences of the existence of such a genre might be, and of its future direction. These are issues which require further examination. Before addressing them, however, we will establish the historico-cultural context out of which the particular texts under discussion emerged, and will address its complex influence upon them.

Eroticism, *Ecriture* and the Social

Rachilde and Colette began writing in the 1890s and the early years of the twentieth century. Each led a life indicative of the relative freedom enjoyed by French women of the privileged classes. Their personal independence partially explains how they came to produce 'desiring discourse' at all. The lot of French women in general was, in any case, becoming (apparently) less restrictive at this time, thanks to reforms relating to education, divorce and female financial autonomy which feminist activity in the closing decades of the nineteenth century and the early part of the twentieth century (the 'Belle Epoque du féminisme en France'[20]) had helped bring about. It would seem that Rachilde and Colette, particularly the latter, were embarking on their literary careers at a moment of sociosexual change which the First World War, with the increased freedoms it afforded women, subsequently consolidated. However, as Michèle Sarde points out, in comparison to what was happening in Britain and America, the French women's movement had achieved relatively little by the eve of the Great War.[21] The war itself, however much of an upheaval in gender relations it may have generated (an upheaval symbolized by the popular image of the 'garçonne', taken from the novel of the same name by Victor Margueritte (1922)), is viewed by some historians as having had the effect of (re)imprisoning women in the role of 'mère-ménagère', in part as a result of the depredations it inflicted on French population statistics.[22] Female independence, specifically female sexual independence, was the focus of considerable male anxiety, particularly during and after the First World War. French society in the late nineteenth and early twentieth centuries was by no means casting off the shackles of sexual conservatism, and was marked by a rigid gender hierarchy.

Bearing this turn-of-the-century sociohistorical situation in mind, what other factors may be considered to have inflected the way in which Colette and Rachilde wrote about female sexuality and desire? Rachilde belongs squarely to the 'entre-deux-siècles' period, while Colette was producing many of her texts within the context of the upbeat 'années folles' (1920s–30s). Both women have, however, a certain literary and sexual heritage in common; a heritage related, most notably, to the female body. Women's bodies were still, in the nineteenth century, a taboo subject for women themselves, including feminists. For feminist activists of the period, fighting for social and educational rights was a matter of course, but many shied away from public debate of issues around 'le corps féminin'.[23] Women writers of the nineteenth century, for all that they had written about love, had avoided foregrounding the body and its sexuality.[24] Male writers of *fin-de-siècle* France, on the other hand, transformed woman, and by extension the female body, into a devouring, demoniacal entity.[25] The hidden/caricatured female desiring body, the body which nineteenth-century women authors had themselves obscured and which certain of their male counterparts had made monstrous, constituted a legacy which women writers of the early modern period could not lightly ignore. Undoubtedly, the shadow of that legacy did not make it easy for Rachilde and Colette to produce an overt, desiring 'body language' or, indeed, to create desiring heroines whose experience of sexuality, of the delights of sensuality, is wholly empowering or exemplary. Neither did the fact that they belonged to an epoch when female textual productions, regardless of their increased numbers and popularity, were still derided by the male literary establishment.[26]

The four remaining authors analysed in this book belong to a more 'liberated' time. At the time of writing, Cixous, Wittig and Duras are still alive, and may be conveniently labelled as writers of the mid/late twentieth century, while Leduc, who died in the early 1970s, is clearly identifiable as a post-war author. What of the sociocultural context of these writers' textual productions? As the feminist historians Maïté Albistur and Daniel Armogathe point out in their illuminating *Histoire du féminisme français*, the problem of female alienation seemed to be firmly on the sociopolitical agenda by the end of the 1940s.[27] In 1938 the married woman had cast off the status of legal minor which the Napoleonic Code had imposed upon her at the start of the previous century, and women got the vote at the end of 1944. It appears, therefore, that by 1945 French women were accessing a liberation that mirrored that of their country. Legal and political emancipation does not, however, necessarily constitute a miracle remedy against prejudice and oppression. French women's ostensible equality after the Second World War, imposed according to Albistur and Armogathe upon a culture and a ruling class unable, any longer, to resist the force of change, was constantly being called into question, on the level of everyday reality.[28]

In the decades that followed the Second World War, French women came to see that legal equality masked a basic, enduring disequilibrium between the sexes: an 'inégalité de fait'.[29] They discovered that women were still inferiorized by virtue of their sex alone. Their 'prise de conscience' was fuelled in part by the revolutionary fervour of May 1968 – and by the sexism which women none the less encountered during that explosive, anti-authoritarian moment. It provoked a new upsurge of feminist activity, creating a climate in which, simultaneously, women's status as enfranchised, equal subjects came to be taken more seriously than before and women were able to access what Marcelle Marini describes as 'positive narcissism' ('un narcissisme enfin positif') – a new sense of self-love and self-worth, engendered by the collective revaluation of the feminine, and of the female subject, French feminists embarked upon in the 1970s.[30]

It is in terms of the emergence of women's 'positive narcissism' and self-revaluation that Marini contextualizes the 'creative explosion',[31] and the consequent reconstellation of the cultural space, which have in her view characterized the post-1968 period, and women's development within it. For Marini, one of the key gains to emerge, for French women, out of the upheavals of the late 1960s and early

1970s was the possibility of remoulding, on their own terms, the previously male-dominated socio-symbolic domain ('le champ socio-symbolique').[32] In her essay 'La Place des femmes dans la production culturelle',[33] she argues that the *Mouvement de la Libération des Femmes* or *MLF* (the French women's liberation movement) had the effect of legitimizing an alternative female creativity and of impelling women, even those not directly involved in feminist activity, into a new engagement with culture.[34] Marini may be overstating the importance of the 'sociosymbolic metamorphosis' French women have (arguably) effected since the early 1970s. She may also be privileging an issue – women's battle against their exclusion from the hegemonic cultural realm – which has a less than central significance for more politically minded feminists. None the less, the feminine 'insertion into culture' she evokes did take off, and constitutes one element of the 'backdrop' against which the radical transcriptions of female eroticism, sensuality and (homo)sexuality offered by Wittig, Cixous and Duras may be considered to have come into being. However, the work of Violette Leduc, who began writing after the Second World War, published *La Bâtarde* in 1964 and died in 1972, largely predates the neo-feminist 'cultural revolution' of the late 1960s – a phenomenon which explains in part the absence within it of overt evidence of an engagement with sexual politics of the kind discernible in the writings of Cixous and Wittig.

French women of the 1960s and 1970s were not concerned exclusively with breaking down cultural barriers in order to pursue a 'venue à l'écriture', erotic or otherwise. As Janine Mossuz-Lavau remarks in her sociological study of sexuality, *Les Lois de l'amour*, moderate and radical feminist activists alike played a key part in the sexual revolution which ensured that, from 1967 onwards, the highly restrictive post-Vichyist sexual model lost a good deal of ground.[35] In 1967, the *loi Neuwirth*, legalizing contraception, was passed. Radical feminist activism (exemplified in 1971 by the 'manifeste des 343'[36]) helped legalize abortion in 1975, reversing the draconian interdiction against it instituted in France in the 1920s and reinforced by the Vichy régime. Feminists and homosexuals battled in the 1970s to make the point that there was more to sexuality than childbearing, and that the female orgasm was neither inevitably and exclusively vaginal nor a function of heterosexual intercourse alone.[37] Consequently, during and after the late 1960s and early 1970s, French women enjoyed a far greater degree of sexual freedom than hitherto. Being straight no longer appeared wholly compulsory. Women's experiences of (heterosexual) desire no longer needed to be haunted by the dread of missed periods, of backstreet abortions and their terrible consequences.[38] This modification of the sexual status quo, like the feminine 'entrée dans le champ socio-symbolique' chronicled by Marini, may be viewed as a factor inflecting the erotic discourse created by the authors under scrutiny in the final chapters of our study. Women's ability to take charge of their sexuality and their fertility, their freedom to love whom and how they choose, are essential stimuli for the production of untrammeled 'desiring writing'. Without these *acquis*, women's literary representations of the sensual and the erotic can never wholly elude constraint. Once again, this phenomenon is illustrated by the work of Leduc. It is hard not to relate the tortured account of heterosexual love offered in *La Bâtarde* to the fact that this text was written in the early 1960s, at a time when women had only limited control over their reproductive processes.

A third contextual factor which meshes with the emergence of post-war feminine desiring writing relates to the changing fortunes, during the post-war period, of the erotico-literary tradition. We need always to bear in mind that the relationship between the kind of female-authored sexual discourse which is our concern here and that corpus of (normally male-authored) literary texts constituting what Nancy Huston calls 'le mosaïque de la pornographie' is ridden with ambiguity and tension. None the less, there is obviously some degree of 'overlap' between the two bodies of writing, deriving, amongst other things, from the fact that neither can flourish in a climate of moral censure. In the introduction to *Ecrire d'amour*, Claudine Brécourt-Villars observes that the years following the Liberation failed to reverse the oppressive moral order which prevailed during the Vichy régime, with the result that erotic writing continued to be the focus of official opprobrium.[39] During the 1940s and 1950s various erotic texts – the French translations of Henry Miller's *Tropic of Cancer*, *Tropic of Capricorn* and *Sexus*, Vian's *J'irai cracher sur vos tombes*, Réage's *Histoire d'O*, certain texts by de Sade published by Pauvert – were either banned or became the focus of legal wrangles. At the same time, however, textual explorations of the erotic were capturing the imagination of France's intellectual community. Intellectuals 'went wild' about de Sade, and articles about his *oeuvre* were written by Bataille, Blanchot, Lacan and Klossowski. By the end of 1962, Sade's *Oeuvres Complètes* had begun to appear under the aegis of the *Cercle du livre précieux*. Clearly, then, the phenomenon of 'littérature érotique' was the focus of both considerable interest and unremitting repression in the post-war period. It is impossible, here, to give a comprehensive account of the complex evolution of the erotico-discursive tradition. However, Brécourt-Villars isolates two key moments as particularly significant in terms of the counteroffensive against erotic censorship which she associates with the latter part of the twentieth century. These are 1964 (the year of the inception of a 'nouvelle offensive de l'érotisme',[40] after which mainstream publishers such as Gallimard became more receptive to erotica[41]) and 1973, the year in which the trial of Régine Deforges, deemed to have published texts constituting 'an apology for perversion', provoked French writers and intellectuals into an outraged public defence of the freedom of expression. Brécourt-Villars is suggesting, essentially, that in and after the early 1970s, in spite of continuing legal constraints, the French literary scene was witnessing a revival of the erotic genre and that this was a logical extension of the post-war intellectual enthusiasm for erotic literature. A number of the female-authored desiring texts we are considering in the later sections of our book, regardless of the 'disjunctions' they effect *vis-à-vis* the formulae of 'classic' (male) eroticism, may undoubtedly, in terms both of their existence and of the freedom of their content, be placed within the context of the erotic upsurge Brécourt-Villars evokes, an upsurge which, significantly, she considers to have been stimulated in some measure by the publication of Leduc's *La Bâtarde*.[42]

Contextual data help us to read the writings of our authors in a more informed way. However, we need to be wary of establishing overly simplistic causal links between the nature of the treatments of feminine sexuality under scrutiny here and the historical, social and cultural moments at which they came into being. Commenting on the aftermath of debates about *écriture féminine* in her book *Muse de la Raison*, Geneviève Fraisse makes the point that the notion of sexual equality belongs to 'the political space', whereas knowledge about sexual difference can more properly be said to belong to the literary and psychoanalytic domains which deal with the human passions.[43] This comment highlights a distinction between the erotic and the political which is of vital importance to any consideration of the complicated relationship between historical context and the textual representation of sexuality. This distinction is illuminated by two of the texts to which particular attention is devoted here, *La Bâtarde* and *L'Opoponax*. Both overtly address the 'taboo' subject of lesbian love and signal an 'opening up' of the erotico-literary domain. Both appeared in 1964. They were published at a point in history which preceded the sexual revolution Mossuz-Lavau sites as occurring in France in the late 1960s and early 1970s. This phenomenon suggests that the relationship between sexual emancipation and the production of erotic literature is not in fact a causal one and that advances in freedom of (erotic) expression are not directly linked to, and generated by, legal, social and political advances for women. In this context, we should remember Brécourt-Villars's point that in eroticism it is not logical or continuous relationships that are being dealt with, but the unconscious, fantasy and an infinite libidinal territory.[44]

Gender, Genre, Politics: Some Concluding Remarks

Is it the case that an identifiable genre of women's erotic writing is emerging, in French or other Western literatures, in the contemporary period? What are its sources, and what of its effects? A number of women writers and critics, some of whom have already been cited, have noted that an upsurge in erotic writing by women seems currently to be occurring. Recent erotic writing by women could be seen as a continuation of that 'liberation of female writing'[45] which began in the 1960s. In the vocabulary deployed by Michel Foucault in *The History of Sexuality: An Introduction*,[46] what we are witnessing, arguably, is an extension of the discursification of sex as it pertains to women's erotic experience (not a discourse which figured in the material presented by Foucault in 1976).[47]

What of the consequences of this discursive phenomenon? The unhampered publication of texts which focus explicitly on women's sexuality can always be considered to be a victory of sorts. However, it is debatable whether a connection between a 'discursive liberation' (often a victory over censorship) and a liberation of subjectivity and desire can be conclusively established. The appearance of both *La Bâtarde* and *L'Opoponax* in 1964 marks a key moment in the evolving discursification of women's erotic experience. However, when these texts are viewed with hindsight in 1995, is it possible to assert a positive link between their publication and any definite, subsequent 'liberation' of women either as authors or as desiring subjects?

For an author such as Wittig, this question must clearly be answered in the affirmative.[48] Currently, however, there are indications of a continuing tension between the demands of feminism and the kinds of texts women are actually writing. The narrative construction of some of the extracts in a follow-up volume to Françoise Ducout's 1982 *L'Almanach érotique des femmes, Plaisirs d'amour 2*,[49] reveals little or no awareness on the part of the authors concerned of the political significance of the feminist debates alluded to above. In a review of new erotic novels by British and American women which appeared in 1994, the conclusion reached is that although these writings have female narrators and focus on women's erotic experiences, they employ too much of the language and the techniques of 'male' pornography to indicate any real shift in the prevailing ideology of erotic relations between the sexes.[50] The reviewer adopts an optimistic view of the darkly masochistic turn of several of the novels in question, terming them 'the literature of catharsis', the mark of 'a kind of mourning' of painful sexual experience which she hopes is the prelude to 'something more interesting'. Exactly what would qualify as 'more interesting' than the troublingly complex eroticism of the novels she is reviewing remains, however, unspecified. That said, the strong impression created by the selection of contemporary French, British and American fiction referred to here is that the tone and structures of erotic narratives by women, although they sometimes anticipate changes in sexual politics, do not obediently adjust themselves to such changes when they occur.

A further dimension of the sociopolitical questions raised by women's erotic writing is noted by Lucienne Frappier-Mazur when she observes that the setting of many novels of the 1960s, 1970s and early 1980s against a personal and social background of women's everyday life 'places eroticism in the context of social and gender relations'.[51] This *rapprochement* of eroticism with mainstream literature actually relates more pertinently to the first three authors included in this book than to the second three, each of whom has been associated with, and made a major contribution to, formal experimentation in the novel as practised by modernist and latterly postmodernist writers.[52] It is important to note, further, that Wittig, Cixous and Duras have all been embraced by Anglo-American critical theory, both because of their distinct contributions to theoretical discourse and because of the theoretical questions their fictional writings raise. The interest all three women display in innovations of textuality or *écriture* and in the processes of theory, combined with their considerable reputations, could, however, be said to make their erotic writings a significant contribution to the erosion of boundaries between mainstream and more formally complex writing which Frappier-Mazur discerns in recent French erotic fiction by women. As with its blurring of the distinction between erotica and pornography, it seems that women's sexual writing in France is contributing to this important process of cultural change.[53] Women's erotic writing may itself be considered currently to be constructing itself as a genre. If, however, this is so, it seems simultaneously to be participating in the modification of 'generic and cultural models' for the first time.[54]

The final issue raised by Frappier-Mazur at the close of 'Marginal Canons: Rewriting the Erotic' is whether new involvement in the historical shifts in literary and cultural models might lead to the participation of women's erotica in canon formation. In the same volume of *Yale French Studies* (75), Alice Jardine and Anne Menke acknowledge that the canon is itself an Anglo-American concept,[55] an observation they arrive at in part because of the indifference expressed by many of the fourteen French women writers interviewed towards their inclusion in, or exclusion from, the canon. Identifying the canon as an Anglo-American notion implies not that canonical processes do not take place in France, but that their existence and functioning are not (yet?) as politicized an issue there as in Britain and the United States. Debates about the canon may have tended to focus on the question of the transmission of national cultures. However, it could be claimed that the origin of the content of a canon is less important than its destination; a canon is by definition always received by a specific readership or institutional constituency. Since this book is an English study of French women's erotic writing, any claim on our part to be intervening in the French canon might seem misplaced or spurious. We are, nevertheless, seeking to define and promote a canon of French women's erotic writing, whilst recognizing the precariousness and provisionality of that canon's identity. It is to be hoped that this project gives our book the 'qualité de regard' of the few 'very recent and new feminist orientations' on eroticism Claudine Brécourt-Villars was able to identify in 1985.[56]

Notes

1. The selection process anthologization entails can also offer the temptation to formulate superficial truths, what Brécourt-Villars terms 'la tentation spécieuse du florilège', *Ecrire d'amour*, p. 15.
2. There are, of course, exceptions to this trend. The work of Marcelle Marini and Nicole Mozet focuses precisely on the question of a female literary tradition. See, for example, the latter's essay 'La Place des femmes dans l'institution littéraire', in Mireille Calle (ed.), *Du féminin*, Sainte-Foy, Québec, 1992, pp. 251–63.
3. *Anthologie historique des lectures érotiques*, by Jean-Jacques Pauvert, Paris, vol. I, 1979; vol. II, 1980; vol. III, 1982.
4. A recent critical work which also demonstrates this tendency is *Histoire de la littérature érotique*, by Alexandrian, Paris, 1989, of which a whole chapter (pp. 247–90) is devoted to denigrating erotic writing by women.
5. 'la seule métaphore des rapports de domination et de coercition . . . et la condamnent sans appel', *Ecrire d'amour*, p. 18.
6. 'Marginal Canons: Rewriting the Erotic', *Yale French Studies*, vol. 75, 1988, pp. 112–28.
7. Ibid., p. 113.
8. Ibid.

9. All the texts discussed in detail in the author-based chapters of this book are in print, and the following are also available in English translation: Rachilde, *Monsieur Vénus*, trans. by M. Boyd, New York, Covici Fride, 1929; *The Juggler*, trans. by Melanie Hawthorne, New Brunswick NJ, Rutgers University Press, 1990; Leduc, *La Bâtarde*, trans. by Derek Coltman, London, Peter Owen, 1965; Wittig, *The Opoponax*, trans. by H. Weaver, New York, Simon and Schuster, 1976; *Les Guérillères*, trans. by David Le Vay, London, Peter Owen, 1971 and New York, Avon, 1973; *The Lesbian Body*, trans. by David Le Vay, London, Peter Owen, 1975 and New York, Avon, 1976; Cixous, *The Book of Promethea*, trans. by Betsy Wing, Lincoln and London, University of Nebraska Press, 1991; Duras, 'The Seated Man in the Passage', *Contemporary Literature*, vol. 24, no. 1, 1983, pp. 268–75; *The Malady Of Death*, trans. by Barbara Bray, New York, Grove Press, 1986; *Blue Eyes Black Hair*, trans. by Barbara Bray, London, Collins, 1988. For details of the various translations of Colette's writings available, see chapter 2.

10. Extracts from no fewer than five of the books to which particular attention is devoted in this volume (*Monsieur Vénus*, *La Bâtarde*, *Le Corps lesbien*, *Le Livre de Promethea* and *L'homme assis dans le couloir*) were selected by Brécourt-Villars for *Ecrire d'amour*. No extracts are reprinted from the novels of Colette due to the refusal of Colette's heirs to allow their inclusion in an anthology of women's erotic writing, a refusal which is, as Brécourt-Villars notes, a startling reminder of the perceived unacceptablity of the signifier 'érotisme' (or of the incompatibility of 'féminin' and 'érotisme'?) as recently as 1985. The two texts by Colette which Brécourt-Villars selects as being particularly suited to inclusion in her anthology, had permission been granted, are *L'Ingénue libertine* (1909) and *Duo* (1934). Evelyne Sullerot's *Histoire et mythologie de l'amour: huit siècles d'écrits féminins*, Paris, 1974, includes extracts from texts by Rachilde, Colette and Wittig, not being recent enough to take account of the more identifiably 'erotic' texts of Cixous and Duras. Sullerot's exclusion of Violette Leduc is evidence of the widespread judgement of Leduc's work as unacceptably scandalous compared to, for instance, the more politicized eroticism of Wittig, whose *Les Guérillères* (which appeared five years later) finds sufficient favour to be included. For *Plaisirs d'amour: L'Almanach érotique des femmes*, Françoise Ducout selects none of the 'major' writers we have chosen to focus on, her declared intention being to bring to attention the work of unknown and unpublished women writers.

11. 'un tissu continu qui se déroulerait de siècle en siècle', *Ecrire d'amour*, p. 16.
12. An extremely succinct summary of the early history of women's erotic literature is given by Frappier-Mazur in 'Marginal Canons', pp. 116–20. The account given by Brécourt-Villars in the introduction to *Ecrire d'amour* goes into more and often absorbing detail, but interestingly, coincides almost exactly in the periodization or 'archeology' of erotic discourse it offers: Brécourt-Villars's book predates Frappier-Mazur's article by three years and is appreciatively footnoted by the latter at the start of 'Marginal Canons', p. 112, n. 2.
13. 'Reading through the Veiled Text: Colette's *The Pure and the Impure*', *Contemporary Literature*, vol. 24, 1983, pp. 176–89, p. 177.
14. E.g. Judith Butler, *Gender Trouble: Feminism and the Subversion of Identity*, London and New York, 1990; and *Bodies that Matter*, London and New York, 1993.
15. For Butler, homosexuality and its positions are currently compelled to represent the constitutive outside of hegemonic heterosexuality. Analysing these positions, Butler stresses the paradox of their 'abject' status. She makes the point that they are actually *produced* by the social/symbolic, heterosexual order, as a restrictive, 'threatening' spectre of sex/gender otherness, and produced so that that order might safeguard its continuing hegemony. *Bodies that Matter*, p. 104.
16. George Stambolian and Elaine Marks (eds), *Homosexualities and French Literature*, Ithaca, 1979, pp. 353–77, p. 371.
17. At the discursive level, Pierre Guiraud's analysis of the erotic tradition in France notes the existence of a 'veine galante' which exploits silence and obfuscation for the purposes of erotic intensification. 'In contrast to the bawdy [*gaulois*] strand of eroticism, this "galant" strand avoids naming things directly, but relies on allusions that remain more or less veiled', Pierre Guiraud, *Dictionnaire historique, stylistique, rhétorique, etymologique de la littérature érotique*, Paris, 1978, p. 112.
18. A dialogue between psychoanalytic theory and the implication of gender difference in the problem of domination which is helpful in clarifying this dynamic, although it does not directly describe it, can be found in Jessica Benjamin's 'The Bonds of Love: Rational Violence and Erotic Domination', in *The Future of Difference*, ed. by Hester Eisenstein and Alice Jardine, Boston, 1980, pp. 41–70, and is developed more fully in Benjamin's book *The Bonds of Love: Psychoanalysis, Feminism and the Problem of Domination*, New York, 1988.

19. 'il n'y a pas de rapport sexuel', 'Encore', *Le Séminaire livre XX*, Paris, 1975. See also the introduction to chapter 6, 'God and the Jouissance of Woman. A Love Letter', in Juliet Mitchell and Jacqueline Rose (eds), *Feminine Sexuality: Jacques Lacan and the 'école freudienne'*, Basingstoke and London, 1982, pp. 137–8. A succinct explanation of Lacan's account of erotic relations is also to be found in Elizabeth Grosz, *Jacques Lacan: A Feminist Introduction*, London and New York, 1992, pp. 137–40. As Grosz puts it, 'Love relations aspire to a union or unity that is strictly impossible. The two can never become *One*', p. 137.

20. Florence Montreynaud, *Le XXe siècle des femmes*, Paris, 1992, p. 84.

21. See Sarde, *Regard sur les Françaises*, Paris, 1983, p. 590.

22. See, for example, Françoise Thébaud's essay 'La Nationalisation des femmes', in Georges Duby and Michelle Perrot (eds), *Histoire des femmes*, vol. 5, Paris, 1992. Thébaud argues that the changes brought about by the war were limited by the fact that the war maintained and even reinforced traditional sex roles (pp. 49–70).

23. See Duby and Perrot (eds), *Histoire des femmes*, vol. 4 (covering the nineteenth century), 1991, p. 509, for a discussion of this phenomenon. We should not forget, however, that some early twentieth-century feminists, such as Madeleine Pelletier and Nelly Roussel, were actively campaigning around issues such as contraception and abortion.

24. For a discussion of the inability of nineteenth-century French women writers to overcome the taboos surrounding the female body, see Béatrice Slama, in Jean-Paul Aron (ed.), *Misérable et Glorieuse: la femme du XIXe siècle*, Paris, 1980, pp. 234–5.

25. See Brécourt-Villars, *Ecrire d'amour*, and Mireille Dottini-Orsini, *Cette femme qu'ils disent fatale: textes et images de la misogynie fin-de-siècle*, Paris, 1993, for helpful discussions of this Decadent phenomenon.

26. In this context Marini cites a remark made by Léautaud at the beginning of the twentieth century: 'Women are all writing . . . one can no longer even find anyone to do the cleaning', *Histoire des femmes*, vol. 5, p. 284 ('Toutes les femmes écrivent . . . On ne trouve même plus de femmes de ménage'). Dominique Desanti quotes an analogous observation made by Huysmans, in connection with a woman writer, Myriam Harry, whom he briefly considered as a potential recipient of the Goncourt, 'We'll have no skirts here!', *La Femme au temps des années folles*, Paris, 1984, p. 96 ('Pas de jupes chez nous!'). It was in reaction to comments of this kind that a group of women set up what was initially an 'anti-Goncourt', the prix Fémina.

27. See Maïté Albistur and Daniel Armogathe, *Histoire du féminisme français*, Paris, 1977, p. 437.
28. Ibid., p. 437.
29. See Françoise Picq, *Les Années Mouvement*, Paris, 1993, p. 26.
30. See Marini, in *Histoire des femmes,* vol. 5, pp. 282–3.
31. Ibid., pp. 278–83.
32. Ibid., p. 291, p. 281.
33. Ibid., pp. 275–96. This text is invaluable to anyone seeking to contextualize twentieth-century French women's writing.
34. See ibid., p. 281. This is not to say that French women in the twentieth century – particularly after the Second World War – were not turning to literary activity in increasing numbers. However, the *années mouvement* saw a real explosion in women's creative activity.
35. See Janine Mossuz-Lavau, *Les Lois de l'amour: les politiques de la sexualité en France 1950–1990*, Paris, 1991, especially pp. 295–305.
36. This was a document signed by French women, many of whom were in the public eye, declaring that they had had illegal terminations and demanding that the law be changed so that abortion might become available and safe.
37. See Mossuz-Lavau, *Les Lois de l'amour*, p. 302.
38. For a very clear account of the sexual history of French women in the twentieth century, and of their history in general, see Huguette Bouchardeau, *Pas d'histoire, les femmes*, Paris, 1977. We are grateful to Felicia Gordon for drawing our attention to the existence of this study.
39. As Nancy Huston indicates, this opprobrium is exemplified by a dictate passed in 1949 which was designed to protect French youth from exposure to salacious literature, *Mosaïque de la pornographie*, Paris, 1982, p. 38. The 1949 law was reinforced by further statutes relating to the censorship of erotic texts, with the result that, as Brécourt-Villars comments, the years between the end of the war and the early 1970s were marked by a highly stringent censoring of erotica, a 'legal repression of the book even harsher than that under the First Empire, which drew its justification from article 14 of the law of 16 July 1949 and its "repressive arsenal" from the edict of 23 December 1958 and the law of 4 January 1967', *Ecrire d'amour*, p. 48.
40. In 1955, Gallimard refused to publish the prefatory section of Leduc's third novel, *Ravages*, because they feared the legal consequences that would follow. The text – a lyrical evocation of lesbian love in a boarding school – was duly excised.
41. *Ecrire d'amour*, p. 50.

42. Brécourt-Villars associates the early 1970s specifically with a flowering of women's erotic writing, by authors as varied as Monique Wittig and Xaviera Hollander.
43. *Muse de la Raison*, Paris, 1989, p. 301.
44. *Ecrire d'amour*, p. 19.
45. 'libération de l'écriture féminine', ibid., p. 255.
46. Michel Foucault, *The History of Sexuality: An Introduction*, Harmondsworth, 1978, translation of *La Volonté de savoir*, Paris, 1976.
47. Brécourt-Villars notes the relevance of Foucault's theories to the investigation of the history of erotic literature when she refers to the spread of practices for the 'confession of the flesh' in Western societies, *Ecrire d'amour*, p. 20.
48. For an exposition of Wittig's conception of lesbian subjectivity, see 'On ne naît pas femme', *Questions féministes*, no. 8, May 1980, pp. 75–84.
49. *Plaisirs d'amour 2*, Paris, 1994. Authors represented in this volume include Jeanne de Berg, Régine Deforges, Benoîte Groult and Julia Kristeva.
50. 'The pain for pleasure principle', Rebecca Abrams, *The Guardian*, 19 July 1994. The novels reviewed, all published in 1994, are *Exposure*, by Kathryn Harrison; *House Rules*, by Heather Lewis; *Lunch*, by Karen Moline; and *True Romance*, by Helen Zahavi.
51. 'Marginal Canons', p. 128.
52. In her book *Representation in Contemporary French Fiction*, Lincoln and London, 1986, Dina Sherzer picks out Wittig, Duras and Cixous as the three representatives of postmodernist feminist fiction.
53. This relationship between gender and the blurring or erosion of generic boundaries also seems to apply in the field of criticism. Whilst feminist criticism such as Frappier-Mazur's survey of erotic fiction pays attention to the question of boundary-blurring, a relatively recent study entitled *L'Erotisme et l'amour* by Etiemble concentrates on reinforcing the distinction between eroticism and pornography by asserting the value of the former and roundly condemning the latter. 'For pornography is precisely the opposite of eroticism, which should not be lightly condemned', *L'Erotisme et l'amour*, Paris, 1987, p. 19.
54. 'Marginal Canons', p. 128.
55. 'Exploding the Issue: "French" "Women" "Writers" and "The Canon"?', *Yale French Studies*, vol. 75, 1988, pp. 275–307.
56. *Ecrire d'amour*, p. 18. It is worth noting here that Cixous, Duras and Wittig express divergent opinions on canon formation in

their interviews with Jardine and Menke. Cixous's view is that 'the canon' in France is fragmented into multiple categorizations, 'an infinite variety of codes', but that women in French universities are uninterested in promoting women's work or women's issues. Wittig does not share Cixous's conception of the plurality of the canon, and sees the role of the writer as being 'to experiment so as to fight the canon, to break it down', whilst seeming also to agree that inclusion in the canon is a measure of a writer's capacity for innovation. Duras, whilst recognizing her fame/notoriety, expresses the view that her position in France is 'still shaky' on account of her past involvement in Communism and the 'bad taste' often ascribed to her work.

– 1 –

Monstrous Women: Rachilde's Erotic Fiction

Diana Holmes

Any representation of sexual pleasure [jouissance] is inscribed within historically specific social relations, and thus can not fail to refer, implicitly or otherwise, to an ideological norm, even if only to transgress it.

Anne-Marie Dardigna[1]

In a preface to the 1889 edition of Rachilde's novel *Monsieur Vénus* – a preface designed to tantalize the prospective reader – Maurice Barrès emphasized the scandalous contradiction between the youth and innocence of the text's female author and the erotic nature of her story: 'What is most delicate about the perversity of this book is the fact that it was written by a young girl of twenty.'[2] In late nineteenth-century France the phrase 'jeune fille' connoted virginity and sexual ignorance, meanings which are explicitly reinforced by Barrès's description of Rachilde as 'a most gentle, retiring child', 'a virgin', and by his quotation from Jean Lorrain's portrayal of the young writer as 'a schoolgirl whose manner is sober and reserved, very pale, . . . a true "jeune fille", rather slim and frail'.[3]

The preface contrasts the figure of the fragile maiden with the product of her imagination, an 'abominable' yet 'marvellous' work which tells the story of a curiously perverted love affair in a style designed to 'make the reader quiver'.[4] Barrès's device for encouraging sales of his protégée's work was to play on the public's fascination with the paradoxical conjunction of virginal innocence and erotic fantasy. The implied oxymoron of chaste perversity underlay the appeal of both author and text.

Born in 1860, Marguerite Eymery began to publish under the pen-name of Rachilde in 1880, achieving fame and notoriety in 1884 when *Monsieur Vénus* was first published in Brussels and the Belgian Court of Justice banned the book and sentenced its author (in her absence) to a fine and two years' imprisonment. Rachilde's representation of sexual identity and practices, and the scandal this caused, need to be understood within the ideological context of late nineteenth-century France. Since 1804, the differing rights and duties of the sexes had been inscribed in the Napoleonic Civil Code, a document which formed the basis of French law and which put a firm end to the short-lived contestation of patriarchy of the Revolutionary years. The *Code Civil* defined women as the legal equivalents of children and minors, and made the obedience of the married woman to her husband a legal obligation. As the century progressed, the very gradual industrialization and urbanization of France determined a material reality in accordance with this legal differentiation of the sexes, as men became identified with the public world of employment and political struggle, women with the private, domestic sphere.

Though this frontier was regularly crossed by the millions of working-class women who continued, of necessity, to work outside the home, their lack of legitimate status as workers and citizens was clearly marked by their lower pay, their exclusion from trade unions and their concentration in the 'feminine' sectors of textiles and domestic service. France also had a particularly high rate of prostitution: in the 1850s, for example, if London had approximately 24,000 registered prostitutes, Paris, with half the population, had 34,000.[5] The lives of bourgeois women, with very rare exceptions, observed the pattern of a minimal education followed by marriage and motherhood.

Sexually, women were cast as a civilizing, stabilizing force whose purity and devotion held male passions in check. From Right to Left of the political spectrum, and from Catholic Church to anti-clerical Republicans, the good wife and mother was held to be at the heart of a civilized society, and sexual modesty and fidelity to be a central component of her virtue. Adultery by a wife was liable to much harsher sanctions than the same offence committed by her husband. If women's capacity for sexual pleasure was acknowledged and approved by the more liberal authorities of the era, this was very much within the context of monogamous marriage.[6] The *jeune fille*, innocent and fragile, was in apprenticeship for her role as wife and mother, awaiting the man whose love would release her into adulthood.

On the other hand the woman who failed to live up to the ideal of feminine virtue might find herself condemned as a threat to the social order. If the heroines of nineteenth-century French literature play out their dramas in terms of the choice between a stultifying fidelity, or the dangerous indulgence of passion, it is because it was in the sexual arena that women's social legitimacy and indeed material livelihood was most often at stake: thus Stendhal's Madame de Rênal and Flaubert's Madame Bovary (both significantly remembered by their husband's names) risk social ostracism and finally die for having sought love and pleasure outside marriage. Zola's Nana embodies the nineteenth-century nightmare of the sexually active woman whose deliberate provocation and exasperation of male desire destroys the very fabric of society.

To acknowledge or act upon pre- or extra-marital desires represented a material and social danger for most women. The stigma of sexual promiscuity and of illegitimacy attached only to women, and it was in terms of these powerful taboos and anxieties that women's sexuality was lived. It is not surprising that most of the feminist movements in the early decades of the Third Republic campaigned not for women's sexual freedom but for the abolition of the double standard through the extension of the ideals of purity and fidelity to men. Women writers on the whole observed the unspoken conventions of patriarchal sexual ideology, granting to their male characters the role of desiring subject and avoiding explicit representation of the male body as object of desire. In the work of Rachilde's female contemporaries – for example Gyp, Marcelle Tinayre, Colette Yver – female sexuality is responsive rather than proactive, and desire is inseparable from romantic love. Only Colette – who admired and was in turn admired by Rachilde – was to reconstruct the heterosexual scenario with the woman as primary subject, but Colette's first novel was not to appear until 1900.

Thus the very existence of an explicitly erotic work authored by a woman – moreover a young, unmarried and apparently virtuous woman – contravened accepted codes of feminine behaviour. Rachilde's style of writing was none the less not without its literary roots and parallels for, both by inclination and by her choice of literary friends, she was part of a loosely knit tendency in *fin-de-siècle* French literature known as Decadence. The Decadents' major themes and motifs can be traced back to a number of earlier writers including Baudelaire (1821–1867) and Sade (1740–1814), but the development of Decadence as a literary mode between 1870 and the turn of the century can be attributed, at least in part, to the particular social and political circumstances of the period.

Decadent narratives tend to be set in enclosed spaces, exotically furnished to exclude all reminders of the more everyday realities beyond the walls or beyond the pages of the text. This literal and figurative retreat from the social world is exaggerated almost to the point of parody in J-K. Huysman's *A Rebours* (1884), a Decadent novel in which the hero encloses himself within a carefully planned and controlled sensory environment, shutting out all that is natural or contingent. The protagonists of the Decadent text are sometimes cynical dandies, sometimes young men corrupted by evil women, but in either case the narrative centres on the fulfilment or frustration of desires which originate not in nature but in a sophisticated imagination freed from the instincts of common humanity. Macabre trappings recur from one work to another, from skulls and severed limbs to whips and branding irons, signifying both a style of eroticism designed to arouse the jaded senses of heroes and implied readers, and a repressed anger in the text which never clearly defines its object.

This mode of writing with its rejection of both nature and society, its violent but unfocused anger, can be read as the response of a class of men caught, from the birth of the Third Republic in 1871, between their aesthetic and political rejection of the new regime and the impossibility of revolt.[7] The Third Republic, founded as a result of Napoleon III's defeat in the Franco-Prussian war, signified the final triumph of the conservative, commercial middle class, and made a generation of young artists dependent for economic survival and cultural recognition on a ruling class whose rational materialism and complacent faith in democracy and progress they abhorred. The Decadents shared a loathing for the new ruling class, and an inability to identify with its most potent political enemies, the working class – for as the products of a bourgeois élite or of the declining aristocracy they viewed the nascent power of the masses without sympathy. Opposed to the existing structure of power, yet with no focus for their opposition, the Decadents produced an art which is angry, alienated, and sadistically erotic.

Much of the texts' fury focuses on female figures who are used to represent, on the one hand, the degrading servitude of the natural and, on the other, the intrusive power of society. In *The Decadent Imagination*, Jean Pierrot identifies two primary Decadent characterizations of women: the *femme fatale* whose voracious sexual appetite threatens to destroy the hero, and the 'ball and chain', whose concern for material and social security drags him down to the plane of the vulgar and the everyday. In *La Première maîtresse* (1887), Catulle Mendès succeeded in combining these two figures of the female enemy into one, by creating in Madame d'Arlemont a demanding mistress whose perverse desires exhaust and humiliate the hero, yet who also, as 'a very methodical bourgeoise' (p. 153), locks him into a respectable middle-class affluence that stifles his artistic aspirations. The character of Madame d'Arlemont demonstrates with particular clarity the spirit of exasperated misogyny which fuels so many Decadent texts.

Decadence was thus an odd mode of writing for a woman to adopt, but – gender aside – Rachilde largely shared the background and ideological stance of her fellow Decadents, many of whom she frequented in Paris during the 1880s and 1890s, and many of whom were published, from 1889 on, by her husband Alfred Vallette, editor of the literary journal *Mercure de France*. The daughter of an officer in the army of the Second Empire, with aristocratic blood on both sides of the family, Rachilde's political sympathies were firmly reactionary. Though her account of her girlhood and literary debut makes clear how much she suffered from a restrictive female education and from her father's bitter regret that she was not a son, she made no alliance with the emerging French feminist movement of the 1880s and 1890s, maintaining a strictly individualist position: 'I have always acted as an individual, without any desire to found a new society or to undermine the existing one.'[8] There is thus an interesting tension in her work between observance of the misogynist conventions of Decadent writing, and the subversive implications of her position as a female author of erotic texts. Just as the Decadents' social and political alienation led not to analysis and action but to an often bitter and morbid art form, so Rachilde's experience of oppression as a woman led her not to feminist resistance, but to the production of deeply ambivalent literary images of relations between the sexes.

Rachilde's writing career extended from 1880 to 1947 and produced over fifty novels, as well as two volumes of stories, a few short plays, some poetry and two autobiographical essays. Most of her work remains out of print: by the time Rachilde died in 1953 she had been long forgotten by critics and public, and her death went virtually unnoticed. However, a revival of critical – and particularly feminist – interest since the late 1970s has meant the republication of a few of the early novels – novels which made her reputation and whose themes and devices she reworked throughout her life.[9]

Monsieur Vénus (1884, reprinted 1977, henceforth *MV*), *La Marquise de Sade* (1887, reprinted 1981, henceforth *MS*) and *La Jongleuse* (1900, reprinted 1982, henceforth *LJ*), are all novels whose central narrative concern is the nature and the possible satisfaction of sexual desire. In *Monsieur Vénus*, Raoule de Vénérande is seized with sensual longing for the equivocally gendered body of Jacques Silvert, and installs her penniless lover in a flat as her 'mistress', eventually scandalizing her aristocratic friends by marrying him. *La Marquise de Sade* tells the story of Mary Barbe, whose sadistic desire, announced by the book's title, can only be satisfied by the infliction of pain and humiliation. Marriage to a weak and corrupt man allows her to indulge her appetite for sexual domination not only with her husband, but more satisfyingly with an ardent young lover. *La Jongleuse* narrates the arousal and repeated frustration of male desire, that of Léon Reille for the mysterious 'juggler' Eliante, whose own desire can never coincide with Léon's constantly deferred and finally unsatisfied longing for her body.

In a manner typical of the primarily erotic text, these novels operate an elaborate *mise-en-scène* in which all the material elements of the narrative, from the setting to the characters' clothing and possessions, contribute to the foregrounding of desire. All three stories are staged principally in closed rooms, from which, in true Decadent style, the natural world is rigorously excluded. The heroines' bedrooms function as explicit signifiers of their sexual inclinations: thus Raoule's deep red, windowless room is decorated with exotic weapons adapted for her use, and with erotic paintings including a male nude; Eliante's room is draped with the skins and heads of dead animals, framed by a material 'half silk, half metal' (*LJ*, p. 104), indicating both her sensuality and her fascination with death and instruments of death. Rooms are also used to display and frame the object of desire, so that Jacques Silvert appears white-skinned against the pale blue silk of his bedroom or the deep red marble of the bath. Mary Barbe's huge bed, draped in purple and bearing the inscription 'Aimer c'est souffrir' (*To love is to suffer*), recurs several times in the text, framing the white bodies of Mary herself or of her lovers within a setting ambivalently voluptuous and cruel.

Objects and clothing function primarily to heighten the texts' eroticism. Jacques is dressed in increasingly soft, feminine garments which reveal his flesh. Eliante's austere black costume serves paradoxically to focus attention on her concealed nudity, as Léon observes her reflected in a mirror alongside a naked marble statue of a woman: 'Female twins, their backs turned towards each other, the one wholly naked . . ., the other marvellously clothed.'[10] Similarly, later in the text, Léon's desire for Eliante's hidden body will be both exacerbated and symbolically satisfied by the sight of the naked, erotic statuettes made in her likeness. Mary Barbe's dress on the day of her betrothal is designed to cover partially the body in order to heighten its erotic impact, a device echoed in the text itself where the reader is invited to identify with the gaze of a desiring observer, designated by the pronoun 'on' (one), and to imagine what the dress merely implies.

> The dress corresponded exactly to what the cruel girl had intended. . . .
> The bodice was high-necked, but had an unexpected opening between the breasts, which one saw as all the more pink for their contrast with the intense green of the velvet.[11]

The novels conceal, reveal and display the body in strategies designed to maintain the focus on what is also the central narrative concern: the arousal, frustration and possible satisfaction of desire.

In this sense Rachilde's texts obey the rules of the standard erotic narrative in which sexual desire is the focus and its communication to the reader the goal. But most erotic narratives, at least at the end of the nineteenth century, were written by and for men, and thus tended to make active desire a male prerogative and to represent the female sexual role as one of response or submission. This scenario reproduced and endorsed the division of gender roles inscribed in the legal and economic organization of Rachilde's society. The question is, then, since her very authorship of erotic texts represented a transgression of the sexual rules, to what extent do the texts themselves challenge the prevailing normative view of sex and sexuality?

It has already become apparent in the outlining of Rachilde's plots that some reversal of the equation male = subject, female = object is taking place. In fact the reversal of the central structures and tropes of erotic writing is both marked and detailed in these novels. At the narrative level, the role of economic provider and protector is transferred to the female protagonist, so that Raoule de Vénérande plucks Jacques Silvert from sordid poverty to install him as her kept lover in a luxurious apartment, in a situation clearly and provocatively mirroring the more usual scenario of the wealthy man and his mistress. Eliante, the 'Jongleuse', is similarly wealthy and aristocratic, and as the novel closes has succeeded in marrying the impoverished Léon to her niece, thus providing for his future in a manner which evokes the more traditional figure of the ageing male protector.

Paul Richard in *La Marquise de Sade* has all the characteristics of the betrayed and corrupted virgin: he is poor, innocent, romantic and diverted from his honest attempts at self-improvement by a wealthy and cynical seducer, Mary Barbe. Paul suffers from regular and heavy nosebleeds, which hold a curious attraction for Mary: 'Yes, I adore the sight of your blood flowing. Perhaps it's the reason I love you.'[12] This involuntary, debilitating loss of blood contributes to the feminization of the character, since it provides Paul with a figurative capacity for menstruation, construed as a cause or sign of feminine weakness. The financial and cultural inferiority of each male protagonist places him in a position of dependence, in which his only power lies in the capacity to provoke the heroine's desire. The narratives reproduce a very familiar sexual script, but within that script they reverse the distribution of gender roles.

Since she is in the dominant role, the gaze of the desiring subject can be transferred to the female protagonist, which in turn means that the reader is positioned to view the male body as object. This is most radically the case in *Monsieur Vénus*, in which Rachilde focalizes the body of Jacques from the perspective of Raoule's desire in a series of precise reversals of conventionally gendered images. Jacques first appears draped in the artificial flowers he is making, flowers which Raoule has come to buy: 'Around his chest, over the loose smock, hung a garland of wide-petalled roses of flesh-coloured satin touched with deep red, draped between his legs and spiralling back up to his shoulders, curling finally around the collar.'[13] The roses, more commonly used to adorn or to symbolize female beauty, are here strategically positioned ('between his legs') and described ('flesh-coloured satin touched with deep red') to eroticize the male body.

Once installed in the apartment she rents for him, Jacques is completely exposed to Raoule's gaze: his resistance only emphasizes the fact that the gaze (conventionally coded masculine) connotes power, and that to be the passive object of the gaze connotes subordination.[14] In a scene that clearly identifies voyeurism with sexual aggression, Raoule spies on Jacques in his bath, the text detailing the features of his naked body softly lit by candlelight, explicit and sensual in its description and resorting to allusion only before the final taboo of naming the male genitals.

> Between the underarm and a point much lower on the body, she glimpsed tousled golden fronds of hair. Jacques Silvert had been telling the truth – he had hair all over. He would have been quite wrong, however, to swear that this was the only sign of his virility.[15]

Realizing that he is being watched, Jacques cries out and covers himself but then recognizes and accepts his own powerlessness: 'Then, distressed and pale with shame, he let [the bathrobe] slip passively down, for the poor creature had understood.'[16]

In *La Jongleuse* the male body is not displayed in the same way, for though Léon is rendered helpless to realize his desire by Eliante's superior status and will, he remains the subject of desire. But in *La Marquise de Sade* Paul's function is essentially that of prey, seduced rather than seducing: it is Mary Barbe who initiates their relationship and who travels across the city to visit him in his humble room. His reduction to malleable flesh is intensified by the sadistic imagery of the nosebleeds which Mary deliberately provokes: 'Then she would wrap her arms more tightly around him, drunk on the blood that was now smeared over her; . . . each night their passion grew, and she became more intoxicated with this flesh turned to liquid scarlet by their wild embraces.'[17]

Each Rachildean heroine is thus motivated by an intense erotic longing which is sensual, in that it involves the desire to look at and to touch beautiful bodies, but which is also an assertion of power. Rachilde's novels reverse the familiar scenario of man as seducer/ hunter and woman as prey, and make female desire, however rarely satisfied, the narrative's driving force. Raoule pursues her possession of Jacques to the point of engineering his death, so that as the novel ends the living man is replaced by a wax model, adorned with Jacques' own hair, teeth and nails, which she visits by night. Eliante 'vit comme on jouirait' (literally 'lived as one might reach orgasm', *LJ*, p. 130), she is 'the living, suffering poem of a body tormented by strange passions'.[18] Mary Barbe loses Paul when he realizes the extent of her sadism, but as the novel ends she still haunts *fin-de-siècle* Paris in a frustrated search for sexual fulfilment. Women are clearly established as subjects of desire, but as Jacques Silvert innocently asks Raoule in the opening scene of *Monsieur Vénus*, 'Madame désire . . .?' What, precisely, do these women desire? or to echo Freud's question, what does (the Rachildean) woman want?

What they emphatically do not desire is heterosexual intercourse. Each novel makes it clear that this is what they are *expected* to want, once their behaviour has placed them outside the category of the virtuous woman. Raoule's relationship with Jacques takes place against the background of her courtship by a more conventional suitor, the soldier Raittolbe – and Raittolbe seeks above all to become Raoule's lover. Jacques himself at first interprets her sexual advances as an invitation to rape: 'And he thought that what this woman wanted was to be taken by force.'[19] But though Raoule thinks of Jacques as her 'bel instrument de plaisir' (her 'lovely instrument of pleasure', *MV*, p. 34), she makes it quite clear that he may not 'become her lover', subjecting him instead to forms of pleasure which remain unspecified but which exclude his 'possessing' her 'toute et de tout coeur' ('completely and fully', *MV*, p. 104).

When Léon is invited into Eliante's carriage and taken home for supper, he assumes his desires are to be gratified, but Eliante too is opposed to penetrative sex: 'I do not need human caresses to achieve pleasure . . . Physical union disgusts me, destroys my strength, and I find no fulfilment in it.'[20] There, before him, in a curious and highly sensual passage, Eliante reaches orgasm by embracing the smooth form of a tall alabaster vase. Léon is horrified: 'This is scandalous! There . . . in front of me . . . without me? It's abominable!', and in subsequent letters and conversations with Eliante he tries to explain the episode by his own failure to be sexually dominant, redefining Eliante's apparent sexual self-sufficiency as mere compensation or as a strategy designed to seduce him.

If I had beaten you on the night of the great deception, there in front of the vase, you would love me without so much fuss.[21]

I can only interpret your resistance, Eliante, as a desire to be raped.[22]

But Eliante does not want to be forced, she seeks an unviolated and autonomous sexual pleasure: 'to be happy alone, with my arms folded across my chest and my legs hermetically joined',[23] and when, at the novel's conclusion, Léon believes he has finally reached his goal, it is only to discover that Eliante has substituted another, willing female partner for herself and has chosen death instead.

On her wedding night Mary Barbe announces to her horrified husband that their relations will be strictly on her terms and will involve no risk of conceiving a child. In place of virginal modesty, Rachilde's young bride expresses a well-informed repugnance for marital relations: '. . . do not count on my losing control due to passion. I have a horror of men in general and you are particularly far from my ideal',[24] and rejects their implied corollary of motherhood. Like Eliante, Mary Barbe insists on her own self-sufficiency, refusing the notion of female desire as a lack, as a need for completion by man or by the production of a child: 'I do not want to grow ugly, nor to suffer pain. What is more *my being itself is enough*, and if I could make the world end with me, I would . . .'.[25]

This insistence on the primacy of the erotic, combined with a scornful refusal of heterosexual relations in their commonly accepted form, derives in part from the Decadent refusal of the natural in favour of the cerebral and the artificial. The figure of the voraciously sexual woman, in whom the feminine desire to nurture is replaced by a will to inflict pain, is also part of the repertoire of male-authored Decadent texts, appearing for example in Catulle Mendès's *La Première maîtresse* (1887) and recurring in Barbey d'Aurevilly's stories *Les Diaboliques* (1874). But only in Rachilde's texts does the monstrous woman become the focalizer of the narrative, whose quest for fulfilment outside the terms of acceptable female identity is the central dynamic of the story. In *La Première maîtresse* or *Les Diaboliques*, such women appear as evil forces who block or distort the development of the hero, or who must be destroyed in order that he may thrive. In *Monsieur Vénus*, *La Marquise de Sade* and *La Jongleuse*, the evil woman herself becomes the subject of the tale and, viewed from within, her motivations and goals rather than her destructive power over others become the focus of the narrative. Where most Decadent texts represent female sexuality solely in terms of male desires and fears, Rachilde's novels imply the need to pose different questions: what does heterosexual intercourse mean for a woman? What sacrifices or anxieties might it involve? How is female sexual desire conventionally constructed and what might it mean outside the terms of current social orthodoxies?

In late nineteenth-century France sexual relations between men and women were enmeshed within a gendered structure of power which determined very different sexual experiences for each sex. For the male partner, intercourse signified the satisfaction of what was deemed to be an instinctive and positive need, a cultural belief illustrated by the common practice of encouraging middle-class teenage boys to visit brothels.[26] The satisfaction of male desires might have to be gained by the overcoming of female resistance, through seduction or force, since in many circumstances it was in women's interest to avoid intercourse. For her, to engage in a sexual relationship before marriage meant loss of reputation and thus of the 'capital' of virginity, and sex in or outside marriage might carry the danger of a possibly unwanted pregnancy. Thus the female role in heterosexual relations was often construed in terms of self-giving, self-abandonment (*se donner, s'abandonner*), a loss or gift of the self; male sexuality was associated rather with a series of active verbs: *posséder, vaincre*, an affirmation and supplementation of the self.

Rachilde's heroines share a strength of will and a sense of their own importance which is incompatible with self-abandonment. It is precisely those connotations of defeat and possession which they reject in refusing intercourse; thus on the verge of assenting to an assignation in a hotel with the conventionally masculine Raittolbe, Raoule suddenly changes course: 'once faced with the prospect of *sacrifice*, the body . . . rebelled'.[27] Instead she visits Jacques, whose lack of financial and social power ensure that he loves her 'out of gratitude and submission' (*MV*, p. 107), allowing her both to avoid intercourse and to exercise the control and authority normally gendered masculine. The scene of the alabaster vase in *La Jongleuse*, like the wedding night scene in *La Marquise de Sade*, represents a provocative rewriting of a conventional scenario. Léon is invited home by a beautiful woman and anticipates the satisfaction of his desire for her: 'I want you, quite simply that. And I shall have you, that is quite certain';[28] but, far from a display of resistance preceding surrender, Eliante's behaviour proves to be the expression of a desire which specifically rejects 'normal' heterosexual relations. Here, as in the other novels, fundamental male assumptions about female sexuality are articulated only so that they may be refuted.

On the one hand, then, heterosexual intercourse is rejected or avoided by Rachilde's heroines because, within their culture, the act connotes female submission and loss of control, male assertion of power. But there is a further dimension to their refusal: each text implies female disappointment with a male sexuality structured as arousal/erection, leading to orgasm followed by rapid detumescence, an 'economy of pleasure' incompatible with and frequently indifferent to the pleasure of a female partner. This degree of precision about the mechanisms of male and female sexuality is extremely unusual in a female-authored nineteenth-century text, but, though to some extent linguistically veiled, it is a recurring element in the novels.

Raoule, declaring herself representative of the female élite of her era, condemns the inadequacy of men as sexual partners: 'The brutal ones are frustrating, the impotent ones are degrading, and *they* are all in such a rush to get their pleasure.'[29] Jacques' desire to consummate their relationship 'naturally' provokes in her a weary sense of familiarity: 'she knew, word for word, what nature would say through Jacques' voice . . .',[30] for she recognizes in his plea to 'have her completely and all to himself' (*MV*, p. 104) the prelude to a satisfaction which she will not share: 'And when they had all cried and moaned, when they had had their dearest wishes granted, as the expression goes, they all became smugly satisfied, all equally vulgar with their satisfied senses.'[31]

Eliante, 'the juggler', refuses conventional sexual relations in favour of an eroticization of everyday life, a mode of existence which her juggling exemplifies and symbolizes: 'She took an absolute, naive delight in the pleasure she gave them, and she needed the sharp desire of the spectators' eyes on her, she needed that atmosphere charged with love.'[32] Eliante juggles with knives, keeping death at bay by her skill, enjoying both the active pleasure of control and dexterity and the thrill of her audience's attention: '. . . she juggled to amuse herself. One could feel vibrating within her another blade, both perfidious and passive.'[33] Her sustained sensual 'vibration' is compared to Léon's insistence on the need to satisfy and thus provisionally terminate his desire.

Mary Barbe too opposes to Paul's impatience for sexual satisfaction a constant deferral of pleasure: 'I am true love, love which refuses to reach its end!'[34] In each of these novels male desire is a condition of the erotic scenario, heightening the sexual excitement of the heroine and of the text, yet its fulfilment cannot be reconciled with female pleasure. In the recurring implication of an incompatibility between a masculine economy of pleasure, centred on the arousal and gratification of a specific desire, and a more diffuse and less goal-oriented feminine desire, Rachilde points towards French feminists' formulations of these differences almost a century later. Rachilde's heroines live out the difficulty of reconciling what Hélène Cixous terms a 'masculine sexuality [which] gravitates around the penis . . .

and which is inscribed only within boundaries'[35] with a feminine sexuality less clearly focused and structured, more diffuse and open-ended. If Rachilde's male protagonists display, in Irigaray's words, 'the polarization of desire on only one pleasure', her women characters oppose to this 'the multiple nature of female desire'.[36]

There are radical implications in Rachilde's representation of heroines who want intense sexual experience but refuse the terms of existing sexual contracts. The subversive power of such narratives is attenuated, though, by Rachilde's determination to observe the codes of Decadence, and by that refusal of feminism later to be articulated in a lengthy polemical essay entitled 'Why I am not a feminist' (*Pourquoi je ne suis pas féministe*, 1928). Though it is tempting to read Raoule de Vénérande, Eliante Donalger and Mary Barbe as representative of a collective and well-justified female dissatisfaction with existing heterosexual relations, Rachilde repeatedly characterizes them as outside the norm, as monstrously unnatural exceptions to their sex.

Several devices contribute to this effect. Secondary characters are used to deliver authoritative diagnoses, like the doctor in *Monsieur Vénus*, called in to treat Raoule as she reaches puberty, who pronounces her to be 'A special case. . . . A creature of extremes! She will either become a nun, or a monster!'[37] The omniscient narrator also comments directly, defining the heroine's character in terms of exceptional evil, as s/he does in the passage immediately following the doctor's comment: 'That was ten years ago, at the time when this story began . . ., and Raoule had not become a nun . . .'[38] or in *La Marquise de Sade* where the narrator, describing Mary as a child, predicts her future sadism as an inalienable destiny: 'Ah! how the little boy, asleep in some distant corner of the world, must have shivered in his dreams! That little boy who, when he became a man and she a woman, would be fatally destined for her.'[39]

Monstrosity is further signified by physical characteristics – Mary Barbe's peculiarly long thumbs, her dark eyebrows meeting to form a single line (a feature she shares with Raoule), Eliante's singularly white skin and sinuous movements. Physical description is reinforced by implicitly violent imagery: the train of Eliante's dress 'forming silky curves like the ripples left by the fall of a body into deep water',[40] and her hair so tightly drawn back that her ears are blood-red 'as if they were actually bleeding under the weight of a sharp helmet'.[41] Whenever the heroines are focalized externally they are viewed as intrinsically evil, and their search for sexual pleasure is characterized as sinister and inexplicable.

But despite Rachilde's determined designation of her characters as *femmes fatales* whom the reader is to view with fascinated horror, the fact that the narratives are partially focalized from their perspective works against any simple view of them as merely monsters. It is patently clear in each of the novels that, despite their wealth and class status, the heroines live extremely restricted lives in which marriage is the only available path to a limited independence. Both Raoule and Mary Barbe are highly educated, but by virtue of their sex there is no possibility of this leading to any career or activity. The men of their own class are represented as arrogant and complacent, so that whilst the selection of a male lover disadvantaged and *feminized* by poverty and low-class status has little to recommend it as a political solution, this device in the novels does foreground the parallels and the complex interaction between hierarchies of class and gender.

It is in *La Marquise de Sade* that the narrative specifically traces the origins of the heroine's repugnance for 'normal' heterosexual relations and her association of sexual pleasure with the infliction of pain. Like most of Rachilde's writing the novel is overladen with the trappings of the macabre, the letting and drinking of blood being a recurrent motif, and the heroine being repeatedly characterized, in a heavy-handed fashion, as an aristocratic incarnation of evil, misplaced in a mediocre age: 'Had she found herself on a throne she would have done great deeds, but to be one atom amongst all the other atoms who made up this gangrenous country did not seem to her to be a mission in life . . .'[42] But the novel opens with a powerful and significant scene which founds Mary's sexual development very clearly in gendered power relations.

The seven-year-old Mary accompanies her aunt, Tulotte, on an outing to collect a fortifying remedy for Mary's sick mother. Mary believes this to be milk, but it is in fact blood from the slaughterhouse, prescribed to fortify a weak constitution. Believing herself to be at a farm, Mary enjoys visiting the animals, identifying particularly with the little calves whose pathetic plight, though at this point unknown to Mary, is emphasized by the tone of the narration: 'The smallest calves moaned in such quavering little voices that she took them for children, like herself'.[43] Despite her aunt's strict instructions, Mary follows her secretly into the slaughterhouse, where she sees the butcher brutally kill and bleed one of the cattle, a sight so violent and horrible that she faints.

The scene has many of the overtones of transgression, voyeurism and dream associated with the Freudian primal scene, in which the child first sees or dreams sexual relations between their parents. Mary enters the slaughterhouse through a 'sinister hole', aware that she is disobeying a rule ('She thought that she was doing wrong' (*MS*, p. 13)) and watches from the position of an unseen observer, guilty and horrified, the scene distorted by her emotion to dream-like proportions: 'It seemed to the little girl that the scene was blown up to an extraordinary size; the whole slaughter house became a single, horned head, smashed and shattered, grinding its teeth and spurting blood on to her white dress.'[44] This is the founding scene of her development in the sense that she identifies herself with the animals threatened by the huge figure of the butcher, clutching her neck as the blow falls on the ox, and identifies the butcher with men as a sex. '(The) man! . . . I'm frightened of (the) man' ('L'homme' in French translates both as 'the man' and as 'man' as a species or sex),[45] repeats the delirious Mary during the fever that follows this shock, and her friend the cat seems to answer her: 'If you wanted . . . I could teach you to scratch him with your claws, the man who kills oxen . . . man, king of the world!'[46]

The scene has powerful sexual connotations, both in its implication of adult secrets discovered and in the imagery of the blood which spatters Mary's white dress. The killing of the animal is experienced as castration, as a brutal ending to the heroine's childish dreams of omnipotence, and the revelation of her subordinate status as a female excluded from the category of the 'kings of the world'. It is a moment of loss of innocence, and the rest of Mary's childhood will confirm the lesson of a world centred on male power, the legitimacy of which rests finally on physical strength and on violence. Mary's father, who bitterly resents the fact that she is not a son, responds with violence not only to her acts of disobedience, but also to her tears or illness. The birth of a baby brother not only brings about the death of Mary's mother, but also displaces her from the affections and the attention of a household henceforth completely devoted to the needs of the son and heir: 'His deafening yells asserted the privileges of his sex; the three women of the household gave in to that inexhaustible rage. One would bring him a rattle, another some sugar, the third her breast.'[47]

The child's privileged maleness attracts all the nurturing and love of which Mary herself is deprived. Man is the *roi du monde* whom she resents as a rival and fears as a brutal master. When she first forms a relationship with a boy, she is careful to select the peasant Sirocco, whose poverty and lack of status cancel out the superiority of his gender. When the adult Mary chooses lovers weaker than herself, she plays out again the brutal primal scene, with herself in the controlling role. The moment in the slaughterhouse is re-enacted as Mary's lover bleeds profusely, and the blood stains her clothing. Her erotic pleasure arises from the transgressive reversal of the original scene, as she becomes torturer rather than victim.

The corollary of male power is female subservience. When she is alive, Mary's mother is a feeble, ineffectual figure, whose lack of any proper status or activity within the military world of Mary's childhood is signified by her constant illness. She shows neither interest in nor understanding of her daughter, so that when she dies, leaving in her stead the hated baby brother who is to usurp Mary's place, this is only the last in a series of maternal betrayals. There are no good mothers in Rachilde's world: Raoule de Vénérande's parents are dead, and in the mother's place there is only a stupidly pious old aunt; Eliante is orphaned and exiled from her native land. If Rachilde's unorthodox, and in some senses subversive, portrayal of sex lacks any dimension of warmth or tenderness – qualities associated with the maternal – then this is surely connected with the absence of any positive characterization of mothers and the maternal body in her work.

It is in the context of the development of female sexuality that Simone de Beauvoir briefly discusses *Monsieur Vénus* in *Le Deuxième Sexe*. Beauvoir argues that the novel demonstrates the difficulty, for a girl, of making the transition from cherishing the soft, rounded mother's body, her first object of desire and pleasure, to desiring the harder, coarser male body. The transference of desire is difficult on two counts: firstly because early sensuality has a determining effect on the tactile preferences of both sexes; secondly because female as well as male infants first experience eroticism as active desire, and display a 'prehensile', 'possessive' tendency, which the girl will be expected to renounce in order to become the passive object of male desire. Rachilde's heroine, according to Beauvoir, avoids this transition by choosing a man who looks and feels like a woman, and whom she can treat like a woman, thus refusing to relinquish the aggressive eroticism of childhood.[48]

Beauvoir's analysis can be extended to Rachilde's heroines in general, and developed further. It is true that they are drawn to men whose physical attributes have a feminine quality – 'chairs blonds' ('blonde flesh', *MV*, p. 54), 'rondeur solide' ('a sturdy roundness', *MV*, p. 55), 'peau de blond, toute tendre encore sur le cou' ('fair skin, still soft at the neck', *MS*, p. 206). But since each heroine has been abandoned early by the death of the mother, since there is no positive image of the maternal to counteract the degraded status their culture attributes to the feminine, their reaction to these feminized males is not simply one of desire but also one of troubled anger and sadism. When the vulnerability of Jacques' soft white body is heightened by the scars of a beating inflicted by Raittolbe, Raoule at first responds with passionate concern, but this is soon replaced by the desire to inflict further pain and to punish him for his beauty and helplessness: 'All her instinctive human anger, which she had tried to annihilate in her metamorphosis to this new being, now awoke, and the thirst for the blood that flowed over these twisted limbs replaced the pleasures of her fierce love.'[49] The passivity and roundedness of Jacques' body is what attracts Raoule, just as Paul's fair, delicate appearance appeals to Mary Barbe, but because they fear and reject the feminine in themselves these qualities also arouse the heroines' anger.

In Rachilde's female protagonists we can posit an unconscious but significantly recurring connection between the early loss of maternal love, and of the maternal body, and an attraction to sensually feminine bodies as objects of desire. But the negative characterization of mothers, and of the novels' other secondary female characters, means that this attraction is shadowed by feelings of contempt and hatred. Since there are no positive images of mothers, or indeed of feminine identity, on offer to the heroines of Rachilde's texts, whose dealings with the maternal afford them only a sense of betrayal and deprivation, they have no conception of an alternative source of power to that of the father. Thus the heroines' options are limited: accept their own subservience, or usurp the masculine role within the limited sphere available, that of sexual relations with a male partner who is both physically and socially feminized.

Neither of these options constitutes a real threat to patriarchal power, for whilst the reversal of sexual roles does imply a refusal of conventional definitions of female sexuality, a woman's domination of a weak man here simply confirms his inadequacy as a male. The model of eroticism as a relationship based on power and subservience is not disturbed. There is no space for any pleasurable sense of dependency, or merging of the self with the other – aspects of eroticism which reproduce, positively, infantile relations with the mother. Desire remains locked in angry self-assertion, in contempt and fear of the loss of self.

Eroticism is thus inseparable from the acceptance or defiance of male authority. Love or desire between women is either absent from the narratives or is evoked only to be brutally refused, as in *La Marquise de Sade*, where Mary Barbe engineers her own seduction by her husband's mistress, to be secretly watched by the husband himself, then turns on the naked Madame de Liol and brands her with a red-hot poker. This scene contrasts interestingly with Colette's later and very different treatment of a similar episode in *Claudine en ménage*, when Claudine's husband sets up the seduction of his wife by his mistress, but discovers to his confusion that the women's relationship takes on a life and intensity which excludes him. Rachilde's work is closed to any such possibility of sexual or emotional relationships which positively redefine the feminine and marginalize masculine power.

At the end of each novel the limits of the heroine's revolt are signified by her defeat. It is the masculine Raittolbe, alarmed by Jacques' seductive beauty and the threat this poses to his own sexual identity, who kills Jacques and thus reduces Raoule's conquest from that of a feminized man to that of a mechanical dummy. Mary Barbe ends *La Marquise de Sade* as a lonely, sinister figure who haunts the meeting places of male transvestites, fantasizing murder and, significantly, drinking blood just like her sickly, powerless mother at the beginning of the novel. Eliante chooses death rather than risk a relationship with Léon which could only end in her defeat.

There are radical elements in Rachilde's literary treatment of the erotic. If the youth and sex of author and heroines were such important elements in the marketing of her early novels, this was because prevailing ideologies of gender made the conjunction of femininity and eroticism in itself excitingly wicked. The novels scandalized further by their precise, provocative reversals of familiar sexual scenarios, turning the male body into the object of a female desire which drives and fills the narrative, and implying a discrepancy between masculine economies of pleasure and what women might really want. But though Rachilde's narratives often seem fuelled by an anger that can be read as feminist, and though they clearly establish the origins of female sadism in the oppressive conditions of women's lives, she refused the more radical implications of her own stories, 'disowning' heroines by designating them as monsters, and maintaining intact a model of gender which devalued the feminine and privileged the masculine. Rachilde's vision of eroticism is finally cruel and limited, excluding any dimension of reciprocity or trust, tenderness or love. It provides a fascinating commentary on sexual relations in late nineteenth-century France, and a complex representation of the relationship between ideology, desire and sexual pleasure.

Notes

1. 'Toute représentation de la jouissance s'inscrit dans des rapports sociaux historiquement constitués et ne peut donc que se referer, implicitement ou non, à une norme idéologique. Quand bien même ce serait pour la transgresser.' Anne-Marie Dardigna, *Les Châteaux d'Eros ou l'infortune du sexe des femmes*, Paris, 1981, p. 45.
2. 'Ce qui est tout à fait délicat dans la perversité de ce livre, c'est qu'il a été écrit par une jeune fille de 20 ans.' Preface to *Monsieur Vénus*, Paris, 1977, pp. 5–6.
3. 'une pensionnaire d'allures sobres et réservées, très pale . . . une

vraie jeune fille, un peu mince, un peu frêle', ibid., p. 6.
4. 'exciter et aviver des frissons', ibid., p. 17.
5. T. Zeldin, *France 1848–1945*, vol. I, *Ambition, Love, Politics*, Oxford, 1973, p. 306.
6. For example the popular manual *Hygiène et philosophie du mariage* by A. Debray, which went through 173 editions between 1848 and 1888, 'was quite specific about women enjoying intercourse as much as men' within the context of marriage. Zeldin, ibid., p. 296.
7. For a full, closely argued analysis of Decadence within the social and political context of late nineteenth-century France, see Jennifer Birkett, *The Sins of the Fathers: Decadence in France 1870– 1914*, London and New York, 1986.
8. 'J'ai toujours agi en *individu*, ne songeant pas à fonder une société ou a bouleverser celle qui existait.' *Pourquoi je ne suis pas féministe*, Paris, 1928, p. 6.
9. Rachilde maintained the themes and style of Decadence long after the literary mode had passed. In the view of her biographer and critic Claude Dauphiné, 'Le monde de Rachilde, dans son ensemble, apparaît volontairement figé', *Rachilde*, Paris, 1991, p. 11.
10. 'Deux jumelles se tournant le dos, celle-là très nue . . . celle-ci merveilleusement habillée' (*LJ*, p. 26).
11. 'Cette robe incarnait parfaitement l'idée qu'elle avait eue, la cruelle fille! . . . Ce corsage était montant et cependant s'ouvrait par une échancrure inattendue entre les deux seins, qu'on s'imaginait plus roses à cause de l'intensité de ce velours vert' (*MS*, p. 196). I have kept the rather clumsy 'one' in the English translation in order to demonstrate the presence in the text of the desiring observer.
12. 'Oui, j'ai un bonheur à le voir couler, je t'assure. Peut-être je t'aime à cause de cela' (*MS*, p. 234).
13. 'Autour de son torse, sur la blouse flottante, courait en spirale une guirlande de roses, des roses fort larges de satin chair velouté de grenat, qui lui passaient entre les jambes, filaient jusqu'aux épaules et venaient s'enrouler au col' (*MV*, p. 24).
14. In an influential essay on the construction of the gaze in cinema, for example, Laura Mulvey argues that the active pleasure of looking has come to be coded as a masculine activity. 'In a world ordered by sexual imbalance, pleasure in looking has been split between active/male, passive/female. The determining male gaze projects its fantasy on to the female figure which is styled accordingly. In their traditional exhibitionist role, women are

Diana Holmes

simultaneously looked at and displayed, with their appearance coded for strong visual and erotic impact so that they can be said to connote to-be-looked-at-ness' ('Visual Pleasure and Narrative Cinema' (1975) in Laura Mulvey, *Visual and Other Pleasures*, Basingstoke and London, 1989, p. 19). I would argue that this gendered construction of the look was equally present in narrative fiction, but that in Rachilde's fiction the active pleasure in looking is frequently, and unusually, the prerogative of the female protagonist. In a 1981 article: 'Afterthoughts on "Visual Pleasure and Narrative Cinema" inspired by King Vidor's *Duel in the Sun*', (also in *Visual and Other Pleasures*) Mulvey develops and partially revises her thesis without, however, proposing any fundamental revision of the equation between the look, erotic power and a masculine subject position.

15. 'Entre la coupure de l'aisselle et beaucoup plus bas que cette coupure, dépassaient quelques frisons d'or s'ébouriffant. Jacques Silvert disait vrai, il en avait partout. Il se serait trompé, par exemple, en jurant que cela seul témoignait de sa virilité' (*MV*, p. 55).

16. 'Ensuite, navré, tout pâle de honte, il laissa glisser [le peignoir] passivement, car il comprenait, le pauvre' (*MV*, p. 57).

17. 'Alors elle l'enlaçait plus étroitement, s'enivrant du sang qui la barbouillait; . . . chaque nuit voyait s'augmenter leur passion et ce vertige de la chair se liquéfiant, vermeille, sous les étreintes sauvages' (*MS*, pp. 252–3).

18. 'le poème vivant et souffrant d'un corps tourmenté de passions bizarres' (*LJ*, p. 242).

19. 'Et il pensa que cette femme voulait absolument qu'on lui sautât dessus' (*MV*, p. 54). 'Sauter dessus' means to grab, to leap on, but the implied meaning here is that Raoule is inviting rape.

20. 'Je n'ai pas besoin de la caresse humaine pour arriver au spasme . . . J'ai le dégoût de l'union, qui détruit ma force, je n'y découvre aucune plénitude' (*LJ*, p. 49).

21. 'Si je t'avais battue la nuit du grand jeu, devant la potiche, tu m'aimerais sans tant d'histoires' (*LJ*, p. 91).

22. 'Je ne peux traduire votre résistance, Eliante, que par un désir de viol' (*LJ*, p. 99).

23. 'être heureuse toute seule, les bras bien croisés sur ma poitrine, les jambes jointes hermétiquement' (*LJ*, p. 167).

24. '. . . ne comptez pas sur une passion désordonnée, j'ai l'horreur de l'homme en général, et en particulier vous n'êtes pas mon idéal' (*MS*, p. 213).

25. 'Je ne veux ni enlaidir, ni souffrir. De plus, *je suis assez, EN*

ETANT, et si je pouvais finir le monde avec moi, je le finirais' (*MS*, p. 214).

26. See Zeldin, *France 1848–1945*, p. 306. On Thursday afternoons when there was no school Parisian *lycéens* formed a major part of the brothels' clientèle.

27. 'une fois en présence du *sacrifice*, le corps . . . venait de se révolter' (*MV*, p. 71, my italics).

28. 'je vous veux, tout simplement. Je vous aurai, ça c'est sûr . . .' (*LJ*, p. 42).

29. 'Les brutaux exaspèrent, les impuissants avilissent et *ils* sont, les uns et les autres, si pressés de jouir' (*MV*, p. 87).

30. 'elle savait, mot à mot, ce que la nature dirait par la voix de Jacques . . .' (*MV*, p. 105).

31. 'Et quand ils avaient tous bien crié, quand ils avaient tous enfin obtenu la réalisation de leurs voeux les plus chers, selon l'éternelle expression, ils devenaient les assouvis béats qui sont tous également vulgaires dans l'apaisement des sens' (*MV*, p. 105).

32. 'Elle s'amusait naivement, absolument, du plaisir original qu'elle leur procurait, et il lui fallait aussi le désir aigu des regards pointés sur elle, toute la vibration d'une atmosphère chargée d'électricité amoureuse' (*LJ*, p. 144).

33. 'elle jonglait pour s'amuser. On sentait vibrer en elle comme une autre lame à la fois perfide et passive' (*LJ*, p. 143).

34. 'Je suis le véritable amour, celui qui ne veut pas finir!' (*MS*, p. 233).

35. Hélène Cixous, 'The Laugh of the Medusa', in Maggie Humm (ed.), *Feminisms*, Hemel Hempstead, 1992, pp. 201–2.

36. 'La polarisation sur une seule jouissance' as opposed to 'ce multiple du désir . . . féminin', Luce Irigaray, *Ce sexe qui n'en est pas un*, Paris, 1977, p. 29.

37. 'Un cas spécial. . . . Pas de milieu! Ou nonne, ou monstre!' (*MV*, pp. 40–1).

38. 'Il y avait dix ans de cela, au moment où commence cette histoire . . ., et Raoule n'était pas nonne . . .' (*MV*, p. 41).

39. 'Oh! comme dut, au fond d'un rêve, tressaillir le petit garçon dormant en quelque coin du monde, bien loin d'elle. Ce petit garçon qui devenu homme, quand elle deviendrait femme, lui serait fatalement destiné' (*MS*, p. 55).

40. 'formant les mêmes cercles moirés que l'on voit se former dans une eau profonde, le soir, après la chute d'un corps' (*LJ*, p. 26).

41. 'paraiss(ant) vraiment saigner sous le poids d'un casque coupant' (*LJ*, p. 26).

42. 'Elle se serait trouvée sur un trône qu'elle aurait fait de bonnes

choses, mais rouler en atome parmi tous les atomes de ce pays gangrené ne lui paraissait pas une mission . . .' (*MS*, pp. 288–9).

43. 'Les plus petits veaux gémissaient d'une voix si chevrotante qu'elle les croyait être des enfants, semblables à elle' (*MS*, p. 12).

44. 'Il sembla à la petite fille que cette scène prenait des proportions phénoménales; elle s'imagina que tout le bâtiment de l'abattoir était une seule tête cornue, fracassée, grinçant des dents et lui lançant des fusées de sang sur sa robe blanche' (*MS*, p. 14).

45. 'L'homme! . . . j'ai peur de l'homme!' (*MS*, p. 27).

46. 'Si tu voulais . . . je t'apprendrais à griffer l'homme, l'homme qui tue les boeufs . . . l'homme, le roi du monde!' (*MS*, p. 30).

47. 'La priorité de son sexe s'affirmait dans des cris étourdissants; les trois femmes de la maison s'inclinaient devant cette rage inépuisable. L'une apportait un hochet, celle-ci du sucre, celle-là son sein' (*MS*, p. 102).

48. Simone de Beauvoir, *Le Deuxième Sexe*, vol. 2, Paris, 1949, p. 137.

49. 'Toutes les colères de la nature humaine, qu'elle avait essayé de réduire à néant dans son être métamorphosé, se réveillaient à la fois, et le soif de ce sang qui coulait sur des membres tordus remplaçaient maintenant les plaisirs de son féroce amour' (*MV*, p. 145).

– 2 –

Colette and the Hidden Woman:
Sexuality, Silence, Subversion

Margaret Callander

Colette has been viewed with some annoyance by committed feminists, because she consistently evaded making general political or social statements about the position of women or joining women's movements or making firm gestures of solidarity. This was all of a piece with her life-long refusal to pronounce overtly upon any kind of public issue, or even to confess to having any general or abstract ideas at all. However, what she did do was to create a rich textual web of female sexuality, in which she often shies away from direct, explicit commentary but which is none the less highly telling and, on occasion, subversive in its reworking of gender norms and relations. Through a series of artistic projects, Colette articulates a surprisingly varied sequence of erotic discourses (focusing on male as well as female sexuality), and these I would like to deploy in parallel in this chapter. Colette is often assumed to have a single artistic and very personal mode of writing, but her styles of erotic discourse turn out to be most diverse. Examples of them considered here range from publications of the 1890s to those of the 1940s, cover many genres, and feature male as well as female voices.

Approaches to Sexuality

In fact, Colette's role as commentator on and narrator of the erotic is always marked by paradox, reticence and sometimes apparent contradictions. Men's and women's sexuality is constantly being defined according to timeless traditional norms, reinforced by animal imagery and metaphors of hunting and siege. In *Le Blé en herbe* (1923), for example, Philippe is the predestined male 'born hunter and pre-destined deceiver',[1] Vinca shares 'the survival-mission, inherited by all females'.[2] This writing mode suggests a fatalistic reversion to stereotypes, diminishing the free will of the characters and sealing an inevitable compliance with established patterns. But the shifting surface of Colette's writing also displays fluctuating gender identities and behaviour, and unexpected responses to new situations. The freedom bestowed upon the adolescents of *Le Blé en herbe* by the fact that they have not yet acceded to adult eroticism allows them to play the whole gamut of roles, so that Vinca moves from tomboy to pliant or dominant female, Phil from comrade to leader to captive.

To childhood and early adolescence is attributed an exciting androgynous energy and freedom. 'You can have no idea what a queen of the land I was at twelve years of age . . . Ah! how you would have loved me when I was twelve and how I miss this self.' So says the 'Colette' narrator as she dialogues with the fictional 'Claudine' of her own novels. Puberty is not so much access to the new, therefore, as loss and diminishment – notably for the female (desiring) subject. 'Alas, Claudine, I have lost almost all of that, so as to become after all nothing but a woman.'[3]

The dialogue referred to in the previous paragraph is contained in a sketch called 'Le Miroir' (in *Les Vrilles de la vigne*, 1908). This reminds us that the mirror and its figurations, an omnipresent motif in all of Colette's writing, play a key role in her evocations of female sexuality and desire. The mirror is used narcissistically by a number of Colette's 'amoureuses' who seek to verify, consolidate or discover their identities. The Renée of *La Vagabonde* (1911) expects from 'that painted mentor who gazes at me from the other side of the looking-glass'[4] a lucid intimation of the realities of her situation: a situation predicated upon what Christina Angelfors describes as a 'kind of thraldom that is apparently voluntary'.[5] The Julie of *Julie de Carneilhan* (1941) re-selects and recomposes an elective image of herself: 'In front of a looking-glass in the hall, she put on a certain expression, a sort of contraction of the nostrils, to which she was especially attached. It accentuated, she maintained, the "wild animal" side of her character.'[6] But the most striking direct uses of the mirror itself are those that reveal the ravaging power of sexuality. For Philippe, his erotic encounter with Mme Dalleray (*Le Blé en herbe*) produces a gender-reversal witnessed in a mirror ('He saw . . . those pathetic features, less like those of a man than those of a bruised young girl'[7]), and for Léa in *Chéri* (1920) the mirror reveals the distraught defeated woman abandoned by her lover: 'An old woman, out of breath, repeated her movements in the long pier-glass, and Léa wondered what she could have in common with that crazy creature.'[8]

Related to the scenes of *dédoublement* contained in the specular episodes discussed above are the externalized forms that female sexual desire is given. Renée imagines a physical and emotional escape from the stifling tunnel-vision of sexual passion, but sees her way as being literally barred by her own desiring body.

> But how to achieve it? Everything is against me. The first obstacle I run into is the female body lying there, which bars my way, a voluptuous body with closed eyes, deliberately blind, stretched out and ready to perish rather than leave the place where its joy lies. That woman there, that brute bent on pleasure, is I myself.[9]

The heavy languor of sensuality evoked here is often elsewhere rendered as the 'entrave', the leash or tether that restrains the woman and likens her to a pet or captive animal. More insidious, however, for Renée is the plaintive cry of need: 'Shall I also be able to overcome the lost child, a hundred times more dangerous than that greedy beast, who trembles inside me, weak and nervous and ready to stretch out her arms and implore: "Don't leave me alone!".'[10]

A third image refers to the traditional one of the pagan deity, powerful, alien and mysterious, thus completing an essentialist scenario in which the woman is marked out as victim by being identified with desire: 'Desire, that imperious demi-god, that unleashed faun who gambols round love and does not obey love.'[11] Thus the woman feels subjected to a force that blots out individual feminine identity: 'A female I was and, for better or worse, a female I find myself to be.'[12]

The images evoked here represent various facets of woman's sexuality for Colette, the darkly erotic, the nurturing, and the amorally vital. In spite of the use of the dialogue form – Colette's favoured mode – most of these perceptions are determinedly solipsistic. Even within the highly stylized exchanges which punctuate Colette's writings, if a 'Colette' persona is present she keeps her counsel, remaining content simply to draw conclusions, or to suggest inferences to the reader. Moreover, most characters' fears and insights are not shared in any verbal form with the partner who has inspired them.

The Centrality of Silence

In Colette's universe, there is always some kind of silencing or masking going on. Sexuality remains intrinsically mysterious, and a paradigmatic image of its mystery is that of 'The Hidden Woman', the initial story in the book of that name. A husband and wife agree that they will not attend a fancy-dress ball, but secretly both do so. The shock of revelation is suffered by the husband alone, as he watches his beloved embracing a stranger and discovers her alarming alterity while she savours 'the monstrous pleasure of being alone, free, honest, in her native brutality, of being the one who is unknown, forever solitary and without shame, whom a little mask and a hermetic costume had restored to her irremediable solitude and her immodest innocence'.[13] Here sexuality and the need for an autonomous integrity are linked to the desire for a private defensive space, and part of the self-protection is silence.

What is the range of the erotic reticences and suppressions that operate in Colette's writing? There are the silences of her characters, her own silences as actor and writer, and those silences that inhere in her forms of discourse. In her youth her mother Sido, whom Colette often takes as a moral example, treated sexuality with a mixture of frankness and decorum. She would retain a pregnant servant in her household, whilst attempting to protect her child from too early a contact with, for instance, the feverish atmosphere and the innuendoes of a village wedding feast, with the sly and knowing glances at the marriage bed. When the placid people-centred family dog turns into a vengeful jealous projectile the young Colette is disturbed.

> 'Oh! Toutouque! Toutouque!' I would find no other words in which to express my dismay, my alarm, and my astonishment at seeing an evil power, whose very name was unknown to my ten years, so transform the gentlest of creatures into a savage brute.[14]

The confusion Colette's heroine experiences here results no doubt from her mother's obfuscation of certain aspects of sexuality. This stance is presented as protective and as a necessary stage in a young girl's gradual acquisition of sexual knowledge by the narrator of the semi-fictionalized *La Maison de Claudine* (1922). But in the case of an adolescent, attempts to mask the truth of sexuality can savour of hypocrisy. As J. H. Stewart comments, in a patrilinear society, the father's voice gives names, whereas in the fictional world of *Gigi* (1944) 'a matrilinear community attempts to discredit or annihilate them. Custodian of language and sexual knowledge, [Gigi's] grandmother adopts a strategy which makes the female space a linguistic absence.'[15]

In this text, a sixteen-year-old girl is to be invited into the bed of a rich protector, according to time-honoured rituals. However, the essential commodity which she brings to him – her unsullied sexuality – remains unnamed and undefined within her matrilinear household.

Striking linguistic precision is deployed by members of that household in teaching Gigi how to be discriminating in jewellery, dress, food, table manners, deportment, and to all of these is linked an exacting value-system. The same precision does not extend to discussion of Gigi's 'you-know-what':

> 'Have my skirts made a little longer, so I don't have to fold myself up in a Z every time I sit down . . . You see, Grandmamma, with my skirts too short, I have to keep thinking of my you-know-what.'
> 'Silence! Aren't you ashamed to call it your you-know-what?'
> 'I don't mind calling it by any other name, only . . .'
> Madame Alvarez blew out the spirit-lamp, looked at the reflection of her heavy Spanish face in the looking-glass above the mantelpiece, and then laid down the law:
> 'There is no other name.'[16]

Because, as Stewart puts it, 'Gigi's you-know-what is the elusive, problematic centre of a network of financial and sexual exchange'[17] and is to be sold intact to a male owner, it must remain outside language. To name it would be to infringe the strict codes dominating Gigi's world, to subvert the proprieties of that world. But Gigi will break these codes, on the level of the linguistic and the social, and this is perhaps the real triumph of her marriage.

In *Gigi*, sexual obliqueness is the focus of Colette's irony. However, elsewhere Colette sets out to demonstrate that, within the domain of desire, the word can kill. The Michel and Alice of *Duo* (1934) are a sophisticated couple in their late thirties, professionally involved in the theatre world. Alice's decision to tell her husband of a brief affair with a colleague, and, more fatally, his reading of this man's letters, drive him to drown himself. 'A horrible dream, but a short one'[18] is how Alice sums up her liaison, but the physical explicitness of the written word makes it for Michel a searing reality. Although he destroys the letters instantly, 'mentally he began to read those three letters again, forgetting nothing, changing nothing'.[19] The very shapes of the letters suggest to him Alice's body and its movements and this is consolidated by a little drawing. This is therefore the objectivization of his private world. For Ketchum[20] it is because Alice fails to play the role of the tearful repentant wife that Michel collapses; for Berthu-Courtivron[21] it has to do with his having been betrayed for an unworthy partner of the family estate where they are staying, already neglected and secretly mortgaged. Michel's collapse reveals too that recurrent economy in Colette's work by which men succumb to crisis while women endure and survive. 'All the coarse anxiety and febrile weakness are his, all the refinement of sense, healthy tenacity, and vitality are hers. In Colette's fictional world there is no coming to terms.'[22] However, it seems a stronger argument that Michel is murdered by the articulation of the sexual in language. In *Gigi*, words – and words that convey adequately the sexual realities behind them – are needed. In *Duo*, on the other hand, words prove fatal, and reticence is posited as desirable.

The Power of Reticence

But of Alice's letters no words appear on the printed page for us, the readers. And this is all of a piece with Colette's own reticence when describing physical encounters and her avoidance of sexual explicitness (especially as far as female homoeroticism is concerned). When as a writer she began to move out of the orbit of her husband Willy and to seek an individual style and control of her own, she particularly wanted to dissociate herself from a portrayal of sexuality that, in the 'Claudine' and 'Minne' books (written between 1900 and 1905), now seemed to her to be shallow, knowing, provocative and sometimes salacious. It was, after all, Willy who had constantly urged her to 'spice up' her first narratives, and so bring them in to line with the type of commercially successful publication that normally appeared under his own signature. In no case, however, were any of these books written by himself, so Colette had a double reason for her wish to dissociate herself from this doubly deceitful discourse, because of its false eroticism and its false signature. Her dissociation takes the form of a move towards an erotics of reticence. Various extracritical observations made by Colette make this apparent.

'I enjoyed the moderate but honourable satisfaction of not talking about love'[23] she said in *Mes Apprentissages* (1936) of her earliest animal book, *Dialogues de bêtes* (1904). In *Les Vrilles de la vigne*, published in 1908, there is already evidence of her need to produce 'livres chastes': 'the books I want to write are melancholy and chaste, where there will only be landscapes, flowers, sadness, pride and the frankness of delightful animals who shun mankind'.[24] Clearly, a contrast is being implied here between the kind of discourse from which Colette sought to detach herself and the 'livres chastes' evoked above. But readers would be much mistaken if they expected to find a kind of pastoral innocence in Colette's 'chaste' writing just as they would in expecting Colette's Parisian scenarios to stage nothing but jaded, salacious eroticism. In *Claudine en ménage* (1902), for example, Colette had already shown Claudine entering into a lesbian relationship with the more experienced and fascinating Rézi, and finding a deeper and more subtle sexual pleasure than she had ever felt with the more shallow and febrile Renaud, her 'mari-papa'. In fact, this particular text, which has some biographical basis, is a much more complex and experimental piece of writing than anything normally published under Willy's imprint. This does not, of course, mean that she is producing the kind of politicized discourse of lesbian sexuality that appears in the works of later, more radical women writers. She is, however, doing something new. Especially significant is the aestheticization of sexuality *Claudine en ménage* effects; an aestheticization which points towards the reticent mode of erotic writing Colette sought subsequently to elaborate.

Claire Dehon has noted in her 'Colette and Art Nouveau'[25] the similarities of style between Colette's descriptions and the products of that movement in their sinuosity and their merging of human with animal, insect and plant forms. These motifs recur constantly in Claudine's evocations of Rézi.

> All her supple body followed my game with a treacherous compliance. Her hair, tossed back from the head that lay on my shoulder, brushed against my face like the twigs I had invented to distract me from my inner turmoil.[26]

> From time to time a glint of light, like a sun-gleam on a river, shone on her teeth as she talked. She talked in a fever of gaiety, one bare arm raised and her forefinger drawing what she said. In the twilight I followed that white sinuous arm whose gestures made a rhythmic accompaniment to my languor and the adorable sadness that drugged me.[27]

Passion is delineated through the partner's visual, physical and aesthetic fascination with these arabesques, until memory and anticipation become obsessive and render the rest of life insipid and meaningless. The contrast, too, is between the half-light of interiors and the unshaded light of day, the secret and the public.

Colette constructed lesbianism rather differently from 1906 onwards, when her relationship with 'Missy', the Marquise de Belboeuf, had begun. As her acquaintance with women's circles developed, she began to see these as refuges for the like-minded, and notions of sameness, nurture and escape attached themselves to such unions. Renée in *La Vagabonde* (1910) broods on her lover Max's insensitivity:

Two women enlaced will never be for him anything but a depraved couple, he will never see in them the melancholy and touching image of two weak creatures who have perhaps sought shelter in each other's arms, there to sleep and weep, safe from man who is so often cruel, and there to taste, better than any pleasure, the bitter happiness of feeling themselves akin, frail and forgotten.[28]

The plaintive gentle tone of this image of withdrawal and solidarity is also characteristic of the sketches and lyrical pieces that Colette placed among the short fictions of *Les Vrilles de la vigne* (1908). With hardly a pronoun or agreement to signal gender, these brief poetic evocations suggest the warmth, exaltation, surprises and comforts of intimacy. 'Jour gris' traces the limits of sharing, when the narrator stifles an intense nostalgia for the landscapes of her childhood and dispels the jealousy of her partner by opting for the present. But the most delicate lyricism is in monologue form. In 'Nuit blanche' this intimacy is focused through an invocation to the shared bed: 'O our bed, completely bare! . . . Fixed star, never rising or setting, our bed never ceases to gleam except when submerged in the velvety depths of the night.'[29] Thus indirectly is the radiance and the security of the relationship conveyed. It relates to the natural world through vivid impressions of the past day spent in the summer heat, and the aromatic herbs through touch, taste and smell construct the correspondents of its sensuality.

The shoots of the blackcurrant bush that you brushed against, the wild sorrel dotting the grass with its rosettes, the fresh young mint, still brown, the sage as downy as a hare's ear – everything overflowed with a powerful and spicy sap which became on my lips mingled with the taste of alcohol and citronelle.[30]

With bodies it is arms, shoulders, faces, knees that are described. Arms support, shoulders are comforting, knees are cool, and the motif of the welcoming shoulder is a common physical referent in all of Colette's work. 'Your knees are two cool oranges . . . Turn towards me, so that mine can steal some of that cool freshness.'[31] It is easy for this kind of grave, gentle lyricism to move from the sexual to the maternal. The speaker is the cherished, the receiving partner, and plays the role of the child in addition to that of the lover. Sanctified by Nature, private and absorbing, this relationship harmonizes a series of needs. 'You will accord me sensual pleasure, bending over me voluptuously, maternally, you who seek in your impassioned loved one the child you never had.'[32]

More striking, more original – and, more pertinently, more 'chaste' still – is the 'Chanson de la danseuse', where attraction, ecstasy, joy, as well as the passage through life are translated metaphorically through the medium of the dance. This translation into a fluid abstract form conveys the possibility for Colette of a vital union of body, emotion and spirit, under the stimulus of the word. It is the partner who selects the word and in bestowing it creates the reality. But the piece begins and ends with the subject's disclaimer 'You who named me the dancer, you must know today that I have never learned to dance.'[33] 'You have called me dancer, but I do not know how to dance.'[34] This enigmatic closure is in fact a tribute to the power and creativity of the partner who has willed and elicited this response, and acquiescence signifies the recognition of affinity with other images of dance. So there are echoes of the Greek and Virgilian eclogues, just as Daphnis and Chloe are signalled as antecedents in *Le Blé en herbe*. A stylized natural scene of water, sand and flowers escorts the dancer, and in an exchange of sexual passion she reaches the climax of the dance: 'But naked in your arms, linked to your bed by the fiery ribbon of pleasure, you have nevertheless named me the dancer, since you have seen the inevitable ecstasy rush under my skin from my curved breast to my tensed feet.'[35] It is in these forms, rather than within a narrative fiction, that Colette evokes, mimics and transposes most inventively physical pleasure and physical union. Here, in contrast to *Duo*, the word can give life.

These texts certainly speak of love, but in increasingly experimental forms whose delicate lyricism would make them for Colette 'livres chastes'. Colette uses this notion as she later used the distinction between the 'pur' and the 'impur'. It is not intended to convey a moral judgement but to suggest depth and integrity. A further manifestation of her desire to create 'livres chastes' is her employment of animal figures to create a *displaced* sexual discourse and a stark rhetorical verbalization of sexuality as an anonymous obsessive power. Her use of animals chimes in with the personifications of Renée as animal in *La Vagabonde*; in 'Nonoche' (*Les Vrilles de la vigne*) it entails giving a voice to the animal as the unheard and the unspeaking. Only Nonoche, a female cat, hears or senses the power of the male that compels her away from her maternal duties towards the unknown mate; a power which is given a formal rhetorical shape. It is striking that this most overt sexual discourse is imputed not to a human but to a beast. Striking too is the fact that the animal is male, and that Colette exerts her female authorial power and autonomy to accord him a voice: 'Come to me! Come! When I appear before your eyes you will only recognise in me – Love!'[36] Elsewhere, in more naturalistic animal stories, for example 'Chats' in *La Maison de Claudine* (1922), Colette uses animals – cats of the same gender and of different genders including the neutered – in order to trace subtle and changing power-relationships. In 'Nonoche', however, the pattern is an unvarying and fated one of dominance and submission, with the inference that human sexuality has a similar core to it.

> My teeth will hold down your rebellious neck, I will soil your pelt, I will inflict upon you as many bites as caresses, I will suppress within you the memory of your home and during the nights and days you will become my wild and screaming companion . . . until the dark hour when you will be once more alone, for I will have mysteriously fled, tired of you, drawn by the one I know not, the one that I have not yet possessed.[37]

Because the voice speaking here is not human, there is none of the relativity, the cynicism and irony found in the Don Juan-figure Damien of *Le Pur et l'impur* (1932). Its use of the unmitigated future tense closes off any variation or escape for the female. With this in mind, let us turn finally to a discussion of Colette's exploration of sex/gender interaction, and of its multifarious manifestations and consequences.

Evasion, Subversion and Survival

As we saw earlier, the notion of the 'entrave', the leash, is intimately bound up with Colette's vision of the sexual. In *La Vagabonde* we saw a heterosexual woman feeling not so much the victim of a man as of her own sexuality. When, within the heterosexual relation, the man is more exclusively posited as dominating or controlling, Colette explores the strategies used by the woman to survive. One such strategy is deception: 'Fighters! It is the fight that keeps you young.'[38] Employment of the artifice of make-up is another, since it indicates not vanity but a moral toughness and self-respect.

> Heroically hidden behind her orange-tinted make-up, her eyes emphasised, a small red smile painted over her pale mouth, woman, thanks to her daily dissimulation, puts together a daily modicum of fortitude, and her pride in never making any kind of concession.[39]

Colette also presents silence – once again – as a strategic mode of self-protective deception. In 'La Main' a young wife who is watching her sleeping husband becomes aware of his hand as an apparently detached entity, spider-like and all too material with its menacingly convulsive movements and its ability to concentrate in itself the whole physique and being of the man. 'Then she concealed her fear, bravely subdued herself, and, beginning her life of duplicity, of resignation, and of a lowly, delicate diplomacy, she leaned over and humbly kissed the monstrous hand.'[40] This lucid hypocrisy is given a moral value by Colette, just as a pretence of happiness is consistently put forward as a necessary concomitant of marriage. But are there strategies to be used by women that involve more than patience and a silent acceptance of sexual enslavement? There are, for example, certain types of reversal of roles, although these will tend to occur in out-of-the-ordinary contexts.

Marie McCarty writes in 1981: 'women can only overcome their Otherness by becoming consciously marginal, by revelling in marginality'[41] and she sees a number of situations in Colette's fiction as best interpreted as 'a refusal of the androcentric community'.[42] This point provides the prelude to her analysis of 'Le Tendron'. In this novella the experienced and sophisticated Albin assumes that he will be able to dominate and seduce the very young Louisette whom he views as charmingly gauche and simple but whose affinity with the secluded natural scene and whose ultimate solidarity with her mother he does not comprehend. He is routed, verbally by the mother's pitiless anatomizing of his 49-year-old appearance, his grey hairs and the incongruous and shoddy nature of his pretensions to possess Louise (as her mother calls her), and then physically by the stones that fall upon him as he flees from the menacing duo on the bank above. Louise asks her mother if they should not run him down, using the same term that described her goat's attack on him at their initial meeting. Albin is unnerved by the unpredictable. 'We can never foresee what a woman may do when she loses all control',[43] he says, as a world without rules opens before his feet. This anecdote is recounted by him to a 'Colette' narrator, who allows his self-revelation to unfold in a silence as devastating as the mother's discourse. With touches of the Furies, or, as McCarty suggests, of a Demeter succeeding in protecting her Persephone, these women can be seen as elemental disturbing figures in an unresolved sexual drama.

Less belligerent, more serpentine is the stance of Charlotte, a figure in Colette's most ambitious and enigmatic exploration of sexual roles, *Le Pur et l'impur* of 1932. In the drug-house that is the currently fashionable haunt of journalists and writers Charlotte's rough and possessive young lover prevents her from singing in public. What is heard later in the night, however, are the throaty melodious trills of her orgasmic pleasure.

But from the depths of this very silence a sound imperceptibly began in a woman's throat, at first husky, then clear, asserting its firmness and amplitude as it was repeated, becoming clear and full like the notes the nightingale repeats and accumulates until they pour out in a flood of arpeggios.[44]

This aesthetically accomplished construct is linked to the natural through the nightingale reference. The instructive here becomes the artistic and would seem to suggest a harmony of expression and joy.

Further conversations with Charlotte, however, reveal the insecurity of this analysis. The little veil that she wears by day under her hat signals the ambiguities of her position. Circumspectly she reveals to the narrator the true basis of her musical recital. 'It would be too wonderful, the love of such a young man, if only I didn't have to pretend.'[45] A rapid revision will produce in readers a new portrait of Charlotte: this stout-hearted woman not only tends her lover's tubercular body but caters for his egotistic sexual satisfactions as well. This, however, is not all. From their carefully phrased formal discourse, in which they call each other 'madame' and 'Madame Charlotte', and out of the equivocal semi-dark of the night, there emerges Charlotte's perhaps final statement about herself: that she need not dissimulate, in fact, but chooses to do so because she wishes to retain control of herself and of the situation. 'Just imagine, madame – if I were to let myself go like a fool and not even know what I was doing or saying . . . Oh! I can't bear the idea!'.[46] So we come back to self-respect, integrity and power over the immediate context, achieved in ways that are both subtle and surprising.

When in the same volume Colette turns to the historical eighteenth-century figures of the Ladies of Llangollen, the possibility of deception may seem far-removed. Contemplating the tranquil seamless idyll that is the diary of Lady Eleanor Butler, the aristocratic chronicler of this life-long female/female companionship, Colette casts a searching gaze at their reclusion and its reticences. 'A vow of seclusion descended on this couple of young girls, separating them from the world, veiling and changing and remaking the universe in their eyes.'[47] Harmony characterizes all of their recorded dealings, with each other supremely, with neighbours, friends, visitors, servants, animals, Nature. Is this miraculously transparent, or does it veil a number of hidden complexities? Colette is quick to ward off prurient sexual curiosity about the couple, disputing the views of her friend Renée Vivien, here seen as immature and off-beam. 'In living amorously together, two women may eventually discover that their mutual attraction is not basically sensual – in contradiction to the cynical opinions expressed by Renée Vivien. Oh, the pathetically infantile and distraught cynicism of Renée!'.[48] But she certainly perceives here, as elsewhere, a power relationship. The silence of Sarah Ponsonby prompts her to the reflection that a lesbian couple, in the end, can never be a wholly female entity in a female-defined space, since one partner will, inevitably it seems, adopt the traditional male role. Lady Eleanor's diary, then, is presented by Colette not as an exercise in deceit, but as evidence of a probably shared self-deception; that of 'two sweet, foolish creatures, so intensely loyal to a delusion'.[49] In this perspective, the diary can retain the wholeness and integrity of its purity. Clearly, however, Colette's view seems to have shifted from the figuration of previous lesbian texts where the older or stronger partner was given maternal characteristics. Colette may still be denying the dominance of sexual passion within homoerotic relations, but she is accepting the presence within them of other types of pressure, if only the compulsion to happiness. For if Eleanor is to be cast as 'the prudent warden – the masculine element',[50] with the Bien-Aimée enmeshed in the limpid veil of words, Colette is no longer adhering to the image of lesbianism that she seemed to be sharing with Simone de Beauvoir. 'Between women love is contemplative, caresses are intended less to gain possession of the other than gradually to re-create the self through her.'[51] However, inconsistency is a dangerous word to be using in Colette's case; *Le Pur et l'impur* offers a kaleidoscope of perspectives, and in any case Beauvoir could be also signalling a non-vital circular narcissism in such a relationship – in which case her model would be negative.

In fact, a number of commentators see in *Le Pur et l'impur* a particularly subtly unified text. For Ann Cothran this is revealed by an analysis of its semiotic coding. Using light and dark as fundamental code-words she links in a number of other 'signs', so that eventually, after similar exercises, she can claim that: 'Colette presents a vast, circular panorama of human sensual behaviour wherein traditionally separated or opposed types actually share significant characteristics'.[52]

With such codes in mind we can work out how Charlotte dissimulates to her lover but conceals her deeper secret, whereas La Chevalière and her lesbian associates conceal themselves in dark, close rooms, and dissimulate through their cross-dressing. Meanwhile, a connection between the light-code, illusion, violence and consumption allows for a link between the Don-Juan figure whose confident discourse and plural lust hide from him his own misogyny, and La Lucienne whose attempt to impose herself on other women as a man is done imperiously and disastrously. So for Cothran there is in *Le Pur et l'impur* a particularly rich interplay of semantic signals. 'Every term exists in some kind of relationship to numerous others: nothing in *The Pure and the Impure* is gratuitous.'[53]

This, however, does not disguise the fact that, for most commentators, a fundamental question being explored is whether sexual satisfaction is possible within a homosexual relationship. Colette's answers seem to veer between the hesitant and the negative. If for Sherry Dranch the unifying stylistic factor is 'clearly stated covertness'[54] the repeated suppressions and self-censorship of speech in Colette's text lead her to the conclusion that it represents 'a virile and sensual woman writer's capitulation to silence, to censorship, to the unsaid'.[55] Elaine Marks supports these findings in that she sees Colette's view of female homosexuality as a substitute for a learned model, and so lacking its own autonomy. 'Lesbianism is a *pis-aller*. It is a copy of either mother–daughter or male–female love or both.'[56] In this scenario the 'Colette' observer-narrator, aloof herself from sexual activity, could seem perilously close to the lascivious male *voyeur* of the all-female sphere.

However, it is possible to interpret many aspects of *Le Pur et l'impur* in a more positive fashion. The role of the narrator is to infiltrate a number of sexual situations and to prompt sympathetically those who confide in her. She is a protean figure who extends her sexual knowledge cumulatively and comparatively by absorption into each context. Sometimes, as with the male homosexual group, she mocks her status as 'a nice piece of furniture'[57] at their interchanges. Elsewhere she is more tested and disturbed, and by Damien, the 'Don Juan', she is wounded. 'You, a woman? Why, try as you will . . .'.[58] He snubs her when she has offered comradeship. But in the end she is not daunted and pursues her explorations, by this means liberating herself from conventional roles and positions. This could be seen as her subversive challenge.

The question of gender is a pervasive one. Colette as observer and not actor risks being neutralized or masculinized, and she herself refers to her 'masculine side'. In other texts she is referred to by her mother as a boy sewing, and during her pregnancy a male remarked that hers was a 'male' pregnancy. This was construed by Colette more in terms of androgyny than of gender-reversal, and she certainly perceived an area of virility in the act of artistic creativity. When Dranch comments on an exchange between Colette and Marguerite Moreno she sees an effect of self-censorship, relating, she thinks, to the narrator and her mixed audience. Colette had wondered 'who will realize we are women?' to be answered reassuringly by Moreno 'Other women. Women aren't offended or deluded by our masculine wit.'[59] Dranch uses the translation 'masculine wit', but this phrase is probably to be understood at further levels and so would be better rendered 'masculine spirit', conveying as it does these women's perception of their action upon a public stage and the relation of the professional to the creative. Their challenge to the patriarchal mode, then, will only be misinterpreted by its defenders, and this could be seen as a relative rather than an essential phenomenon.

Colette's 'hidden woman' (the fictional, the historical, the actual and the self-referential) emerges as a figure of considerable force and resilience. 'Ellipses are the connection, it will be seen, between Colette's style – the subliminal style of the flesh – and a forbidden obsession'[60] Dranch says, and this is an acute judgement. But the style of half-iterated communication between Moreno and Colette can also be seen in terms of intellectual confidence and intuitive quickness: 'We had the comfortable habit of leaving a sentence hanging midway as soon as one of us had grasped the point.'[61] Displaying this communication-mode gives it positive status, and extends an endorsement to the covert semiotics of La Chevalière and her friends.

> I revelled in the admirable quickness of their half-spoken language, the exchange of threats, of promises, as if, once the slow-thinking male had been banished, every message from woman to woman became clear and overwhelming, restricted to a small but infallible number of signs.[62]

This could be seen as the secret language of a slave-culture, the creole of the lesbian community. But it can also signify, more positively, the triumph of Colette's writing strategy, the valorizing of attitudes and expressions that she does not overtly seek to transform but that her lucid gaze opens up and defines irreversibly.

Notes

All texts are by Colette unless otherwise stated.

1. *Le Blé en herbe*, my translation: 'né pour la chasse et la tromperie' (*Le Blé en herbe*, Paris, Garnier-Flammarion, 1969, p. 32).
2. Ibid. 'la mission de durer, dévolue à toutes les espèces femelles' (p. 163).
3. *Les Vrilles de la vigne*, my translation. 'Vous n'imaginez pas quelle reine de la terre j'étais à douze ans! . . . Ah! que vous m'auriez aimée quand j'avais douze ans, et comme je me regrette! Hélas, Claudine,

j'ai perdu presque tout cela, à ne devenir après tout qu'une femme' (*Sido; Les Vrilles de la vigne*, Paris, Le Livre de poche, 1908, p. 204).

4. *The Vagabond*, trans. E. McLeod, London, Secker & Warburg, 1954, p. 5. 'cette conseillère maquillée qui me regarde de l'autre côté de la glace' (*La Vagabonde*, Paris, Le Livre de poche, 1983, p. 5).

5. 'une espèce de servage, apparemment volontaire': Christina Angelfors, *La Double Conscience: la prise de conscience féminine chez Colette, Simone de Beauvoir et Marie Cardinal* (Lund, 1989), p. 34.

6. *Julie de Carneilhan*, trans. P. Leigh-Fermor, London, Penguin Books, 1957, p. 79. 'En passant devant le miroir de l'antichambre, elle rétablit sur son visage une contraction des narines à laquelle elle tenait beaucoup, et qui accentuait, disait-elle, son caractère fauve' (*Julie de Carneilhan*, Paris, Le Livre de demain, 1952, p. 8).

7. *Le Blé en herbe*, my translation. 'Il vit . . . des traits plaintifs, et moins pareils à ceux d'un homme qu'a ceux d'une jeune fille meurtrie' (p. 107).

8. *Chéri and the Last of Chéri*, trans. R. Senhouse, London, Penguin Books, 1954, p. 136. 'Une vieille femme haletante répéta, dans le miroir oblong, son geste et Léa se demanda ce qu'elle pouvait avoir de commun avec cette folle' (*Chéri*, Paris, Le Livre de poche, 1976, p. 190).

9. *The Vagabond*, p. 203. 'Comment y parvenir? Tout est contre moi. Le premier obstacle où je bute, c'est ce corps de femme allongé qui me barre la route, un voluptueux corps aux yeux fermés, volontairement aveugle, étiré, prêt à périr plutôt que de quitter le lieu de sa joie . . . C'est moi, cette femme-là, cette brute entêtée au plaisir' (*La Vagabonde*, p. 226).

10. Ibid., p. 203. 'Vaincrai-je aussi, plus dangereuse, cent fois que la bête goulue, l'enfant abandonnée qui tremble en moi, faible, nerveuse, prompte à tendre les bras, à implorer: "Ne me laissez pas seule!"' (ibid., pp. 226–7).

11. Ibid., p. 62. '. . . le désir existe, demi-dieu impérieux, faune lâché qui gambade autour de l'amour et n'obéit point à l'amour' (ibid., p. 70).

12. Ibid., p. 158. 'Femelle j'étais, et femelle je me retrouve' (ibid., p. 179).

13. 'The Hidden Woman', trans. M. Ward in *The Collected Stories of Colette*, ed. R. Phelps, New York, Farrar, Strauss and Giroux, 1983, p. 238. 'le monstrueux plaisir d'être seule, libre, véridique dans sa brutalité native, d'être l'inconnue, à jamais solitaire et sans vergogne, qu'un petit masque et un costume hermétique ont

rendue à sa solitude irrémédiable et à sa déshonnête innocence' (*La Femme cachée*, Paris, Folio, 1974, p. 17).

14. *My Mother's House*, trans. U. V. Troubridge and E. McLeod, London, Penguin Books, 1966, pp. 98–9. '– Oh! Toutouque . . . Toutouque . . . Je ne trouvais pas d'autres paroles, et ne savais comment me plaindre, m'effrayer et m'étonner qu'une force malfaisante, dont le nom même échappait à mes dix ans, pût changer en brute féroce la plus douce des créatures' (*La Maison de Claudine*, Paris, Le Livre de poche, 1960, p. 100).

15. J. H. Stewart, *Colette*, Boston, 1983, p. 88.

16. *Gigi*, trans. R. Senhouse, London, Penguin Books, 1958, p. 8.

' Qu'on me fasse des jupes un peu plus longues, que je ne sois pas tout le temps pliée en Z dès que je m'assois. Tu comprends, grand-mère, tout le temps il faut que je pense à mon ce-que-je-pense, avec mes jupes trop courtes.

– Silence! Tu n'as pas honte d'appeler ça ton ce-que-je-pense?

– Je ne demande pas mieux que de lui donner un autre nom, moi . . .

Mme Alvarez éteignit le réchaud, mira dans la glace de la cheminée sa lourde figure espagnole, et décida:

– Il n'y en a pas d'autre.

(*Gigi*, Paris, Ferenczi, 1952, p. 10).

17. Stewart, *Colette*, p. 89.

18. *Duo and Le Toutounier*, trans. M. Crosland, London, Peter Owen, 1976, p. 121. 'Un rêve sale, mais court' (*Duo*, Paris, Le Livre de poche, 1960, p. 102).

19. Ibid., p. 122. 'dans sa mémoire fidèle il commença, sans oubli ni faute, de relire les trois lettres' (ibid., p. 104).

20. A. Ketchum, 'Colette and the Enterprise of Writing: A Reappraisal', in E. Eisinger and M. McCarty (eds), *Colette: The Woman, the Writer*, Pennsylvania, 1981, p. 29.

21. V. M-F. Berthu-Courtivron, *Espace, demeure, écriture*, Paris, 1992, pp. 100–3.

22. Stewart, *Colette*, p. 75.

23. *My Apprenticeships*, quoted in R. Phelps (ed.), *Earthly Paradise*, London, 1970, p. 133. 'Je me donnai le plaisir, non point vif, mais honorable, de ne pas parler de l'amour' (*Mes Apprentissages*, Paris, Ferenczi, 1936, p. 141).

24. *Les Vrilles de la vigne*, my translation. '. . . je veux écrire des livres tristes et chastes, où il n'y aura que des paysages, des fleurs, du chagrin, de la fierté, et la candeur des animaux charmants qui s'effraient de l'homme' (*Sido; Les Vrilles de la vigne*, p. 146).

25. V. C. Dehon, 'Colette and Art Nouveau', in Eisinger and McCarty (eds), *Colette*, pp. 104–15.
26. *Claudine en ménage*, my translation. 'Tout son corps souple suit mon jeu, avec une complaisance traîtresse. De sa tête, renversée sur mon épaule, les cheveux s'envolent et me frôlent comme les ramures qu'invente mon inquiétude en quête de diversions' (*Claudine en ménage*, Paris, Mercure de France, 1954, p. 145).
27. Ibid. 'De temps en temps, si près de ma bouche, aux dents de Rézi, qui parle, un reflet luit comme une ablette. Elle parle dans une fièvre gaie, un bras nu levé, dessinant de l'index ce qu'elle dit. Je suis dans le demi-jour ce bras blanc et sinueux, dont le geste rythme ma lassitude et l'adorable tristesse qui m'enivre' (ibid., p. 160).
28. *The Vagabond*, p. 188. 'Deux femmes enlacées ne seront jamais pour lui qu'un groupe polisson, et non l'image mélancolique et touchante de deux faiblesses, peut-être réfugiées aux bras l'une de l'autre pour y dormir, y pleurer, fuir l'homme souvent méchant, et goûter mieux que tout plaisir, l'amer bonheur de se sentir pareilles, infimes, oublieés' (*La Vagabonde*, pp. 211–12).
29. 'Sleepless Nights', trans. H. Briffault in *The Collected Stories*, p. 91. 'O notre lit tout nu! . . . Astre sans aube et sans déclin, notre lit ne cesse de flamboyer que pour s'enfoncer dans une nuit profonde et veloutée' (*Sido; Les Vrilles de la vigne*, p. 104).
30. Ibid., p. 92. 'Les pouces des cassis que tu froissais, l'oseille sauvage en rosace parmi le gazon, la menthe toute jeune, encore brune, la sauge duvetée comme une oreille de lièvre, – tout débordait d'un suc énergique et poivré, dont je mêlais sur mes lèvres le goût d'alcool et de citronnelle' (ibid., p. 105).
31. Ibid., p. 92. 'Tes genoux sont frais comme deux oranges. Tourne-toi de mon côté, pour que les miens leur volent cette lisse fraîcheur' (ibid., p. 104).
32. Ibid., p. 93. 'Tu me donneras la volupté, penché sur moi, les yeux pleins d'une anxiété maternelle, toi qui cherches, à travers ton amie passionnée, l'enfant que tu n'as pas eu' (ibid., p. 107).
33. 'Chanson de la danseuse', my translation. 'O toi qui me nommes danseuse, sache, aujourd'hui que je n'ai pas appris à danser' (ibid., p. 99).
34. 'Tu me nommes danseuse, et pourtant je ne sais pas danser' (ibid., p. 100).
35. 'Mais nue dans tes bras, liée à ton lit par le ruban de feu du plaisir, tu m'as pourtant nommée danseuse, à voir bondir sous ma peau, de ma gorge renversée à mes pieds recourbés, la volupté inévitable' (ibid., p. 99).

36. 'Nonoche', my translation. 'Viens! Viens! . . . Quand je paraîtrai à tes yeux, tu ne reconnaîtras rien de moi – que l'Amour!' (ibid., p. 141).

37. 'Mes dents courberont ta nuque rétive, je souillerai ta robe, je t'infligerai autant de morsures que de caresses, j'abolirai en toi le souvenir de ta demeure et tu seras pendant des jours et des nuits, ma sauvage compagne hurlante . . . jusqu'à l'heure plus noire où tu te retrouveras seule, car j'aurai fui mystérieusement, las de toi, appelé par celle que je ne connais pas, celle que je n'ai pas possédée encore' (ibid., p. 141).

38. 'Maquillages', my translation. 'O lutteuses! C'est de lutter que vous restez jeunes' (ibid., p. 165).

39. 'Héroiquement dissimulée sous son fard mandarine, l'oeil agrandi, une petite bouche rouge peinte sur sa bouche pâle, la femme récupère, grâce à son mensonge quotidien, une quotidienne dose d'endurance, et la fierté de n'avouer jamais' (ibid., p. 164).

40. 'The Hand', trans. M. Ward in *Collected Stories*, p. 246. 'Puis elle cacha sa peur, se dompta courageusement, et commençant sa vie de duplicité, de résignation, de diplomatie vile et délicate, elle se pencha, et baisa humblement la main monstrueuse' (*La Femme cachée*, p. 43).

41. M. McCarty, 'Possessing Female Space: *The Tender Shoot*', *Women's Studies, an interdisciplinary journal*, vol. 8, no. 3, 1981, p. 367.

42. Ibid., p. 369.

43. 'The Tender Shoot', trans. A. White in *Collected Stories*, p. 445. 'Nous ne pouvons rien prévoir d'une femme déchaînée' (*Le Képi*, Paris, Le Livre de poche, 1968, p. 107).

44. *The Pure and the Impure*, trans. H. Briffault, London, Secker and Warburg, 1968, p. 21. 'Mais du sein de ce silence même un son naquit imperceptiblement dans une gorge de femme, un son qui s'essaya rauque, s'éclaircit, prit sa fermeté et son ampleur en se répétant, comme les notes pleines que le rossignol redit et accumule jusqu'à ce qu'elles s'écroulent en roulade' (*Le Pur et l'impur*, Paris, Hachette, 1979, p. 12).

45. Ibid., p. 33. 'Ce serait trop beau, l'amour d'un si jeune homme, si je n'étais pas forcée de mentir' (ibid., p. 22).

46. Ibid., p. 35. 'M'abandonner comme une imbécile, ne plus seulement savoir ce qui vous échappe en gestes ou en paroles . . . Oh! je ne peux pas supporter cette idée-là' (ibid., p. 22).

47. Ibid., p. 121. 'Un voeu de clôture descend sur ce couple de jeunes filles, les sépare du monde, voile, change et refond l'univers à leurs yeux' (ibid., p. 93).

48. Ibid., p. 114. 'A vivre ensemble amoureusement, deux femmes peuvent découvrir enfin que l'origine de leur réciproque penchant n'est pas sensuelle, – n'est jamais sensuelle, ô pauvre cynisme enfantin et égaré de Renée!' (ibid., p. 88).

49. Ibid., p. 130. 'deux folles et douces créatures, si fermement fidèles à une chimère' (ibid., p. 100).

50. Ibid., p. 128. 'le prudent géôlier – le mâle' (ibid., p. 99).

51. *The Second Sex*, trans. H. M. Parshley, London, 1953, p. 406. 'Entre femmes l'amour est contemplation; les caresses sont destinées moins à s'approprier l'autre qu'à se recréer lentement à travers elle' (S. de Beauvoir, *Le Deuxieme Sexe*, Paris, 1949, vol. 1, p. 499).

52. A. Cothran, 'The Pure and the Impure: Codes and Constructs', *Women's Studies, an interdisciplinary journal*, vol. 8, no. 3, 1981, p. 336.

53. Ibid., p. 356.

54. S. Dranch, 'Reading through the Veiled Text: Colette's *The Pure and the Impure*', *Contemporary Literature*, vol. 24, no. 2, 1983, p. 179.

55. Ibid., p. 189.

56. E. Marks, 'Lesbian Intertextuality', in G. Stambolian and E. Marks (eds), *Homosexualities and French Literature*, Ithaca and London, 1979, p. 369.

57. *The Pure and the Impure*, p. 139. 'meuble agréable' (*Le Pur et l'impur*, p. 108).

58. Ibid., p. 67. 'Vous, une femme? Vous voudrez bien . . .' (ibid., p. 50).

59. Ibid., p. 69. 'qui nous tiendra pour femmes? . . . Des femmes. Seules les femmes ne sont ni offensées, ni abusées par notre virilité spirituelle' (ibid., p. 52).

60. Dranch, 'Reading through the Veiled Text', p. 177.

61. *The Pure and the Impure*, p. 69. 'c'est entre nous un usage nonchalant que de suspendre la phrase en son beau milieu, dès que celle qui écoute a compris celle qui parle' (*Le Pur et l'impur*, p. 52).

62. Ibid., p. 85. 'je me plaisais à la promptitude admirable dans le langage muet, dans l'échange de la menace, de la promesse, comme si, le lent mâle écarté, tout message de femme à femme devînt clair, foudroyant, limité à un petit nombre infaillible de signes' (ibid., p. 64).

- 3 -

Desire and Its Discontents: Violette Leduc/*La Bâtarde*/The Failure of Love

Alex Hughes

When *La Bâtarde* was published in 1964, it was nominated for a number of France's prestigious literary prizes, but was awarded none of them. A prominent member of the 'prix Fémina' jury, Mme Simone, went so far as to declare that if Violette Leduc's first autobiographical volume ('the kind of book one couldn't leave lying around'[1]) were to be 'couronné' by her fellow jurors, she would resign from the panel on the spot. Mme Simone was not alone in perceiving *La Bâtarde* as somehow unsuitable for perusal by the right-thinking. A significant minority of Leduc's reviewers, typically in the right-wing press, likewise articulated feelings of distaste *vis-à-vis* her text. The literary critic on *Minute* spoke for a number of his fellows when he described *La Bâtarde* as a 'boucherie intime'; a brutally sordid farrago of personal revelation.[2]

What kinds of signals were those 1960s critics who condemned *La Bâtarde* as a 'boucherie intime' sending out? On the one hand, they were voicing their dislike of the self-absorbed tenor of Leduc's first autobiographical production and their disapproval of the 'exhibitionism' they imputed to her *récit*;[3] sentiments symptomatic of a broader distrust of the autobiographical genre *per se*. There was, however, another, more particular issue at stake. Members of this group of hostile critical readers were clearly signposting *La Bâtarde*'s *sexual* dimension (the text chronicles a number of love relationships, both hetero- and homoerotic), and were suggesting that the presence of this specific feature of the personal history Leduc offers her readers 'corrupts' her tale, by infusing it with salaciousness.

The negative reception, by these critics, of Leduc's efforts to transcribe sexual experience ensured that *La Bâtarde* was remembered by many as a text 'reeking of sulphur, in which schoolgirls made love and a woman talked crudely about her own sexuality'.[4] Their reaction was, in part, an inevitable consequence of the cultural context within which they were operating; a context that was wary of signs of sexual frankness in the fictional works of women writers, let alone in their autobiographies.[5] It was also, context notwithstanding, contemptible in that it was born out of prurience and prejudice. Nevertheless, the disquiet which, in 1964, was evidenced by certain of the reviews and critical glosses of Leduc's first 'voyage au bout d'elle-même' is not *wholly* incomprehensible today. *La Bâtarde* is, undoubtedly, a disturbing book, and the unease it generates is related to its representation of things sexual. This is not, however, because it offers an account of sexual congress that is an excessively explicit or obscene 'boucherie'; a highly coloured catalogue of what Henri Peyre labelled 'the Passions of a Gallic Sappho'.[6] In actual fact, Leduc's *récit* contains only a limited number of (intensely figurative) passages in which erotic activity is the direct/exclusive focus. The 'shocking' aspect of Leduc's first autobiographical *récit*, if we choose so to perceive it, derives rather from its extremely negative elucidation of the dynamics of desire. *La Bâtarde* addresses, with a considerable degree of pessimism, the nature and more precisely the impossibility of erotic love. If, in other words, the reader (even the emancipated, liberal reader of the late twentieth century) closes the pages of Leduc's text with a sense of relief or revolt, this is because a key 'message' of the work is that desire, in the last analysis, is a matter not of communion and communication but of self-preservation, of the denial and destruction of the other and, ultimately, of an ineluctable failure of mutuality. This failure, and the complexities of Leduc's charting of it, will provide the focus of my chapter. However, before the textual specificities of *La Bâtarde* can be addressed, we need to consider what we understand exactly by the 'dynamics of desire'.

In his excellent introduction to postmodernism and poststructuralism, Madan Sarup offers a concise definition of the Hegelian model of desire; a model which was drawn upon by Sartre and Lacan, amongst others, and which will serve as a point of departure for the reading of Violette Leduc's elaboration of the perils of love which I intend to offer here. Desire, writes Sarup, 'is directed towards another Desire, . . . another "I". Desire is human only if one desires not the body but the Desire of the other; that is to say, if one wants to be "desired" or, rather, "recognized" in one's human value.'[7] In Hegelian terms, then, desiring the other (within the love relation and indeed within all modes of human exchange) means wishing to be recognized by him/her, and the confirmatory desire of the other constitutes the foundation-stone of our humanity. So how do relations of desire-as-recognition function? As Jessica Benjamin explains in her essay 'The Bonds of Love',[8] such relations revolve around two fundamental needs which exist within each of us: the need to assert our selfhood as absolute and the need, in so doing, to negate the other. We assert ourselves by desiring/'acting on' the other in such a way as to elicit his/her recognition/desire; however, this essentially negatory act risks the 'destruction' of the other, exposes us to the concomitant risk of a damaging loss of his/her recognition/desire (on which we depend), and must not therefore be taken too far. Ideally, for interpersonal relations, relations of recognition, love and desire, to work effectively, it is necessary, as Benjamin points out, to have 'both negation and recognition simultaneously between self and other'; to have, in other words, 'mutual recognition between subjects'.[9]

The scenario which Benjamin is outlining here turns on the notion of 'intersubjectivity'.[10] Intersubjectivity involves both tension and equilibrium. It rests upon a 'wholeness' that derives from the (paradoxical) preservation, between and by two desiring subjects, of the contradictory elements of self-assertion and acknowledgement of other. However, the wholeness and mutuality Benjamin privileges may – and, in the Hegelian schema, inevitably does – break down. Within the dualistic, desiring relation, for Hegel at least, what ultimately transpires is that one partner 'must fear the other, must give in to the other, . . . must give up his desire and satisfy the desire of the other: he must "recognize" the other without being "recognized" by him'.[11] Within (for instance) the love relationship, in other words, mutuality can (or, according to Hegel, must) be displaced by a dynamic of domination and subordination, in which one lover becomes object (and an object deprived of recognition) to the other's desiring and negating subject. When a breakdown of this kind occurs, we no longer get two equal, differentiated beings; beings whose differentiation, according to Benjamin, 'proceeds through the movement of recognition, its flow from subject to subject, from self to other and back'.[12] What emerges, instead, is a 'false' and excessive differentiation, an intersubjective 'splitting' that replaces wholeness and exchange, a subject/object polarity predicated upon mastery and enslavement.[13]

If I have glossed the Hegelian model of desire relatively extensively, it is because the vision of love Violette Leduc offers in *La Bâtarde* echoes the notion of a fight for control and autonomy, a fight to the 'death' between self and other, which subtends it. Simone de Beauvoir, Leduc's literary mentor and friend, makes this apparent when, in her preface to *La Bâtarde*, she analyses her protégée's engagement with other people and her textual documentation of her 'éducation sentimentale'. 'Her misfortune', Beauvoir observes, 'was that she never experienced a reciprocal relationship with anyone: either the other was an object for her, or she made herself into an object for the other. . . . Even in love, especially in love, any exchange is impossible' (p. 7).[14] The (existentialist) gloss Beauvoir provides of the model of human (and specifically sexual) interaction which she discerns within *La Bâtarde* is highly pertinent, but it is also insufficiently precise. Leduc's first autobiographical opus certainly does stage desire as an oscillation between domination and subordination, as a struggle for mastery. However, this struggle exceeds the confines of the binary self/other relation. Desire, in *La Bâtarde*, is presented as generative of a recurrent structure of triangulation; a structure which is intended to shield the text's autobiographical heroine from harm but which habitually leaves Violette more damaged than she might otherwise have been.

Isabelle de Courtivron, who is primarily responsible for rescuing Leduc's work from the penumbra of critical disregard in which it languished in the 1970s, was the first to signal the significance accorded to triangulation in *La Bâtarde*.[15] She summarizes the role of the Leducian triad as follows: 'One of the strategies developed by Violette . . . is the establishment of triangular relationships that can result only in betrayal. Because of her fundamental attraction to the illicit, but especially because of her emotional claustrophobia, Violette repeatedly creates affective stalemates in order to avoid one-to-one relationships which, for her, represent enslavement.'[16] In the discussion of Leduc's autobiographical treatment of desire which follows, my intention is to provide a close reading of the workings of the triadic erotic bonds that are chronicled in *La Bâtarde* and of the motives which lie behind Violette's compulsive construction of them. I shall begin with an account of the rejection, by Leduc's narrator-heroine, of the dyadic relation; a rejection which is not articulated explicitly but which is charted in the early stages of her *récit*.

Violette's youthful initiation into the realm of erotic love takes place in the course of an episode in which she is not personally involved but which she observes with an intense, voyeuristic fascination. This incident is recounted almost as an aside, but is in fact highly telling. It turns upon the relationship between Cataplame, a simpleton living in the Northern French town inhabited by Violette and her mother and grandmother, and a neighbour, Mme Armande. Superficially, the episode is merely one of a number of baroque adventures which punctuate Violette's childhood years. It constitutes also, however, a premonitory and revealing moment; a kind of 'mise-en-abyme' which provides the reader with an intimation of why Leduc's protagonistic self comes to eschew one-to-one bonds.

The section of Leduc's narrative which describes 'l'affaire Cataplame' opens with the disconcertingly bald statement: 'A half-wit fell in love with the woman who lived next door' (p. 42).[17] In the pages that follow, we are told of Cataplame's feeble-mindedness, his comic and pathetic courtship of the distant Mme Armande, his supplication, his mistress's teasing play with the duster that serves them as an object of erotic exchange, and her eventual acceptance of his overtures. We learn also of the intensity of his desire, the account of which is ominously interspersed with adjectives such as 'funereal' and 'sombre'. Finally, and cataclysmically, we are informed of the outcome of the lovers' passion: 'One sunny morning I saw people clustering in front of the house. I questioned a group of young girls who were bubbling with excitement. "Cataplame has slit his mistress's throat" one of them told me' (p. 44).[18]

So why might this event, observed by the young Violette and retold by her older, narrating persona without comment or analysis, be interpreted as a symbolic, annunciatory and even, perhaps, catalytic stage in her own sexual evolution? What lessons does it have to offer? For one thing, it makes apparent, to Leduc's child-heroine and to her readers, that the dyadic erotic bond is fraught with dangers; dangers of the kind illuminated by the Hegelian account of self/other desiring interaction. It reveals love to be a matter of folly and inequality. The relationship between the desiring inequality evoked here and the hierarchized power relations that subtend traditional gender roles is less than straightforward, however. In this Leducian replay of the courtly love scenario, it is after all Cataplame, the male, who is cast as a devirilized and self-abasing clown, dancing like Salome before a woman who manipulates him, while the object of his love, ensconced in a high window as she gazes upon his desperate cavortings, may be classed amongst the various, generally cruel 'phallic females' who people the pages of Leduc's texts.[19] In addition, the episode, closing as it does with a decapitation (an act of symbolic 'castration'[20]), suggests that sexual disequilibrium must, inevitably, have fatal consequences. Ultimately, its message is that whenever love is degraded into a master/slave polarity, the 'slave' – in this case the emasculated Cataplame – will always seek to regain (phallic) mastery, in a reversal that must end in death.

Violette's own first sexual relationship – a love affair with a schoolmate, Isabelle – confirms the model of erotic interaction she witnessed in childhood and consolidates the lesson it afforded her. On the surface, this liaison – like the adolescent lesbian bond depicted in Leduc's 1966 novella *Thérèse et Isabelle* – represents an initiatory idyll, albeit a transitory one. However, in contrast to the bond between the protagonists of that later text, the Violette/Isabelle relation in *La Bâtarde* is in fact no less corrupted during its brief duration by issues of domination and subordination than that which obtains between Cataplame and his sweetheart. Once again, the erotic relation is instigated by an ostentatious display of supplication and 'courtship' (constituted by Isabelle's petulant antics in the cloakroom of the *collège* she and Violette attend; antics which are a plea for the other girl's attention/'recognition', even though they seem to signal hostility), enjoys an interim phase during which love appears to bloom harmoniously, and closes with the 'murder'/decapitation – symbolic this time – of one (dominant) partner by the other. This occurs at a fair when Isabelle, grieving at the tangible diminution of Violette's desire for her, 'strangles' her lover with a paper ribbon. The erotic tie which binds Isabelle and Violette is more complex than that generated by 'l'affaire Cataplame'. On occasion, especially early on in their union, Violette is the subject instead of the object of supplication, and Isabelle, sexually at least, is the assertive, controlling ('phallic') partner: 'She was thrusting, thrusting, thrusting . . . She was putting out the eye of innocence' (p. 95).[21] Consequently, the master/slave dynamic, within the Isabelle/Violette relation, is not as rigidly unidirectional as before. Nevertheless, it is manifestly present and Violette, sensing the trap it represents, acts to elude it, even though it is not in fact she but rather Isabelle who is in the last analysis relegated to 'slave' status. Violette's action damages irreparably her bond with her partner. Her efforts at evasion take the form of a competition for her own affection and attention which she generates between her mother – who is also, at this point at least, 'courting' her – and her lover. This contest is palpably exploited by Violette in order that she might emerge· from a (by now) stifling erotic union, but is disingenuously presented by her older, narrating self simply as the product of a situation over which she had no control. It does not last long, and is not accorded a particularly significant place in Leduc's narrative. However, it intimates to the reader the future use which, in her affective and erotic life, Violette will endeavour to make of triadic relational configurations.

In summary, then, by the time Violette enters into adulthood, she has come to intuit (or, more precisely perhaps, is presented by her older, wiser narrating self as intuiting) that splitting and disequilibrium inevitably characterize binary love-bonds, that such bonds can be 'fatal' – even though she herself has survived 'murder' by Isabelle – and that they are to be treated with circumspection. She has also been afforded the perception that the intervention of a third party offers, at the very least, a means of release from them. These discoveries determine the nature and the direction of her dealings with the two characters who, after Violette, are the key 'players' in *La Bâtarde*: Hermine and Gabriel. The next part of my discussion will trace the evolution of her relations with these individuals and will explore in detail the vision Leduc offers of the fight for desiring mastery. It will indicate also the extent to which Violette's manipulation of triangular relationships constitutes a strategy that is doomed to disappoint her.

Violette's relationship with Hermine, a former teacher at the *collège* she attended with Isabelle, lasts nine years. In the course of the account Leduc's narrator provides of this lesbian liaison, very little space is given over to descriptions of the pleasures of desire or of physical intimacy. What we get instead is a tortuous chronicle of power games; games from which Violette eventually emerges as both victorious – because she has achieved 'the end of a love affair . . . the end of a tyranny' (p. 239)[22] – and abandoned. The reader is left with the sense that at no stage is there any lasting equilibrium or mutuality between Leduc's lovers. Within the Hermine/Violette dyad, it initially appears that Hermine, a 'self-sacrifice addict' (p. 156)[23] bent upon satisfying the whims of her imperious and needy lover, is always the subservient partner; the 'negated', confirming other whose function is to shore up Violette's sense of selfhood and supremacy. This is not, however, the case. For much of the time, Violette is in reality compelled into a position of subordination; a position which Hermine imposes by virtue of her acts of apparent (but only apparent) self-abnegation. Hermine's self-suppression – signalled *inter alia* by the gifts she insistently offers her mistress – constitutes a trap for Violette. It represents in fact a (masochistic, ineluctable) demand for recognition and love on Hermine's part; a demand which oppresses Violette and lures her into passivity and objectification. Leduc's narrator intimates as much when she comments, early on in her recollections of her affair with Hermine: 'I had to become a whore: she wanted to be a martyr' (p. 155).[24] This observation – whose context will be made apparent below – suggests the self-interested deliberation which subtends Hermine's loving martyrdom, indicates that Violette finds this burdensome, and hints that it is actually she who is consigned, as a result of her lover's (seemingly) self-sacrificial stance, to a subordinated state; a state that is symbolized by her role as Hermine's whore/ 'putain'.

So what are the precise modalities of Hermine's 'enslavement' of Violette? Why should Leduc's narrator equate the subordination her lover's desire inflicted with a vision of herself as a tart? As Isabelle de Courtivron points out, 'during the years she spends with Hermine,

Violette explores the process of feminization, the pressures of the commercial machinery that mass-produces "femininity"'.[25] The feminization to which de Courtivron refers is in fact a key strategy employed by Hermine in order to 'prostitute' and entrap Violette as her object/other; an entrapment which is facilitated by Hermine's exploitation of mirrors and of a kind of vestimentary 'negation' of her lover.

When Hermine sews for Violette, or buys her clothes, it seems at first that this is simply an expression of her capacity for generosity and selflessness, and an indication that, within the love relation which binds her to her partner, it is she who is the object/victim of Violette's need to be dominant and desired. This is suggested, for example, during the episode in which Hermine is forced by the fractious Violette to make a shirt for her: 'I had wanted a collar so tight it would almost grow into my flesh. Hermine said that she would alter it . . . Forgive my sleepless night, forgive the wretched results, her eyes begged' (p. 168).[26] Here, evidently, it is indeed Hermine who emerges as (sexual) victim, mendicant and 'recognizer'. However, as Leduc's narrative proceeds, it becomes apparent that the production and/or the gift of various (feminizing) costumes affords Hermine the opportunity to reverse the master/slave dynamic evidenced in the above extract and to accede to a position of control *vis-à-vis* Violette. Her loving 'gifts' – ostensibly, the symbol of her self-denial – are, in other words, a vehicle for self-assertion rather than self-abnegation, and are harmful to her lover. Habitually, Hermine's offering of them is witnessed and confirmed by a mirror, whose presence propels Violette into the alienating, immobilizing domain of the Imaginary, imposing identifications/constraints which prove inimical to her autonomy.[27]

The first occasion on which the mirror/clothes/whore topos surfaces in the narrative is during a visit Violette makes to the country village in which Hermine is teaching. In the course of this visit, Hermine produces the first of the vestimentary tokens she offers her lover: a delicate lace nightgown. It is a gift of love, a gift indicative of the erotic attraction Hermine feels for Violette and, seemingly, a gift that suggests the older woman's willingness to make herself into a martyr of generosity. It is also, however, as Violette senses, a gift designed to transform her into her lover's creature, into a passive, fetishized object whose presence serves to substantiate the supremacy of the other woman: 'I had to get into bed, I had to powder my face, I had to wear a luxurious nightdress. I had to become a whore . . .' (p. 155).[28] The objectification which Violette intimates and fears here is rapidly consolidated by Hermine, who uses a glass in order to reify

Violette's (inadequate, 'prostituted') femininity and to highlight her status as the inferior, confirmatory reflection/reflector of her mistress: 'She ran in, she held the mirror higher, lower, more to the right, more to the left. Of the two, she was the prettier, the more feminine, the more courageous. . . . I was her relic, her looking glass' (p. 155).[29] Hermine's generosity, in other words, masks an unacknowledged desire to elicit recognition and achieve mastery; a mastery which is signalled by Violette's vestimentary metamorphosis into a 'whore', and which Hermine confirms through her manipulation of the mirror. It is shortly after this that Leduc's narrator articulates explicitly the noxious dimension of her lover's 'generosity', evoking, significantly, Hermine's fondness for sewing as she evokes the sapping of her own independence that is effected by her *maîtresse/martyre*: 'Hermine devours me, Hermine pricks me all over with a needle and pours all she has to give me into every pore of my skin' (p. 155).[30]

We find the same conjunction of the ('loving') gift of clothes, the (harmful) presence of a mirror and the palpable generation of subordination (Violette's, *vis-à-vis* the superficially self-denying Hermine) in a key scene of *La Bâtarde* which takes place in a salesroom in the Schiaparelli fashion house. By this point, Violette has fallen ill and has been persuaded by Hermine to abandon her job, to become her lover's 'little woman'. Her autonomy has already, in other words, been exposed to serious threat by the love relation in which she finds herself. It is, however, during and after the Schiaparelli episode that her 'negation' is consolidated. What happens here is that Hermine offers Violette a new costume; one, this time, which is not of her own making, and which the lovers buy with their savings. Like the lace nightdress, this garment (an eel-coloured suit) represents, ostensibly, a token of love and, like the nightdress, it constitutes in reality a kind of enclosing and demeaning carapace. As Violette tries it on, she is left with such a sense of paralysis, such a feeling that she is being 'robotized' and absorbed into a quagmire of helplessness, that she is compelled to appeal for Hermine's help: '"It should suit you. You have a mannequin's figure" said a voice behind me. . . . Mannequin, mannequin . . . I'm a mannequin, I said to myself, and felt disheartened. I was in a quicksand. Help me Hermine, I implored. I'm a mannequin standing all naked in a fashion house, I'm sinking into a quicksand and soon you'll see nothing but my head' (p. 196).[31] Rather than providing the succour she craves, however, Hermine accompanies Violette to another glass which, like the mirror in her rural schoolhouse, serves to strengthen the mastery over her lover which the purchase of the Schiaparelli suit − another fetishizing, 'prostituting' item of apparel − affords her. The outfit transforms

Violette into a kind of 'super-putain', as her subsequent, highly comic man-hunting antics on the boulevards of Paris reveal. Concomitantly, it secures and symbolizes Hermine's victory over her lover/whore; a victory that is reinforced by her own 'selfless' decision not to purchase anything for herself from the fashion house. The description Leduc's narrator provides of Violette's besuited mirror-image clearly signals the imprisoning, reificatory function of her tight-fitting costume and of the glass which reflects it: 'I didn't dare sit down, I didn't dare look at myself in the triple mirror. I just remembered the perfection of the cut: the wide shoulders and the pinched in waist' (p. 197).[32] Observing her strait-jacketed self and the reflective space which contains her image, observing Hermine, the 'martyr' who has wisely refused to be tempted into vestimentary metamorphosis/objectification, Violette is left feeling lifeless. Not unsurprisingly, her lover, scenting the other's defeat, declares herself to be overjoyed.

In an essay entitled '*La Bâtarde* or Why the Writer Writes',[33] Jean Snitzer Schoenfeld argues that the Schiaparelli mirror scene conveys a profound desire on the part of Leduc's narrator/heroine to achieve, by means of the manipulation of her reflections in the three-sided glass, an Imaginary totalization of the fragmented parts of her psyche. For Schoenfeld, in other words, this episode situates Violette at a kind of (failed) Lacanian Mirror Stage, albeit of an adult variety, and is indicative of her enduring quest for coherent selfhood. Schoenfeld's analysis of the Schiaparelli incident is undeniably illuminating. However, it obscures the fact that what is taking place here is in reality the culmination of a *loss* of subjectivity; a loss that is forced upon Violette by a more powerful, if apparently self-abnegatory, loving other. The Schiaparelli mirror is not, then, the site of an initiation of self-consciousness. It is rather, as Violette senses, a 'vampire', a glass which entraps and encloses. It is a mirror whose alienating function cannot be dissociated from the struggle for control and domination that characterizes the desiring bond between Hermine and Violette, a bond which makes a harlot of the latter.

In the course of her liaison with Hermine, Violette is driven to collaborate in the negation that is attendant upon her feminization. Increasingly, she becomes rapacious, avid for the gifts and gender-tokens her lover has to offer. She even stoops, on one occasion, to stealing silk underwear from a department store in order to demonstrate her acceptance of her 'putain' status ('I was stealing . . . in order to rob the other women of the things that made them feminine' (p. 179)).[34] She also, however, resists the sexual enslavement to which her dealings with Hermine subject her. Her strategies of resistance revolve in the first instance around her exploitation of the presence, and the gaze, of a (male) other: Gabriel. This character, with his gentleness, his feminine airs, his unthreatening physical presence, seems to Violette to furnish the ideal interventionary element with which to alleviate Hermine's mastery and her own consequent inferiorization. Gabriel's absence of virility, his undemanding, masochistic stoicism in the face of Violette's sexual skittishness, indeed the lack of desire which she doggedly imputes to him all render him appealing to Violette because she believes, evidently, that these characteristics preclude the alarming possibility that he might in his turn dominate her sexually and become the source of further subordination. Because Gabriel is Violette's supplicant, because she can play male to his (subordinated) female, because in his company she can even 'drag up' and escape the vestimentary manipulations of her mistress ('The necktie I wore, my sex for Gabriel; the carnation in my buttonhole . . ., my sex for Gabriel' (p. 167)),[35] Violette perceives him as offering some kind of solution to her predicament. This is made clear, for instance, in the account we are given of a visit Hermine and Violette make to a concert. In the course of the evening, during which Gabriel plays spectator to the lesbian lovers' interaction, his voyeuristic presence is shown to 'obliterate' the oblivious Hermine and consequently to delight Violette, even as it causes her to experience feelings of intense guilt: 'We are murdering Hermine while she smiles at the violas . . . I'm going to turn my head round, I'm going to murder Hermine a little more. . . . Gabriel, is that what it means to enjoy your beloved? Hermine, is that what it means to die in blissful ignorance . . .? Violette, is that the meaning of betrayal?' (pp. 130–1).[36]

The triangular relation which Violette is establishing here has little or nothing to do with the erotic triad as it is constructed by Marguerite Duras in texts such as *L'Amant* and *Le Ravissement de Lol V. Stein*, in which the presence or image of a third party permits a kind of circulation of desire.[37] It offers no occasion for communion or pleasure, save that generated for Gabriel by his inexplicable, masochistic longing for exclusion. There is only betrayal and tacit revenge here. Nevertheless, because Violette is driven by the nature of her bond with Hermine to pursue such ends, the triadic scenario she sets up, and the vital place it accords to Gabriel, appear to her, for a while at least, to be desirable. In the long run, however, the Gabriel/Violette/Hermine trio fails to provide her with the enfranchisement she seeks. There are a number of reasons for its failure to satisfy her.

For one thing, despite Violette's determination to situate Gabriel, her interventionary third, somehow outside the realm of desire – because desire creates the potential for enslavement, and must therefore be distanced – she must recognize that she *is* the object of his erotic attentions, that this fact exposes her to a kind of sexual colonization, and that the threat of subordination is therefore present once again. Leduc's narrator makes this apparent when she recalls Gabriel's gaze; the gaze which was supposed to function disruptively, to effect a mediatory attenuation of her domination by Hermine (as during the Châtelet concert), but which is also in fact the vehicle for his 'penetration'/possession of her: '[His] gaze. His ecstasy: gentler than an erection. His gaze: semen, against his will, against my will' (p. 159).[38] There are further problems, for Violette, with Gabriel and more specifically with his gaze. His position as excluded voyeur is, as we saw earlier, initially pleasing to Violette because his scopic intrusiveness allows her to 'betray' Hermine and thereby to alleviate her own slave-status. However, Gabriel's eyes function also for Violette as a mirror in which her union with Hermine – and her own inferior situation within it – are confirmed and preserved. It is in the truth-mirror of Gabriel's objectifying gaze that Violette, shortly before the Schiaparelli episode, is presented with incontrovertible proof of the negation/prostitution to which Hermine's loving 'generosity' relegates her: 'His eyes brushed my legs and turned away. When he looked at me again, his eyes said: you're turning into a whore, she's making you into a whore' (p. 188).[39] In Sartrean terms, the 'other's look' here, far from furnishing Violette with the liberation she craves, is annihilatory: the source of a (shameful) 'solidification and alienation of [her] own possibilities'.[40]

In effect, Violette succumbs to a state of quasi-dependence *vis-à-vis* Gabriel which reflects that binding her to Hermine and illuminates the failure of her attempt to make him into her interventionary tool. He may seem as self-denying, in her company, as Hermine does, but his (sexual) martyrdom, like Hermine's, ultimately constitutes a constraint. Consequently, the triangle Violette forms with Gabriel and Hermine provides her with no lasting support. If anything, it reinforces her servitude instead of diminishing it, and she is not unhappy when Gabriel disappears. She is driven, however, in the wake of the Schiaparelli incident and its aftermath, to construct a new sexual triangle. This second triad involves an anonymous (and, therefore, more malleable) stranger Violette picks up in the street. Its creation brings about the end of her union with Hermine in a way that the trio which included Gabriel failed – and was not indeed intended – to do. The mechanics of this further triangle are predicated upon the same basic elements – specularity, voyeurism – as the Gabriel/Hermine/Violette trio. Before they can be explored, we need to establish what it is that provokes Violette into exploiting erotic triangulation in order to shatter her relationship with Hermine rather than simply to alleviate its discontents.

Shortly after her acquisition of the Schiaparelli suit, Violette undergoes a cathartic experience, which takes place one evening as she strolls besuited with Hermine on the Pont de la Concorde. This event is so cataclysmic, and so shocking to her, that the reader is not, for some considerable time, made privy to what stimulates it. What we see instead are the consequences of its stimulus, consequences which bring Violette close to a kind of self-immolation. Clad in her 'tailleur', she begins by sensing that she has received a stunning blow to the chest. Subsequently, she feels as if she is vomiting up her guts as her suit/carapace falls away, she loses control over language, then loses even the power of speech so that she can only groan like an animal or a baby. Finally, she narrowly avoids succumbing to the temptation to hurl herself into the Seine which, like a woman lover, beckons her invitingly into its engulfing, deathly bosom.[41] During all of this, she feels as if she is caught in a vice; a vice that is of Hermine's making, since it is Hermine who is the source of the gripping movements which exacerbate her extreme distress. It is only after the lovers manage to embrace that Violette can tell the by now distraught Hermine what has happened, and can explain that her crisis has been provoked by words thrown in her direction by a female passer-by: words which cruelly draw attention to Violette's baroque features.

Clearly, the key to this episode is Violette's near-total subjective disintegration. On the surface, what seems to be occurring is a demonstration of her enduring difficulties with her unfortunate physical appearance (specifically her large nose), which the anonymous woman has elected to mock, and which the elegant Schiaparelli outfit has failed to ameliorate. There are, however, other, more serious issues at stake in this scene. What we see here, arguably, is Violette's ultimate *prise de conscience* of her enslaved, de-subjectivized state, a state for which Hermine is responsible and which is symbolically staged by the drama of Violette's physical, linguistic and vestimentary collapse on the Pont de la Concorde. This *prise de conscience* is evidently generated by the casual remark made by the woman passer-by ('If I looked like that, I'd kill myself').[42] We can, if we choose, read her observation both as an articulation of Violette's degraded 'putain' status and its deadliness, and as the emancipatory catalyst which forces her into casting off the whoredom/subordination her sexual liaison imposes. This interpretation is justified, *inter alia*, by the fact that much later on, after Violette has liberated herself from Hermine's thraldom and is reflecting upon her liberation, she recalls explicitly the intervention by the woman on the Pont de la Concorde, referring to it, tellingly, as 'Providence' (p. 240).[43]

Ironically, the events glossed above generate the only moment of real affective mutuality between Violette and Hermine. Faced with her lover's distress, Hermine demonstrates authentic generosity and selflessness by weeping in her turn, with the result that we see, briefly, the realization of a genuine sexual and emotional intersubjective equilibrium: 'We wound our arms around each other and we wept. We moved in a circle as we stood, we circled on the deserted bank, the tears from Hermine's nose running down on to my neck, my cheek. And the tears from my nose on to her cheek, on to her neck. . . . Sex and charity. Our ovaries, our clitorises were melting too' (p. 221).[44] Divisive grief and pain afford Leduc's protagonists access to a dynamic in which each palpably manifests recognition of/desire for the other-as-subject, and is rewarded in her turn with the other's recognition/desire, so that there is for once no threat of inequality or domination. However, this interruption of the normal modalities of her subordinating bond with her mistress is not enough to deter Violette from breaking with Hermine. The break – which is not presented by Leduc's narrator as the product of intention but which is nevertheless clearly sought out by Violette – is achieved as a result of the triangular 'partie fine' that takes place in the Rue Godot-de-Mauroy.

Violette ostensibly sets up the episode that occurs in the Rue Godot-de-Mauroy in order that she might buy a green lacquer table for which she longs. In actual fact, her desire for the table – which, significantly, contains a mirror-panel – serves as a pretext for the vengeance she seeks to wreak upon the previously ascendant Hermine. Violette's revenge incorporates what is obviously a deliberate replay/reversal of Hermine's earlier, negatory exploitation of mirrors, and is all the more violent as a result. During the 'partie fine' which is its vehicle, she forces Hermine to make love with her in a Parisian 'maison de rendezvous', in a room which contains a mirrored ceiling and a three-sided mirror. This last is not unlike the glass which witnessed her own vestimentary debasement, and Hermine's unacknowledged joy at it, *chez* Schiaparelli. This time, though, it is Hermine who is exposed to (specular/Imaginary) debasement, within the confines of the brothel mirrors and before an anonymous voyeur, who is paying to watch the lovers' sexual play. On the surface, Violette tolerates the presence of this individual because his money will enable her to acquire her table; in reality, however, she countenances and exploits it in order to hurt Hermine and overturn the master/slave dynamic that binds the two of them. Violette's venality and her manipulation of the mirror/voyeur conjunction offer her, in other words, a way back to domination and an opportunity definitively to 'obliterate' Hermine (who is caught, here, in the snare of her own self-martyrization): 'He sat down on the satin bedcover. . . . I was promising Hermine the most extravagant sensations. Broken in my arms, she listened and watched me in the mirror' (p. 231).[45]

There is no suggestion at this point, as there was in the interventionary scenario involving Gabriel, that ascendancy is in any way acceded to the male desiring spy. Leduc does not reproduce here the conventional (i.e. male-authored) version of the lesbian/voyeur topos, which, as Lucienne Frappier-Mazur explains, relies generally upon the creation of 'a threesome during which the male observer secures active control of the situation'.[46] The nameless voyeur Violette manipulates is clearly presented as so needy and so 'castrated' that supremacy is hers alone. In his study of voyeurism in Proust, Michel Erman argues convincingly that the delights of the voyeuristic act can be summed up in the motto 'see without being seen'[47] and that voyeuristic mastery is predicated upon the total self-dissimulation of the spying subject. The voyeur of the Rue Godot-de-Mauroy is too involved, and too submissive, to access the distanced mastery Erman evokes, so it is Violette who is uniquely victorious here. Her victory over Hermine is signalled by her perception that her lover has become her sacrificial victim, and by yet another evocation of symbolic decapitation, which recalls the annunciatory throat-slashing activities of Cataplame: 'I stood rooted to the spot as I wiped away Hermine's tears. I was supporting the weight of her head on my shoulder' (p. 231).[48]

In the months and years which follow this episode, Hermine – understandably enough – detaches herself from Violette. Her eventual defection grieves her abandoned lover deeply, but needs none the less to be interpreted as a function of Violette's will and of her longing to liberate herself from the 'tyranny' of desire. Unfortunately for Violette, her liberation proves to be short-lived. The re-entry into her life of Gabriel, coupled with her encounter with the homosexual writer Maurice Sachs, ensures that the same affective and sexual patterns which circumscribed her bond with Hermine reassert themselves, leaving her stricken and, in the long run, alone once more.

As soon as she becomes involved with Gabriel for a second time, Violette is granted the perception – which she endeavours to ignore – that subordination and submission are back on her sexual agenda. Initially, she seeks to avoid the fate she intuits by establishing with Gabriel an ersatz male homosexual bond: 'I asked Gabriel to make love to me as a man makes love to another man' (p. 289).[49] She does so, presumably, because the pseudo-male same-sex relation she envisages embarking upon, constituting as it does (i) a counterpoint to the female/female link she previously shared with Hermine and (ii) an (imaginary) erotic space in which she need no longer play the little woman/whore, seems to Violette to be potentially free of the inequalities that dogged her lesbian liaison. Despite her efforts to 'homosexualize' her marriage to Gabriel, however, and despite the erotic pleasures it affords her at first, it becomes as much of a prison for Violette as her relationship with Hermine. She succumbs to a state of extreme subjective annihilation, which results from Gabriel's negatory reluctance to offer her the sexual attention she so badly needs. Narcissistically self-protective, and highly wary of Violette's emasculatory erotic demands, Gabriel increasingly abstracts sexual recognition. Violette, re-entrapped in (a new form of) erotic enslavement – signalled by the various references to her sexual mendicancy that are contained in the text – resorts once again to triangulation.

Violette's belief, to begin with, is that the establishment of a 'trio' incorporating herself, her husband and Sachs, to whom she has become close, will prove emancipatory. However, she is disabused of this view as she is gradually forced to accept that all she achieves by involving Sachs in her affective machinations is a greater degree of sexual alienation from Gabriel. The Gabriel/Violette/Sachs triangle, like the triadic link between Gabriel, Hermine and Violette, offers Leduc's autobiographical heroine no comfort and simply exacerbates her difficulties. Eventually, as in her union with Hermine, she is driven to seek out another, anonymous male third – on this occasion, somewhat ludicrously, a besmocked almond seller – in order to bring about the (liberatory) destruction of her deteriorating relationship with her husband. This second triadic cataclysm, like that which distanced Hermine, brings in fact no real release for Violette who, moreover, fails once again to acknowledge explicitly the extent to which her own intentionality generated it. It simply ushers in the 'farce' of the 'mariage blanc' she contracts with Sachs after they retreat to Normandy, during the Occupation.

The dynamics of her bond with the homosexual Sachs are complex in the extreme. In his company, Violette is impelled into a relationship in which she must be a 'woman without sex', undesired and undesiring. In her other dyadic love-bonds, Violette has either demanded or withheld sexual favours; here, sex – which is always, in *La Bâtarde*, a function of the master/slave paradigm, regardless of the gender of Leduc's desiring protagonists – is completely off the agenda. The consequences, for Violette, of the asexual nature of her union with Sachs are manifold. Deeply infatuated with the writer who encourages her own literary début, Violette experiences their bond as a torment of erotic denial. It seems therefore, on first reading at least, that this new manifestation of the self/other relation is, once again, fraught with difficulties for her, difficulties which derive on this occasion from the absence of sexual intimacy rather than its actualization. On the other hand, the 'hell' in which she finds herself also offers her access to a 'paradise of impossible love' (p. 403).[50] The reader is left with the sense that this paradise enchants Violette even as it frustrates her because it precludes, definitively, the possibility of desire, and therefore (in theory, at least) means that she faces no renewed risk of sexual enslavement. Sachs, on one level, effectively constitutes for Violette the 'ideal' partner Gabriel failed to incarnate; the non-desiring male subject who cannot and will not subordinate her – hence the gratification which his homosexuality and their celibate liaison secretly afford her: 'She could never imagine him otherwise than as a homosexual. His sex rising for her would be a masquerade' (p. 387).[51] However, Violette can never completely forget that Sachs, for all his sexual detachment, is capable of leaving her demeaned and diminished (notably as a result of the jealousy his intimacy with other males provokes in her). Consequently, she fails to gain enduring satisfaction from her dealings with him – which are, in any case, predicated upon a masochism that cannot fail, she senses, to harm her in the long term. This is why eventually, when Sachs – having fled his creditors and gone to Germany as a 'travailleur volontaire' – seeks to come home to Normandy and asks Violette to fake a pregnancy in order to facilitate his return, she refuses. Her refusal ensures, finally, her liberation from the maze of love-bonds which have oppressed her hitherto. Equally, it announces her embrace of an affective solitude that will prove to be more or less unrelieved,[52] and, moreover, helps to bring about Sachs's death.

By the end of *La Bâtarde*, Violette has dedicated herself to the pursuit of unattainable love objects – because, as de Courtivron comments, impossible love-relations allow her to 'avoid the polluting effects of sexual contacts'.[53] However, with the exception of her bond with Sachs, the desiring relationships which Leduc's first autobiographical work stages are not exemplary of her future 'passion de l'impossible' (*LB*, p. 462). Violette's erotic liaisons with Isabelle, Hermine and Gabriel are all potentially functional bonds. If they fail, it is because their participants (especially, but not exclusively, Violette) never manage to achieve an equilibrium in which the needs of the self and the demands of the other are harmonized, so that a mutual 'recognition' of equal, desiring subjects is realized. Leduc's charting of their disintegration – and its (needless) inevitability – is a key contributory factor to the disquiet *La Bâtarde* arouses in its readers, transforming as it does her narrative into a tale whose 'truth', essentially, is that desire always and ineluctably comes to grief.

My last point rather begs the question 'Why include a chapter on Leduc, or, at the very least, why include a reading of *La Bâtarde*, in a collection of essays subtitled *Desiring Writing?*' By illuminating the detours and difficulties of her physical and affective relationships, Violette Leduc's first autobiographical volume undoubtedly breaks new ground. For all its pessimism regarding self/other bonding – indeed, because of it – *La Bâtarde* has something compelling to say about the labyrinth of desire. We need to remember also that Leduc's autobiography, whilst devoid of the vulgar exhibitionism it was accused by some of displaying, is a text which places openly on display a woman's *personal* experience of feminine – and more particularly lesbian – sexuality. We may, Elaine Marks argues, include *La Bâtarde* in the pantheon of innovatory, female-authored French works that have engendered a 'sexual and textual revolution' precisely because its autobiographical character means that in it, for the first time, 'the lesbian is no longer the object of literary discourse seen from an outside point of view. She is her own heroine.'[54] *La Bâtarde* undeniably poses problems for (radical) feminist readers, in so far as it represents feminine homoerotic interaction in almost as negative a light as heterosexual relations.[55] By presenting the Violette/Isabelle bond and (especially) the Violette/Hermine relationship as marked by a master/slave dynamic which is parallel to, if less inflexible than, that circumscribing Violette's marital union with Gabriel, Leduc's autobiography anticipates Kristeva's depressing contention that even in a lesbian encounter, women cannot avoid the domination/submission paradigm characteristic of phallocentric eroticism.[56] There are few signs here of an attempt on Leduc's part at celebrating alternative erotic modes or libidinal economies. In spite of this, *La Bâtarde*, appearing at the historical moment that it did and chronicling what it does, undoubtedly constitutes a landmark on the road towards what Leduc herself viewed as a necessary 'opening up' of female sexuality ('la mise à jour nécessaire d'une sexualité trop longtemps maintenue secrète'[57]). Her own belief was that she had extended the scope of women's sexual discourse, but that she had not, in the final analysis, been bold enough in *La Bâtarde*. After its publication, she commented to the journalist Madeleine Chapsal that she had sought to be radically 'daring' – more daring than Colette – in her transcription of the erotic, that she had failed in her task, and that her failure should serve to encourage younger women writers to go further

than she herself had.[58] To those of us who have been, and continue
to be, captivated by Leduc's writing, the lack of self-confidence, the
characteristic self-flagellation which she manifests in her discussion
with Chapsal appear sadly misplaced.

Notes

1. In his review 'Elle aura été bâtarde jusqu'au bout' (*Le Match de
   Paris*, 12 December 1964) Roger Mauge suggests that it was Mme
   Simone herself who described *La Bâtarde* as 'un livre qu'on ne
   pourrait pas laisser sur la cheminée'. Leduc, however, attributed
   the remark to a member of the Goncourt jury. Leduc's biographer,
   Carlo Jansiti, believes that the latter version is the correct one.
2. 'Cette Violette ne sent pas bon', *Minute*, 30 October 1964.
3. It is worth noting here that many of their colleagues chose rather
   to laud the 'sincérité intrépide' of Leduc's autobiography – a trait
   which Simone de Beauvoir isolates as the key to the unique flavour
   of Leduc's text, in her preface to *La Bâtarde* (Paris, Gallimard
   (édition blanche), 1964, p. 8). Henceforth, all page references to
   the original, French version of *La Bâtarde* will be to this edition.
   Page references for, and quotations from, the English version of
   the text will relate to the 1965 translation by Derek Coltman,
   published in London by Peter Owen, and will be contained in the
   body of my chapter.
4. 'Un roman sulfureux où des collégiennes s'aimaient et où une
   femme parlait avec crudité de sa sexualité.' René de Ceccatty, *La
   Sentinelle du rêve*, Paris, 1988, p. 95 (my translation). This novel, a
   fictionalized account of de Ceccatty's experience of working on
   Leduc and of his relationships with her devotees, makes compelling
   reading for students of her writing.
5. Two related observations may be made here. First, the fact that
   Leduc's text is an autobiography undoubtedly helps explain the
   furore it provoked in certain critical quarters. Because we interpret
   autobiographical works as governed by a commitment to the
   referential/factual and as tied, however problematically, to a real,
   flesh-and-blood person, autobiographical accounts of sexuality are
   more prone to be read as 'scandalous' than their fictional counterparts. Second, it is most unlikely that sexual openness of the kind
   contained in *La Bâtarde*, had it been in evidence in a *male-authored*
   autobiography published contemporaneously, would have engendered the fuss that surrounded the publication of Leduc's text.
6. Henri Peyre, 'Passions of a Gallic Sappho', *Saturday Review*, 30

October 1965, pp. 46–7.

7. Madan Sarup, *An Introductory Guide to Poststructuralism and Postmodernism*, New York and London, 1993, p. 18.

8. Jessica Benjamin, 'The Bonds of Love: Rational Violence and Erotic Domination', in Hester Eisenstein and Alice Jardine (eds), *The Future of Difference*, New Brunswick and London, 1985, pp. 41–70, see especially pp. 48–9.

9. Ibid., pp. 48–9.

10. For Benjamin's discussion of this see her full-length study *The Bonds of Love: Psychoanalysis, Feminism and the Problem of Domination*, London, 1990, p. 19 and *passim*.

11. Alexandre Kojève, *Introduction to the Reading of Hegel* (trans. James H. Nichols), New York and London, 1969, p. 8.

12. Benjamin, *The Bonds of Love*, p. 36.

13. The paradox here being, as Judith Butler explains, that of 'the unexpected dependency of the master on the slave in order to establish his own identity through reflection'. Judith Butler, *Gender Trouble*, New York and London, 1990, p. 44.

14. 'Son malheur, c'est de ne connaître avec personne un rapport de réciprocité: ou l'autre est pour elle un objet, ou elle se fait objet pour lui. . . . Même en amour, surtout en amour, l'échange est impossible' (*La Bâtarde*, p. 9).

15. Michael Sheringham also provides helpful insights into this phenomenon in his *French Autobiography: Devices and Desires*, Oxford, 1993, pp. 216–17.

16. Isabelle de Courtivron, *Violette Leduc*, Boston, 1985, p. 86.

17. 'Un fêlé devint amoureux de sa voisine' (*LB*, p. 42).

18. 'Un matin de soleil je vis un rassemblement devant la maison. Je questionnai un groupe de jeunes filles en effervescence. – Cataplame a tranché la gorge de sa maîtresse me dit l'une d'elles' (*LB*, p. 44).

19. For an account of Leduc's representation of the phallic woman and of male devirilization, see Ghyslaine Charles-Merrien, *Violette Leduc ou le corps morcelé*, unpublished *thèse de doctorat*, *Université de Rennes* II, 1988, pp. 197–8. Charles-Merrien argues here that all Leduc's phallic women constitute avatars of her mother Berthe, who is consistently represented as masculinized. According to this critic, Berthe's 'virility' is conveyed, for example, by references to her hard blue gaze, which indicates that Leduc accepted the Freudian equation of the eye and the penis (see 'The Uncanny', *Standard Edition*, vol. XVII, pp. 217–53 (p. 231)). The phallic mother, in Leduc's writing, is also associated with elevation, towers etc., which likewise connote masculinity. Mme

Armande's elevated state, as well as the emphasis placed upon her gaze, strengthens the reader's sense that she is one of Leduc's various 'femmes phalliques'.

20. The link between decapitation and castration is established by Freud in 'The Taboo of Virginity', *Standard Edition*, vol. XI, pp. 191–208 (p. 207). As other parts of my discussion will indicate, this association recurs throughout Leduc's writing, which is full of scenes of throat-cutting, strangulation, asphyxiation etc.

21. 'Elle donnait des coups, des coups, des coups . . . Elle crevait l'oeil de l'innocence' (*LB*, p. 94).

22. 'la fin d'un amour, . . . la fin d'une tyrannie' (*LB*, p. 238).

23. A 'droguée de sacrifices' (*LB*, p. 155).

24. 'Je devais devenir une putain: elle voulait être une martyre' (*LB*, p. 154).

25. De Courtivron, *Violette Leduc*, p. 87.

26. 'Je voulais un col serré à l'incrustation. Hermine dit qu'elle le modifierait . . . Pardon pour ma nuit blanche, pardon pour ce triste résultat, suppliaient ses yeux' (*LB*, p. 168).

27. Imaginary identifications, as theorized by Lacan, involve an 'erotic relationship between an individual and an image which alienates him': Anika Lemaire, *Jacques Lacan*, London and New York, 1977, p. 178. In *La Bâtarde*, Violette certainly succumbs to an alienation that derives from her 'fixation' upon/transformation into an image; however, her movement into the Imaginary derives primarily from the deleterious effects upon her of the desires/needs of another – Hermine – rather than from her own embrace of specular reassurance/stasis.

28. 'Je devais me coucher, je devais me poudrer, je devais porter la chemise de nuit luxueuse. Je devais devenir une putain . . .' (*LB*, p. 154).

29. 'Elle accourait, elle tenait le miroir plus haut, plus bas, plus à droite, plus à gauche. De nous deux, c'était elle la plus jolie, la plus féminine, la plus valeureuse. . . . J'étais sa relique, son miroir' (*LB*, p. 154).

30. 'Hermine me dévore, Hermine me pique partout avec une aiguille, elle donne ce qu'elle a à donner entre les pores de ma peau' (*LB*, p. 155).

31. '– Il doit vous aller. Vous avez la taille mannequin, dit une voix derrière moi. . . . Mannequin, mannequin . . . Je suis un mannequin, me disais-je, découragée. Je m'enlisais. Sauve-moi, Hermine, implorai-je. Je suis un mannequin tout nu de maison de confection, je m'enlise et tu ne verras bientôt que ma tête'

(*LB*, p. 195).

32. 'Je n'osais pas m'asseoir, je n'osais pas me regarder dans la glace à trois faces. Je me souvenais de la perfection de la coupe: épaules larges et rembourrées, taille resserrée' (*LB*, p. 196).

33. Jean Snitzer Schoenfeld, '*La Bâtarde* or Why the Writer Writes', *French Forum*, vol. 7, 1982, pp. 261–8.

34. 'Je volais . . . pour dérober aux femmes ce qui les féminise' (*LB*, p. 179).

35. 'Ma cravate, mon sexe pour Gabriel, l'oeillet à ma boutonnière . . ., mon sexe pour Gabriel' (*LB*, p. 167).

36. 'Nous assassinons Hermine pendant qu'elle sourit aux altos. . . . Je vais tourner la tête, je vais assassiner un peu plus Hermine. . . . Gabriel, c'est cela jouir? Hermine, c'est cela mourir au paradis de l'ignorance? Violette, c'est cela trahir?' (*LB*, p. 130).

37. See Marguerite Duras and Xavière Gautier, *Les Parleuses*, Paris, 1974, p. 47.

38. 'Le regard. Son extase: plus doux que bander. Son regard: du sperme, malgré lui, malgré moi' (*LB*, p. 158). As this extract indicates, the look, in Leduc's writing, is intimately and specifically bound up with *male* desire and masculinity. Clearly, Leduc endorses the Freudian eye/penis link, and it is as a result of this that those of her female characters who are shown to indulge in scopic activity may be read as phallic women. In spite of this fact, Leduc's reader must ensure that s/he does not automatically (and oversimplistically) equate the visual with the masculine. As Elizabeth Grosz points out, feminist critics and scholars who take this link as read should remember that 'vision is not, cannot be, masculine (nor the tactile or the auditory, feminine); rather, certain ways of using vision (for example, to objectify) may confirm and help produce patriarchal power relations': Elizabeth Grosz, in Elizabeth Wright (ed.), *Feminism and Psychoanalysis: A Critical Dictionary*, Oxford, 1992, p. 449.

39. 'Ses yeux frôlaient mes jambes, ses yeux se détournaient. Après, son regard m'exprimait: tu deviens une putain, elle fait de toi une putain' (*LB*, p. 188).

40. Sartre, *Being and Nothingness*, trans. Hazel E. Barnes, London, 1958, p. 263. As Elizabeth Grosz observes, for Sartre 'the look is fundamentally objectifying: by means of the look the subject is capable of being transformed into an object, reduced from a self-conscious subject, a being-for-itself, to a being-in-itself and for-others. The look can induce in the subject a sense of unmitigated shame at his/her being': *Feminism and Psychoanalysis*, p. 448. Clearly, Gabriel's gaze is functioning in the way Grosz

describes when it confirms Violette's status as 'whore'. However, the objectification of which it is the vehicle is secondary, Violette's primary objectification/'prostitution' having been inflicted by Hermine.

41. The scene of near-drowning which Leduc creates in this part of the text recalls (i) Violette's sense of being swallowed up before the mirror/vampire she encounters during the Schiaparelli episode and (ii) her perception, during her visit to Hermine's country schoolhouse, that her lover is devouring her. These three textual moments – all of which are of key significance as far as Violette's bond with Hermine is concerned – are linked by the notion of absorption and obliteration. This recurring theme constitutes a leitmotif that is indicative of the subordination and negation to which Violette's erotic relationship exposes her.

42. 'Moi, si j'avais cette tête-là, je me suiciderais' (*LB*, p. 221). Coltman gives 'If I had a face like that I'd kill myself' (p. 222), which renders 'tête' in too limited a way.

43. 'Cette monstrueuse passante du pont de la Concorde? La providence' (*LB*, p. 238).

44. 'Nous pleurions enlacées, nous tournions sur place, nous tournions sur la berge déserte, la morve d'Hermine coulait sur ma joue, dans mon cou. Ma morve coulait sur sa joue, dans son cou. . . . Charité du sexe. Fondaient aussi nos ovaires, notre clitoris' (*LB*, p. 221).

45. 'Il s'est assis sur le lit en satin. . . . Je promettais des sensations extravagantes à Hermine. Brisée, elle m'écoutait, elle me regardait dans le miroir' (*LB*, p. 229).

46. Lucienne Frappier-Mazur, 'Marginal Canons: Rewriting the Erotic', *Yale French Studies*, 75, 1988, pp. 112–28 (p. 116).

47. See Michel Erman, *L'Oeil de Proust: écriture et voyeurisme dans 'A la recherche du temps perdu'*, Paris, 1988, p. 100.

48. 'Je végétais pendant que j'essuyais les larmes d'Hermine. Je portais le poids de sa tête sur mon épaule' (*LB*, p. 229).

49. 'J'ai demandé à Gabriel de m'aimer comme un homme aime un autre homme' (*LB*, p. 287).

50. A 'séjour au paradis de l'amour impossible' (*LB*, p. 398).

51. 'Elle ne peut pas l'imaginer autrement qu'en homosexuel. Son sexe dressé pour elle serait une mascarade' (*LB*, p. 383). There are a number of passages in Leduc's autobiographical texts where the third person is used to replace the normal, first-person narrative mode. This substitution habitually occurs at moments of crisis and/or when Violette's older, narrating persona is subjecting her younger self to mockery or irony. Leduc's

employment here of this type of distancing technique is hardly surprising, given the glaring silliness of the (self-flagellatory) relationship Violette shares with Sachs, and of the secret contentment its asexuality affords her.

52. For Leduc's account of this, see volumes II and III of her autobiography: *La Folie en tête* (Paris, 1970) and *La Chasse à l'amour* (Paris, 1973).

53. *Violette Leduc*, p. 89.

54. Elaine Marks, 'Lesbian Intertextuality', in George Stambolian and Elaine Marks (eds), *Homosexualities and French Literature*, Ithaca and London, 1979, pp. 353–77 (p. 371, p. 373). In this essay, Marks contrasts Leduc with the more dissimulatory Colette (who obscures the issue of her own lesbianism in her writing) and positions her as a kind of 'foremother' of the more radical Wittig.

55. This is a point which Marks's discussion of the revolutionary potential of Leduc's personalized lesbian discourse fails to take sufficiently into account, in my view. It is worth noting here that in her novella *Thérèse et Isabelle*, Leduc presents lesbian love in a much more positive light, and attemps to envision a mode of feminine homoeroticism which departs from a heterosexualized, master/slave model. For a discussion of Leduc's utopian treatment of lesbianism in this later text, see my *Violette Leduc: Mothers, Lovers and Language*, London, 1994.

56. See Julia Kristeva, *Histoires d'amour*, Paris, 1983, p. 80. Kristeva's argument reflects her belief that the nature of the libido and the construction of human psychosexuality mean that the erotic domain is irredeemably phallic and that an 'érotique du féminin pur' (ibid.) devoid of 'les ravages du jeu maître-esclave' (ibid., p. 81) is a chimera.

57. Interview with Pierre Descargues, *Tribune de Lausanne*, 18 October 1964, p. 8.

58. Interview with Madeleine Chapsal, *L'Express*, 19 October 1964, p. 71.

– 4 –

Sophie Ménade: The Writing of Monique Wittig

Jennifer Birkett

Revolutionary Eros: The Utopian Body Politic

Of the many innovations of the 1960s, that revolutionary decade when the work of Monique Wittig first appeared, one of the most productive has been the reappropriation by women of the right to represent the nature of their own desire and the form of their own sexual pleasure. Equally, one of the most intense debates to arise in that context has focused on the position in which women writing desire find themselves in relation to a cultural tradition constructed in a masculine problematic.

One characterization of that position which has attracted substantial critical attention is that offered in, for example, the earlier work of Hélène Cixous. In her prose fiction *Angst* (1977), Cixous presents the woman writer, constituted in masculine culture, as 'wrestling' with a sense of non-being. She evokes the debilitating operation performed on the nascent feminine subject by the texts of a culture dominated by the masculine voice, which write her out of autonomous existence even as they summon her into a fiction of being. As she reads, she receives 'the truth about myself, not a truth I already knew, but that I recognised as the story developed, tightened its grip, pursued me and drove me through nations and centuries, stopped me ever finding rest and peace . . . had me . . . escaping from a trap to end up in a cage . . .'[1]

The instrumental narratives of entrapment are identified in *Angst* as Kafka's *The Trial* and the medieval romance, *Tristan and Isolde*: the tale of the mystery of power and its hierarchical exclusions and the tale of the fatal charm of transgressive love. The two work together to lock the female into an emblematic function as the incarnation of erotic seduction, permanently accused, essentially guilty. In a movement which reworks the theses of Denis de Rougemont's influential study, *L'Amour et l'Occident* (1938), *Angst* evokes the process by which the political and erotic grand narratives of Western culture 'frame' the feminine, in every sense, making of her the means by which generations enact the conflicts which reproduce patriarchal power. The masculine voice of these texts pins down the feminine to the beds that are the focal point of *Angst* – the birth-bed, marriage bed, deathbed on which sexual and social contracts are written. Seduced into the masculine eros, woman disappears from sight. She is the victim of a voice that 'stopped me, frightened me, made me want to run away, stopped me running, clamped me of my own free will to the bed I could no longer leave, down on the ground, sinking, getting smaller . . .'[2]

Interpellated by the language of such a sexual politics, the narrator of *Angst* finds both her creative powers and her sexual energies in deadlock. Any attempt to write her own desire in such a voice is futile to the point of obscenity. Her attempt to find pleasure in pushing her lover's letter, on his instructions, inside her vagina produces only frustration (*Angst*, pp. 229–31). Later texts break the deadlock with the creation of a distinctive *écriture féminine*. In the violent blaze of energies which is *Le Livre de Promethea*[3] (1983), the book becomes the safe haven, the rhetorical enclosure where the representation of feminine creative desire, in the language of the maternal body, is the sole object, subject and bounds of writing, a liberating end-in-itself.

For the materialist feminist Monique Wittig, the sense of disempowerment by an inherited masculine rhetoric has never been an issue. Like Cixous, Wittig identifies the oppressive elements of traditional discourses of sexuality. She does not, however, begin with the perception of desire as an alienating void. Rather, her starting-point is the knowledge of desire as identity, a place of one's own, and her work represents the writing of female desire in the language of the sociocultural tradition as a matter of confident negotiations. Wittig embarks on her writing project as one who already knows herself as a bearer of substantial difference, constituted in the distinctive sexual terrain of the lesbian body. Like the American Djuna Barnes, whose short story collection *Spillway* (1962) she translated in the early 1980s, or like Proust, whom they both admire, Wittig presents herself as entering the world of heterosexual desire at an angle, from the margins, fired with a sense of obligation to bring her marginalized discourse into the mainstream of contemporary textuality, in a way that will change both mainstream writing and the sociological 'realities' it represents:

On the one hand, the work of these two writers [Proust and Barnes] has transformed, as any important work should, the textual reality of their day. But as representatives of a minority their texts also have a responsibility – which they do indeed discharge – of changing the categorising perspective that affects the sociological reality of their group.[4]

Wittig's writing offers a dynamic conjunction of eros and politics. Writing eros for her is a multi-functional operation, involving awareness of the analytical, subversive and seductive force of language. All three aspects are intimated in an interview she gave to Laurence Louppa on the publication of *Le Corps lesbien* (1973). Wittig explains the graphic convention (the split 'I', 'j/e') by which she marks in that text the double act of violence by which the desiring female subject, entering masculine language, tears that language and is itself wrenched into being. She indicates the special status of lesbian desire, which is confident of its identity before it can communicate its difference in terms of the heterosexual 'reality' in which it is immersed. And she notes the power to challenge limits, in the name of desire, which writing sets at the disposal of the lesbian subject:

With 'I/I' as subject, the writing of *The Lesbian Body* functions primarily as a work of seduction. My writing has always been inseparably bound to a forbidden sexual practice: lesbianism. I began to write when I was 12 or 13 years old, having fallen in love with a little girl: I gained access in that way to a doubly-forbidden domain: female homosexuality and writing. Language for me was the only way to give reality to an experience denied existence, declared impossible. And to be honest, I wrote then, as I do now, mainly to seduce . . .[5]

In Wittig's view, the concept of *écriture féminine*, with its emphasis on the metaphors of the maternal body, is too easily appropriated by conservative ideologies which confine women to the sphere of biological reproduction and reserve the privilege of intellectual production for men. It fuels the myth, she argues, in the Preface to her translation of Barnes's stories, that artistic creation is a natural secretion. Consequently, it prevents the revolutionary recognition of writing as material production, a transformative act of labour and a conscious intervention within history. In her essay 'The Mark of Gender', Wittig criticizes writers who do not understand that language is a material, transformative element of social praxis: 'I say that even abstract philosophical categories act upon the real as social. Language casts sheaves of reality upon the social body stamping it and violently shaping it.'[6] In a voluntarist declaration of the power of the locutory subject, which she refers to the linguistician Emile Benveniste, she presents entry into language not as an entrapment in the prison-house but as a political act, a taking on of conscious subjectivity which is of itself a reappropriation of power. It is in the saying of 'I', in the exercise of language, 'that hierarchies within language can be dissolved, a fresh syntax introduced that by changing the relationships of words reorganises the fundamental structures of meaning' (p. 69). At the same time, she recognizes the two-way connection between world and book: '[L]anguage does not allow itself to be worked upon, without a parallel work in philosophy and politics, as well as in economics, because as women are marked in language by gender, they are marked in society as sex' (p. 67).

The hierarchies in need of change are not only ones of gender. In their invocation of the language of Marxist ideology (a reference to Marx and Engels' text, *The German Ideology*, noting that a special interest can only be furthered if it represents itself as carrying other interests with it), the woman-focused theses of 'The Mark of Gender' imply a wider awareness of social imbalances of power. Bringing the lesbian 'I' into the mainstream of textual discourse involves Wittig in the reconfiguration of the whole set of relationships between the body individual and the body politic.

Writing the female body means, therefore, in Wittig's case, a sustained and confident negotiation with the discourses and texts, especially the erotic texts, of the cultural mainstream, the carrier of masculine desire, to unlock the transformative energies contained in language. The best single model of the process appears in *Les Guérillères* (1969), in the tale of Sophie Ménade (pp. 72–3). Sophie Ménade evokes the archetypal female body, Eve, the traditional embodiment of desire, walking through Eden, the archetypal scenario of desire. This Eve is not the traditional object of the masculine desiring gaze. In Sophie Ménade's version, she is the originating centre of a web of new meanings, resonating through the landscape, that reorganizes itself around her to establish new centres, which in their turn create fresh resonances. The rippling hair which is the fetishistic focus of the medieval icon-makers and their generations of imitators is still the centre here, but its erotic force is simultaneously highlighted and transformed with an overlaying of the Medusa myth which reworks the deadly gaze of the *femme fatale* and makes it the source of life. Each hair is a mobile delicate serpent, that makes music as she moves. These are the first notes in a sequence of variations on the serpentine theme that present the female body as active and creative subject, combining the energies of body and mind. This Eve is attended by Orpheus, the musician-poet who put nature into fresh harmonies and, in the tradition, was torn apart by frenzied maenads; here, he appears in new form, as a serpent, and new function, as one of Eve's advisers. Around the remade body of desire, new discourses come into being, liberated from the disabling associations of the old words. The serpents 'speak' to Eve through music and movement. Sophie Ménade, Eve's mediator, speaks of Eve to her female audiences in images, first in prose, and then in the rhythms of a surreal poetry that touches on hysterical frenzy. The audiences respond collectively in the rhythms of the Dionysian dance. Bodies, words, rhythms and landscape are bonded in the equal relations of a new syntax organized by the ultimate mediator of the whole process, Wittig herself, around a new collective locutionary subject: *elles*. Intractable to conventional logic, the significance of the dance clarifies in the course of the rest of *Les Guérillères* as the dancing subjects, in the practice of their discourse, establish it. The liberating equality of the Dionysian dance supplies the power that brings down the walls of the men's city, draws the young men into the women's triumphal procession, and finally turns into the song of the *Internationale* in which the text closes. The maenadic frenzy of sexual instinct which tradition marks as the driving-force of female inspiration is rewritten as a self-regulating, creative and expansive eros. The key to the whole process is the female artist who combines, as her name implies, two modes of knowing, of both body and mind.[7]

Wittig's project makes clearest sense when considered in the light of the influences of its originary moment in the 1960s. The major figure here is not Foucault, though Judith Butler in her *Gender Trouble*[8] has made useful connections between the two writers. Far more important is the work of the radical social philosopher Herbert Marcuse (1898–1979), disseminator of the work of Wilhelm Reich and Erich Fromm, who became a major influence on the student movement in the 1960s with his Freudo-Marxist analyses of the repressive mechanisms of the closed society and his explorations of the role of the aesthetic as a catalyst of revolutionary change. A member of the Frankfurt School before fleeing Nazism in 1933, Marcuse settled into the university network in the United States. He was in Paris in 1959, where he gave a seminar at the *Ecole pratique des hautes études* whose themes he wrote up for the journal *Arguments* in 1960.[9] Wittig translated his *One-Dimensional Man* (1964) for publication in France in 1968. *Eros and Civilization* (1955), published by Minuit in 1963 (with Marcuse's dedication to the students who had followed his courses in France), is one of the points of negotiation she signals in her important Bibliography to *Les Guérillères*. The composition of *Les Guérillères* began in 1968 and was interrupted by the May events and the formation of the first women's groups. Wittig went back to the book at the end of the year and finished it at the beginning of 1969.[10] Its structure and philosophy clearly rest on Marcuse's analysis of the relationship of eros and society, which needs now to be set out in some detail.

Eros and Civilization offers a political analysis of Western consumer society which Marcuse argues, after Freud, functions on the basis of libidinal repression: the denial of eros, which is both life-instinct and sexual drive. He summarizes Freud's analysis of the process of repression that makes the modern individual, and his thesis of the connected process by which modern repressive civilization was constructed and is sustained. Freud's *Moses and Monotheism* (1939) is invoked by Marcuse not, he emphasizes, as anthropological fact but for its symbolic value as a representation of the historical dialectic of domination, said to rest on the control of sexual pleasure. Freud's text evokes the domination exercised over the primal horde by the authoritarian father through his monopoly of the females, and the subsequent overthrow and murder of the father by the brother-clan, who then go on to internalize the father's values and interdictions instead of replacing them with non-hierarchical structures. The subsequent rise of a matriarchy, associated with erotic freedom, is in reality the embodiment of displaced patriarchal values. Effectively, a rebellion intended to liberate eros was followed by remorse and guilt and installed instead the cycle of revolt and (self-) repression which is the founding structure of contemporary civilization. Marcuse goes on to argue that the nature and intensity of repression vary depending on the structures of a given society (whether the society operates on the basis of use or profit, as a free-market or planned economy, whether property is conceived as private or collective, whether there is a hierarchical division of labour, whether the monogamous-patriarchal family is preserved). He identifies the mark of excess of contemporary civilization as the strict coercion of libidinal energies into genital pleasure, with the emphasis on procreative purpose, and the desexualization of zones of sexual pleasure with no procreative connection. In this society, intensity of physical pleasure is deemed perversion, and is feared for its ability to collectivize or divide individuals, to distract them from their primary social function as alienated labour and to set them against the procreative order and paternal domination. The coercive mechanisms are said to be organized in contemporary consumer society to serve the interests of the military-industrial complex. Society's grip on individuals' time, the division and regulation of their work- and leisure-time, begins with the control and reification of individual libidinal energy.

Marcuse asks whether Freud is right to see an inevitable connection between civilization and the repression of libidinal energies or whether this is a matter of historical organization. He considers the possibility of inventing an alternative non-repressive social form which could, he thinks, be found through the liberation of repressed life-energies and the reworking of the relationship of eros and thanatos. Thanatos, the death-drive, should be rethought not as a destructive principle but as the impulse to Nirvana, a return to rest which is followed by fresh affirmations. Art is the means of making the revision of ethical and political perspective; the artistic imagination has a Utopian function, in its ability to produce models of the non-repressive society. His own philosophical imagination, he points out, has already produced its own Utopian vision of the end of scarcity, the end of the cult of productivity, and the increase of leisure. Artistic imaginations should now be seeking to open up the energies locked in the images of art, and to exploit them to subvert social reality with a view to its reconstruction. He proposes that Orpheus and Narcissus be instated as icons of the artistic revolution, new cultural heroes offering representations of the capacity for resurrection, the possibility of joyful unity with nature, and the regenerative power of the concept of identity, all of which can work together to reconfigure the death drive. Alongside art he invokes homosexuality. He links homosexuals with Orpheus and Narcissus as participants in the 'great refusal' of revolution, which he characterizes as the refusal to be separated from the object of desire. This is the point where Wittig's project finds its place: in writing the texts invoked by Marcusan erotico-socio-aesthetics, she aligns the writing of lesbian desire with the desire of other sectors of contemporary society for radical social change.

The remainder of this essay will characterize some of the variants Wittig plays on her theme in three texts: *L'Opoponax* (1964), *Les Guérillères* (1969) and *Le Corps lesbien* (1973). The aim will be to pick out key texts of contemporary culture from within which Wittig seeks to liberate repressed eros in terms of her own desire, and to highlight some of the distinctive practices of her own erotic writing. Particular importance will be given to Wittig's effort to release from words and phrases their rhythmic energy, a process that in many ways recalls Julia Kristeva's speculations on the operations of the chora.[11]

L'Opoponax (1964)

Intertextuality is central in this presentation of childhood sexuality, positioned in the matrix of the cultural texts of the school canon and constructed through them to simultaneous consciousness of the power of desire and the power of language, to the point where the locutionary 'I' can begin to identify a place of its own in the interstices of the texts. In the beginning, the written word is the means by which modern society calls its children to order. Wittig foregrounds the role of the school, which treats learning to read and write as a physical discipline that enforces an order on infant anarchy (figured by the wild-haired, torn-stockinged Reine Dieu), in the same way and at the same time as it makes little boys and girls aware of sexual difference and gender roles. Polymorphous perversity is channelled into genital-focused sexuality, in a process that prepares children to receive and reproduce their society's authoritarian and hierarchical ideology. The child's capacity to respond at a later stage to the sublimations of the texts of high culture depends in a large part on the successful imposition of linguistic discipline at that early stage when language most conspicuously 'casts sheaves of reality upon the social body stamping it and violently shaping it'.

Wittig's account is cast in a Dionysian mode, using techniques that involve the reader in an orgy of intellectual and emotional identifications. Her text sets up a theatre of sexuality, constructed in terms of voices and dramatic movement and with a décor of precisely observed but selective visual and tactile detail. The result is a sequence of dream scenarios sharp-edged and vivid enough to create an effect of authenticity, inviting readers to recognize and reconstruct their own initiation into desire in the liberating drama of Catherine Legrand's voyage into self-discovery. The narrative subject of this drama is the child body, receiver and interpreter of sensuous impressions. Seeing and hearing condition the interpellation of Catherine Legrand into self-consciousness, which begins as she exchanges her mother's hand for that of her (female) teacher. In the scenarios of classroom and playground, the child rapidly acquires bodily understanding of gender hierarchies. Catherine sees and hears herself being placed in relation to authority figures in a very different way from Robert, the little boy who dominates the scene by always coming late, paying no attention to the teacher's voice or to his mother calling from the school gate. ('She shouts so loud everyone can hear her, but Robert Payen doesn't answer, so everyone goes on hearing the voice that calls Robert.')[12] The voice calling the Roberts of this world subtends all Catherine's subsequent experience. The sight of Robert's willy ('ma quéquette', p. 7) is significant in this context, fixing the association of gender difference, genital marker for gender difference, and social power. The lesson is ironically undercut by Robert's death; but its point is later reinforced in a series of death-tableaux which makes a fresh and more potent constellation of masculinity, death and power. The ritual of the bishop's funeral is the highpoint of a process that fixes in the childish imagination the symbol of invisible authority – the Hidden God – as a masculine power.

The link between genital sexuality and oppressive power relationships is reinforced in the playground by a detailed and unusually lengthy account of the dramatic rite of passage, a game of doctors and patients in which the big girls make the little ones display their private parts, as the teacher patrols unnoticing (pp. 54–6). This interpellation into collective female sexual experience is marked by features which will recur in later accounts of adult sexual pleasure. The experience is designated 'frightening' and the emphasis is on the necessity of submission, but at the same time the writing conveys a sense of pleasure at being included in a ritual game and, particularly, a ritual that involves covert rebellion against authority. The episode is followed by a series of other vividly visualized incidents in which Catherine's growing sense of herself as a sexual and gendered individual is marked by negative experiences which will later be repeated in adult play: fear, embarrassment, humiliation, exposure, the perception of self as victim and as dependent.

This learned knowledge competes with another kind of body-knowing which the child practises of her own initiative in the less policed playspaces of family garden, woods and fields, presided over by the other, unnamed deity of the text, the hardly-spoken Mother. Here she experiences the pleasure of confident physical contact with the earth, part of a non-hierarchical landscape where the only difference she sees is that which she herself establishes, patiently observing and noting with scientific curiosity species identity and difference in pond-creatures, birds and leaves, enjoying the sight and smells of nature and her own body. This detailed seeing, touching, smelling remains as the mark of Utopian pleasure through *L'Opoponax* and subsequent texts, an infantile eros looking for the chance to resurface.

In school, the death-drive is reinforced with the texts of high culture bearing the ideology of the bourgeois self: heroic, heterosexual and laden with guilt. The teachers present that self in religious mode, through the moralists and mystics (Pascal, Corneille, St Vincent de Paul), while the girls pass round clandestinely the erotic variant (Rousseau's novel *La Nouvelle Heloise*, Baudelaire's poem 'L'Invitation au voyage', with their complex representation of passion as longing for freedom and guilty pleasure). Baudelaire will continue to make a major contribution to the form of Catherine's (and Wittig's) erotic fantasies. But interestingly, the first 'I' of the text, carrying the declaration of love which appears in the closing line ('I loved her so much that in her I still live'),[13] is drawn from an earlier tradition, the highly conventional neo-platonist code of Maurice Scève's *Délie*. The more obviously constructed the language, the easier it is for the speaker to slip in and out of its forms without finding herself caught in the ideologies they carry.

The classroom, then, is both the place where interpellation begins and the place of resistance. Catherine engages in creative appropriation of the classics. Some readings simply reinforce her homosexual longings. Unable to follow the Latin narrative of Orpheus and Eurydice, she concentrates on the picture of the sculptured bodies in her book and sees not difference but identity, in the curve of the stylized arms (p. 251). Other texts provide her with the means to give those longings form. Catherine discovers Pascal, with his advocacy of faith over reason – the transformation of reality by desire – and his model illustration of the power of rhetoric to stir the will for change. Immediately afterwards, she creates her Opoponax, the thrilling monster of her own repressed desire, which moves in ways not dissimilar to those of Pascal's Hidden God, and through the fascination it exerts over her contemporaries helps her transition from periphery to centre of her classroom world.

The final chapter of Wittig's book is a lengthy evocation of the growing creative independence of Catherine's language in the realization of first love. The force of the erotic struggles to pierce through and renew inherited discourse. To begin with, Catherine's text is threaded through with lines from Baudelaire's 'L'Invitation au voyage'. By the end, Baudelaire's voyages, still quoted, share equal space with the girls' own journey of erotic discovery, travelling together in the back seat of a car, through the rain and dark, or on the train that carries the class on a school excursion. The vehicles are still man-made, and there's a warning joke between the lines, as the girls stick their heads out of the windows of the speeding train, but something new is happening. Simple metaphors from their own everyday experience renew the inert energies of the cultural inheritance and assign them to fresh purposes.

The chapter moves through two phases. In the first, where Catherine's erotic responses are still coming into focus, she speaks from the margins of knowledge and experience. The freshness of childish perception invigorates the presentation of erotic pleasure. The passive pleasure of watching a film unroll is the underlying metaphor, shot through with increasing frequency by the delighted shock of self-awareness as the watcher 'recognizes' herself in and between the frames. It's a rough-edited film, all action and movement, non-reflective, visual and dramatic. It represents the freshness of sensuous experience that doesn't yet know itself as sexual, the first shock of emotions that will be the recurrent focuses of Wittig's texts of adult love (the thrill of mystery and taboo, anticipation, longing, suffering, waiting, jealousy, rejection, reconciliation). An unparagraphed sequence of juxtaposed incidents, a montage of variously cut lengths, recreates the liberating timelessness of long adolescent days. Monochrome reportage suddenly takes on intensity and colour at highpoints of feeling, marked also by changes of rhythm (a change of balance between short and long sentences, or a sudden sequence of short clauses building to excitement) or changes of angle of vision, or the inclusion of unexpected images drawn from experience that is peculiarly Catherine's own.

'On dit' or 'On dit que' recurs frequently at this point, framing Catherine's initiation into erotic experience. The phrase has a double effect: it conveys the sense of alienation which is part of the horrid thrill of desire, and it also carries, by implication, the intense longing to articulate a desire of one's own. Desire and language are liberated together, as Catherine struggles to transcend what Wittig elsewhere describes as 'The smothered, silent "you" ["one"] of childhood'.[14] Erotic pleasure is identified as an intellectual (textual) work, in which Catherine learns to structure and foreground her own perceptions.

Her anticipation of Valerie's return from vacation is a sequence of short, breathless clauses, building up to the delight of the brief statement: 'You run to meet Valerie Borge.'[15] The two bodies are inseparably entangled in a string of unmarked verbs (infinitives in the French), in a mock ritual fight of welcome: 'You see them rolling on top of each other in the dust, pulling, pushing, hitting, struggling apart, Valerie Borge and Catherine Legrand are locked in combat.'[16] The passage is worth comparing with Catherine's fight with Léon Torpusse later in the text (pp. 272–3), where infinitives are replaced by finite verbs, evoking abrupt, clumsy, actions which drive the two bodies apart instead of weaving them together. The buried eroticism of the contact between the girls emerges subsequently in brief snapshot images, where selective detail underlines the pleasure of seeing. Catherine glimpses Valerie's breasts and watches her cheeks redden (p. 257), or sees her hair frame her face, caught at an unexpected angle in the light of the cinema projector (p. 259). Valerie takes tactile initiatives, pressing Catherine's arm in the darkness, and holding her hand (p. 260) – at which point the narrative veers wildly away to describe the images in the film they are watching (two heroes, shot in the chest), to represent Catherine's panic at an unfamiliar and untranscribable emotion. Lesbian love is shown subverting the traditional social discourses, grown stale with familiarity, by reinstating the body at their centre. Picking flowers together for a religious procession, Valerie and Catherine whirl into an orgy of destruction, tearing and shredding the damp red petals, in four sentences of panting, regular rhythms which culminate and collapse with the substitution of their faces – flashed into selective focus on brows, hair and cheeks – for the monstrances carrying the Body of Christ which are at the centre of the religious rite (pp. 262–3). Immediately afterwards, they inscribe their adventure onto that other grand cultural narrative, the *Odyssey*. In the wings of the theatre, during rehearsals of the return to Ithaca, Catherine deliberately kisses Valerie on the cheek at the point where the returning King lays claim to his kingdom. The action is simply presented, without comment, but framed into startling and disquieting significance by clinically precise reference to the carnage that accompanies the returning patriarch: the triumphant music of his return distracts from the sight of the blood and brains spattered on the tables (p. 265). As with the gesture towards the broken body of Christ, there are intimations here of the violence of the adult erotic, which will surface in later texts.

In a more intimate mode, a brief, incantatory prose poem presents Valerie as the focal point of Catherine's emotional landscape (pp. 276– 7). The borrowed elements here are very simple: a brief Biblical echo of the Song of Songs, in the vision of Valerie Borge standing on the hills, and a nursery-tale pastoral backdrop of rivers, sheep, fluffy clouds. Most significant is the mode in which Catherine puts them together, experimenting with the power of her own directorial gaze, projecting Valerie into the distance or drawing her into closely magnified relief, implicitly recalling to the reader the exercises in observation in the family garden. The pleasure of seeing is reiterated immediately afterwards on the journey to the cemetery to bury Mademoiselle Caylus, in the evocation of Valerie's sleeping face. Simple play with verbal modes and tenses creates a change of perspective from passive object to active subject which mimics the sudden thrilling shock of sexual awareness. As Valerie's mouth opens, Catherine sees herself – twice – as the seeing subject: 'Her head is bent, her hair is spread out, you see her mouth half-opening, you see her lips and her teeth.'[17] The building thrill is the seductive power of the dominating subject, which the text promptly defuses. Valerie wakes, to reciprocate the gaze; and in the last two pages both seeing subjects are put in perspective, dissolved in the crowd of schoolfriends, teachers and family in the muddy, flower-covered cemetery. Individual sensuality finds a new role within this predominantly female gathering, made over into part of a life-force which challenges the deadly forms which presided at the bishop's funeral. That 'I' borrowed from Scève's *Délie*, on which the text closes, free of any single referent, lives on in an indeterminate beloved, a 'she' which, grammatically, could equally well be Mademoiselle Caylus, Valerie, or the warm light enfolding the scene. The borrowed reference seals a constellation of headily familiar lyrical images (wet poppies, hyacinth and gold sunsets) which turn the love–death motif towards the theme of resurrection.

Les Guérillères (1969)

This second text foregrounds that imbrication of the personal and the collective which is crucial to Wittig's writing of eros: eros, in other words, here appears in explicitly political as well as textual context. From the outset, female erotic pleasure is differently defined and represented, in the opening scene of the women urinating in the rain, watched by the surrounding group of other women. The writing of this sequence is deliberately flat, communicating not the dark voyeuristic thrill of the reifying gaze, but the fascination of intellectual curiosity satisfied, sharing the pleasure of a subject engaged in its proper activity, in harmony with its natural landscape. Such a radical redefinition of eros presumes the radical reconstruction of the sociopolitical context which the text promptly unfolds. *Les Guérillères* is a world apart, physically and ideologically separated from the old world. Women here are not reproducers, idols, or domestics but rather engineers, builders, warriors, strategists, forming a single community, though all with their own names. All activity in such a world is unselfconsciously erotic, undifferentiated pleasure: a Utopian dream of bodies in harmony within a harmonious landscape.

This is the period of Nirvana imagined by Marcuse, from which it is possible to rework the icons of the past. For Wittig, this means rewriting the female body from passive to active, replacing the conventional markers of desirability (breasts, hips, bellies) with a new hierarchy of moving parts, and redesignating women's place and function. The women decide they are not made for beds or pedestals, for sexual reproduction or display (p. 180). It is also the moment to foreground the violence that is an indispensable part of change. The women discover that women who want to change the world must get themselves guns (p. 120). This political violence is represented as intimately connected to the violence of eros. The connection is embodied historically in language. Inherited language, which is an 'outdated language',[18] enshrines the politics of the phallus, hierarchical, acquisitive and possessive; the two are rejected together (p. 153).

The battle on the terrain of language is constantly emphasized within the text. Its full extent is made plain in the Bibliography printed at the end, whose purpose, Wittig notes, is to show the 'socio-historico-cultural' models her writing has inherited and to allow the reader to measure the distance it has created between itself and these authors. The books cited, at first sight an eclectic bundle, are in fact organized according to Marcusan logic. They are the authorities appealed to by contemporary society on matters of sexuality, language and social organization – the icons to be remade. They include the key references on the origins of the feminine myth (the *Book of Genesis*, the *Mahabharata*), women's political place and function (Aristophanes' *Lysistrata*, Laclos's essay, 'De l'éducation des femmes') and women's sexuality (Brantôme, *Les Dames galantes*, Félix Jayle, *La Gynécologie*, Gérard Zwang, *Le Sexe de la femme*, and a *Dictionnaire de sexologie*). Classic forms of discursive representation are invoked at the micro-level of word (the Robert Dictionary) and the macro-levels of genre (Biblical, Greek and Indian epic) and mode (Confucian rationalism). Social organization appears in Marcusan terms as organization for war (Clausewitz). Alternative ideologies and forms of writing are provided by Lacan, Marcuse, Borges, Sappho, Simone de Beauvoir, Flora Tristan and the theoreticians and historians of revolution, John Reed, General Giap, Mao Tse-tung, and Marx. Between them, these texts establish the lines of an argument which opposes two very different ways of conceiving eros, the matrix within which Wittig conceives the fight. The major ally in the progressive camp is Marcuse. The great enemy, standard-bearer of the traditionalists, is the popular sexologist Gérard Zwang. Zwang's *Le Sexe de la femme* (1967)[19] is the original of the tattered 'feminary' in which the women find the traces of the rejected past, with which they try to negotiate, but fail, and on whose fading pages they finally write their own accounts of their sexuality.

Had Zwang not existed, it might have been necessary to invent him; as it is, he provides the ready-made antagonist for *Les Guérillères*. His work offers a fashionably popularizing account of women's sexuality which takes for granted the authority of masculine gaze and discourse. Indeed, Wittig's opening sequence of the urinating women, with its sympathetic identification of watcher, watched and landscape, could well have been written in direct response to his voyeuristic analysis of female urination (Zwang, pp. 131–2). The preface to the second edition combines libertarian attacks on sexual repression (he cites clitoridectomy, campaigns against divorce, campaigns for the censorship of pornography) with violent antagonism to the levelling of social classes and the refusal of sexual difference. His aim is to reassert what he calls the *natural, normal* (his emphasis) heterosexual couple (p. 26).

Zwang's epigraph, taken from Béroalde de Verville's *Le Moyen de parvenir* (1610), nominates eros as the centre of human experience and, by implication, his book as the representative erotic text: 'And I will tell you the greatest of all secrets: OF ALL BOOKS, THIS BOOK IS THE CENTRE.'[20] A quotation from André Malraux's preface for the French translation of *Lady Chatterley's Lover* proclaims the vagina to be man's route to his innermost self. Writers and doctors are named as joint masters of the mystery of female sexuality. Zwang praises the speculum, which he labels a precious instrument (p. 15), and is proud of his ability to name correctly the parts of the female anatomy. But literature is his principal point of reference, and he flourishes his speculum most happily in the name of such writers as Breton, Brantôme, Balzac, Pierre Louÿs and Henry Miller. Their aphorisms throw into relief the power relationships on which his erotic syntax is constructed. The section on 'Morphologie', in which he describes the female body parts, highlights Balzac's celebrated dictum from his *Physiologie du mariage* that no man should marry without having studied anatomy and dissected at least one woman (p. 99). Zwang's account turns the female body into anatomical object in the name of male pleasure and the procreative function. He emphasizes the passive nature of female sexuality and is particularly concerned to deny the clitoris the same status as the phallus which, he stresses, is an active organ (p. 161).

Zwang's discussion of women's sexuality starts from the 'glorious' phallus, whose glory, he says, depends on the concavity of the vagina, without which the First Sex would find itself equipped with a supremely useless tool (p. 10). He regrets the need to use the medical term for the vagina, which in his view, unlike 'phallus', fails to convey the values attached to sexual activity and lacks poetic resonance. Its sound jars, it has no rhymes or assonances, 'the tongue of Ronsard and Rabelais knows nothing of it'.[21] He points to a plethora of euphemisms, all equally unsatisfactory, and states his own preference for 'sexe', because it means, literally, a split, and metaphorically represents the door through which men enter life and regain eternity (p. 12). More elaborately, a chapter on 'Symbolique et vocabulaire' ransacks the poets for representations of the various parts of the female genitalia. Many of these examples pass straight into Wittig's text: seashell (he quotes Mallarmé's 'Une négresse'), Bird of Venus, circle, triangle, oval (he makes special reference to Hans Carvel's ring and the *Histoire d'O*, where the circle is described as the sign of man's possession of the female orifice), sea anemone, sea, and so on.

Zwang's catalogue explains the insistence with which Wittig

concentrates on terminology in *Les Guérillères*. The women claim the right to describe their own sexual organs, refusing the symbols which fragment them into objects of masculine desire (*Les Guérillères*, p. 93). The clinical terms they prefer set their own observations and self-knowledge in contradiction to the myth-making of the feminary (p. 29, pp. 41–3). Hardest to relinquish is language that celebrates the vagina and privileges the female reproductive function (pp. 80, 86, 94). But finally, they cut the symbolic bond that attaches them to a dead culture and become not organs but subjects ('They, marching together into a new world', p. 102). The connection is made here between language, sexuality and the division of labour: this decision leads straight into a sequence where the women burn all the instruments of unnecessary toil, which are those of domestic labour – and turn what is left from the fire into works of art, asserting a liberated creative energy.

Against the struggle with the erotic represented in the feminary, the text sets the blissful community of Utopian eros. The first two-thirds of the text constitute an artistic representation of the erotic community of Marcuse's political imagination, the product of sensuous, linguistic, social and political liberation. The community of eros is the culmination of a fully advanced technological society, free from scarcity, not divided from nature, where work and leisure are indistinguishable. Labour is an erotic experience, as shown in the soundpoem that evokes the making of oil, where every aspect of the process is present in sensuously selective detail (the machine, the crushed flowers, nuts, heat), built to a rhythmic climax in a vision of glowing flesh, a simple statement, stripped of metaphor, of shining hands and arms and bare breasts (p. 50). Erotic energies are totally dispersed over the whole body and entire natural landscape, with no taboos on any sensuous experience. The women watch each other urinate, in the echoing enclosure of the rain (p. 9), play hide and seek by smell in the dark (p. 10), sniff impartially at spicy scents (p. 10) or mud bubbles bursting with sickly scents of decay (p. 19). They find pleasure in erotic display, observing the dazzling sunlight catching the webs of mucus on pubic hair (p. 24 – cf. Zwang's poets, who identify the female genitals with darkness). They take drugs under the full moon to enjoy the loss of control (p. 25: a parodic reworking of the famous passage in Pierre Louÿs's decadent novel, *Aphrodite*). They enjoy fantasies of sadistic and masochistic violence, aggression and fear, frightening each other with tales of wolves and rats, confident in their control of their own stories (pp. 43–8, p. 56). But the line is drawn between sadistic fantasy and real pain. The little girls weep for the birds they've accidentally smothered – an episode which recalls Flaubert's

Saint Julien, deliberately strangling the pigeon he has trapped for the pleasure of feeling and watching its terrified struggles.

The cultivation of control is a feature of this text, despite its poetic references to the pleasures of disorder (p. 133). The dark side of eros is presented as alien to women's sexual pleasure, something found within the masculine economy, the product of oppression and repression (p. 167). The golden mask of love and hate is a rhetorical ornament that women can put on for the battlefield (p. 183); the battlefield swarms with warrior-goddesses, streaming with blood, violating enemy corpses. But these are presented as pantomime grotesqueries, strategic exploitations of the enemy's fantasy terrors. In the new dictionary the women devise, hate can be transformed into erotic energy, but the reverse is forbidden (p. 106).

The epic narrative of *Les Guérillères* is an attempt to allegorize the exchanges between discourse, sexuality and social formations, showing the power of erotic rhetoric, rhythms and images, to construct and reconstruct social energies. The dance of Sophie Ménade, the bacchante rhythms that celebrate the warrior goddess Minerva (p. 141), and the song of the marching women that spills into the Internationale (pp. 206–8) all spring from that same remaking of female erotic energy, redirected from reproduction to original creative act. Conspicuously in this text, the erotic energies are not purely homosexual. The resistance to patriarchal repression in the final analysis cuts across gender antagonisms. The story the women tell to cement the alliance of the young men and the warriors, of the young lovers bound together and drowned (p. 178), writes a version of sexual pleasure whose rhythms aspire to rise above questions of sexual difference. The few concrete references to the body are to sexually undifferentiated parts (limbs and muscles); otherwise, the text relies on generalizing abstracts (touch, pleasure, sweetness, weariness), verbs with a shared non-human subject, representing a shared sense of surrender (relax, soften, freed, float, sleep), and hypnotically lulling, repetitive sentence rhythms that recreate a state of Nirvanic ecstasy. This is the Nirvana proposed by *Eros and Civilization* as the intermediary state to which the artistic imagination should seek to reduce the antagonisms of that death-drive which is lodged in the limits of genitally defined sexual experience. The only false note in the sequence occurs in the context of the masculine pronoun 'ils', associated with death, and even this is resolved as death is redesignated the sleep of pleasure, the moment of rest, from which resurrection can begin.

Jennifer Birkett

Le Corps lesbien (1973)

Le Corps lesbien turns from the reconstruction of the social macrocosm to the reconstitution of the microcosm of the female body and the individual experience of desire. The country of desire, the sweet poisoned country of no return, as Wittig names it (p. 8), is still intertextual, and the voice of the text negotiates with the familiar poisoners of the wells, Ancients and Moderns, to express the confident awareness of a new subject position that has identified its own ways of articulating desire within the contours of old landscapes. The sequence 'Heureuse si comme Ulyssea' (p. 16), for example, which blends echoes of du Bellay's longing for a homecoming into the scents, music and sunsets of Baudelaire's 'La Chevelure', 'L'Invitation au voyage' and 'Soleils couchants' to evoke the pain of waiting for the loved one, is spoken by a double subject who oscillates between the desire of the returning traveller, longing for an impossible harbour, and the despair of the abandoned lover walking to the same harbour to wait for the wanderer's return. Or again, the celebrated dialogue between the Chimera and the Sphynx, Flaubert's representation of the irreducible opposition of male and female, is reworked as another image of the doubled subject, a powerful figure of the profound intimacy of lesbian knowledge of the other, which can be simultaneously ecstatic and self-conscious (pp. 45–6).

Less obvious is the continuing intertextual dialogue with the contemporary authorities on women's sexuality cited in *Les Guérillères*, Gérard Zwang and the gynaecologist Félix Jayle. The title of *Le Corps lesbien* directly refutes Zwang's *Le Sexe de la femme*, presenting not a fragmented sexual object but a self-possessed body. The project of the text – to endow that body with its own speech – challenges Zwang's claim that women lack the authority to speak of their own erotic experience. They are, he says, too repressed and timid, lacking the phrases and the cultural references to frame responses to the questions of therapeute or lover; their experience of pleasure is too intense to permit reflection and they need – he quotes Françoise Dolto – their partner to bear witness to it (Zwang, p. 18). Female sexuality, for Zwang, needs to be interpreted by the experts: poet, lover, anatomist/ doctor. Doctors, descended from sorcerors, have, he says, the magic powers to confront the taboo of the sight of naked flesh (p. 33).

One of the most striking aspects of the erotic voice of Wittig's text is the authority and power with which it speaks, taking on, from the very beginning, the mantle of Zwang's experts and presenting itself as the observing partner who is also the observed. The three opening sequences confront what Zwang called the taboo of naked flesh with the language of lover, prophet and anatomist. The voice is both subject and object ('I suddenly become the place of the darkest mysteries'),[22] capable of describing with clinical objectivity the thrill of sexual pleasure: 'I feel my blood turn warmer in my arteries, I suddenly perceive the circuits it irrigates, a cry rises from the depths of my lungs, fit to explode.'[23] It leaps confidently into the range of cultural references to which Zwang says women have no access, drawing together the sadism of Baudelairean lyric, the cruel curiosity of the surgeon's knife, and a sharply contrasting invocation to Sappho as the gentle, healing lover. The invocation calls for the gift of Sapphic fingers, lips, tongue and saliva: a reference to the instruments of sexual pleasure which, as the text gradually makes plain, are also the instruments of creative language. The link between sexual potency and intellectual creativity, is the implication, is as well established within the cultural tradition for women as it is for men.

The voice of *Le Corps lesbien* takes the power-games of the authoritative masculine voices it mimics to extremes that outplay the originals. The violence of eros is accentuated in this text, whether in the surgical realism of the physical penetrations charted in early sections (which begin in literal anatomical detail and flower into baroque metaphor), or in the pornographic fantasy of those sado-masochistic scenarios of ritualized subjection, torture and exposure to which the lover/beloved obsessively returns. In the hothouse frenzy of this particular lesbian dream, even the gentle Sappho undergoes a grotesque transformation, written into associations which bear little relation to the language of the known fragments of her texts (offered, for example, a necklace of teeth torn from the loved one's mouth, p. 143). Wittig told Laurence Louppa that she was writing to try out a version of lesbian love as a wild, violent practice and out of a deliberate decision to challenge the sentimental version of lesbianism which has, traditionally, its allotted place in heterosexual erotic fantasy: 'There must be an end to the myth of a milksop, decorative female homosexuality, no threat to heterosexuality, even capable of being recuperated to its purposes.'[24] How resistant to recuperation Wittig's text in fact is must be a moot point. Certainly, its violence successfully evades the rosewater fantasies of such soft pornography as Pierre Louÿs's *Les Chansons de Bilitis*. On the other hand, its games with sado-masochistic fantasy can be argued, in a different way, to be reinforcing the unequal power relations of heterosexual culture. Wittig's text is an early point of reference for the controversy which would shortly be focused for lesbian feminists with the publication of Foucault's *Histoire de la sexualité* (*La Volonté de savoir*, 1976).[25] How can desire which defines itself as politically different, seeking relationships based on identity, equality and reciprocity, begin to negotiate with the dark effects of its construction within the 'poisoned country' of heterosexual relations based on dominance? Can sado-masochism be engaged with at the level of game-play and fantasy without compromising hard-fought campaigns for real political change? *Le Corps lesbien* insists that it can, emphasizing throughout the non-fixity of roles in its own games of erotic violence and concluding, like all Wittig's texts, in an egalitarian vision of community, harmonized within shared identity.

Such a ploy is open to charges of speciousness. But arguably, on a more general level, the political force of the text is precisely in the violence of its rhetorical plays, constantly disrupting its readers, turning them into critical receivers rather than passive consumers. The aim is to make visible the effects of form and language, displacing the functionalism of content and achieving the aesthetic subversion of meaning proposed by Marcuse.[26] The process can be seen at work elsewhere, in a less contentious area, in the double structuring of the text between the sequences of prose-poems and the series of noun-lists. In the disruptive cross-cutting of the lyrical and the scientific, speaking as both lover-poet and lover-anatomist, the voice of Wittig's text undertakes to revise both the imaginative celebration and the scientific understanding of the female body and to remake the links between the two.

The strict framework of double-page blocks of capitalized nouns, naming the body parts, emphasizes the importance of accurate knowledge of the material reality that underlies ideologically constructed feeling. The kind of anatomy invoked for *Le Corps lesbien* is that pioneered in Félix Jayle's enthusiastic study *La Gynécologie* (1918), not the autopsy of which Balzac spoke, but biopsy, the knowledge of the separate parts as interdependent and interacting in the living unit, and not merely knowledge of an ideal body, a fantasy of Classical perfection, but a body in time, subject to change, age and decay.[27]

In this scientifically anatomized body, the categories of analysis, like Jayle's, are clear but their contents are interdependent, emphasizing the wholeness of the female body erotic. Words are split over pages or even between sections; some categories are repeated, to emphasize their central or connective function; some words, like some organs, recur in different contexts, with different connections. The catalogue opens with 'LE CORPS LESBIEN LA CYPRINE' – the lesbian body, its sexual fluid and its various secretions, fluids and gases. Then follow the veins, nerves, glands; the different bones and their material; the soft organs; the nails, teeth and hair; the skin, its layers, aspects, diseases; the nerves; the muscles; the cells; the blood vessels; again, the muscles and, juxtaposed, the soft tissues of vagina, anus and soft palate; the skeleton; the lower internal organs; the body functions; emotion, sensation, kinds of utterance; forms of movement. The final double-page unit recapitulates the body from head to foot, reconstituting elements which are now intimately known, ending almost as it began: 'LE PUBIS LE CORPS LESBIEN'. This is the process re-enacted in the prose-poems in the familiar cultural myth of the dismemberment and resurrection of Osiris, to the same effect. The female body observed in the name of female pleasure is disclosed as a creator and producer: generator of secretions, carrier of sensations, producer of movement, sound, speech. Its functional centre is pure erotic energy. Whereas for Jayle, like Zwang, the reproductive organs are the centre of the feminine, for Wittig, reproduction is only one of a cluster of functions (circulation, respiration, nutrition, elimination, defecation, reproduction, pp. 144–5), and is promptly defined not as the reproduction of the species but as the reproduction of female identification in pleasure (XX + XX = XX). From reproduction, Wittig's anatomization passes straight to 'reactions' (pleasure, emotion) and these in their turn lead to words, whispers, song, laughter, exclamations. The linking is deliberate between the affirmation of liberated female pleasure and the creative female voice.

The noun-lists which represent the body deconstructed by the impersonal, anatomizing gaze of the reflective partner are the supporting framework for the prose-poems, which are written in lyrical identification with the body in ecstasy. In this lyrical mode, in the language of the *fin-de-siècle* erotic, the lesbian body enters the textual body of the cultural tradition. Simultaneously, the body becomes communicable and changes the sense of the terms in which it is communicated. The apparatus and the structures of repressive power relationships are turned into a rhetoric whose application consciously undercuts those relationships and replaces them with motifs of liberation, openness and reciprocity. A concluding review of three instances of the reworking of decadent motifs will give an indication of the techniques involved.

The theme of specular pleasure links three juxtaposed proses (pp. 9–13) which transform possession into a dynamic of reciprocity. The first prose works on three layers of reference: the intensity of the lover's desire to know the loved one, the lover gazing into the beloved's eyes, and the lover masturbating her partner to orgasm. It consists of a single long sentence, representing a sadistic surgical invasion conducted by an obsessively reiterated 'I', subject of a sequence of verbs of increasingly violent action. The operation begins slowly with precise, careful motions, 'delicately' peeling back the skin, and builds to a climactic movement with a repeated spotlighting of 'hands' and 'fingers' searching and sinking among soft tissue, bone and fluids to grasp the loved one's 'eye' and fix the moment of ecstatic self-abandonment. In this rhythmic re-enactment, ecstasy is figured as the sudden freezing of frenzied movement, with the beloved reduced to mere adjective, dumb and immobilized, mind and body split apart ('every cry stopped in your throat your last thoughts behind your eyes held fast in my hands').[28] In the next sequence, in contrast, the speaking subject is the object of the lover's gaze, called into life by the myriad eyes of a protective Argus, into a dizzy ecstasy of sensation, sound and movement, a negation of sight, where subject boundaries disappear in an untranslatable pun ('your eyes are not visible where you follow/are me I am too I am not seen by you').[29] Who speaks is no longer clear, and inside and out are impossible to tell apart ('someone says, I tremble, I am dizzy, it echoes on me in me').[30] In the third sequence, the description of physical sensation is replaced by a fantasy scenario, where the taboo on seeing is re-enacted and abolished through the reworked myth of Eurydice and a female Orpheus. In this version, a putrefying Eurydice is brought back to life by a partner who only indulges in the pleasure of looking when looking no longer involves the destruction of the loved object.

The sequence beginning 'Your hair is black and shining'[31] addresses the decadent motif of animal femininity, recast into an unexpected ferocity by the feminization of the wolf of Freudian desire. Wittig's version is a celebration of the capacity of the female body to experience pleasure over its whole surface and is written to evoke the intensity of that pleasure. Selective detail swiftly sketches in the perception of physical threat – teeth, weight, claws – which heightens the sense of bodily presence – sweat-covered flank, hide (fur and rough hairs), hard teats. The heavily verbal syntax follows an awkward sequence of movements through various sexual positions, into a galloping climax in a flood of sweat and foam, the body spelled out from shoulders to thighs, a noun-list of parts, in the rhythms of the licking tongue.

The ultimate challenge must be the decadent fascination with lesbianism itself, figured as the emblem of the deadly desire for self-possession, passive and sterile. Baudelaire is the specific point of reference in a sequence which evokes the reciprocal pleasure of lesbian congress in a blend of clinically precise observations and fantastic colours (pp. 19–20). The perceiving subject, the split 'I', appears only to be decentred, to note herself drowning in a fluid ecstasy of colour and sound. The focus of the poem is the sexual mucus on which it opens, which becomes the sea of ecstasy, more explicit than the discreet referent of Baudelaire's poetic inspiration. The rhythms of this sea foreground the movements, colours and sounds of the body of lesbian desire: flickering fingers, swimming legs, dishevelled hair, pale cheeks, ringing ears. The frenzy of movement refutes the gloomy passivity of the 'Femmes damnées' sprawled on Baudelaire's beach. The long pulsations of the final sentence of the sequence mimic the rising tidal rhythms that lift the swimming lovers towards the heavens. The surge towards transcendence is Baudelairean, except for the urgent violence that accompanies it in the evocation of the 'brutal' movement of limbs flailing in ecstasy, beating open the window to heaven. With pointed irony, the text closes in a harmonious resolution that merges its erotic energies with those of Baudelaire's 'Voyage à Cythère', confidently appropriating his ambivalent version of Lesbos:

> Submerged to my facial orifices I/I see the mass of liquid grow and swell with mucus in suspension pearly elastic filaments, the golds the reds are now the same colour and consistency as the clouds, the rising tide spills into the sky, farewell dark continent of wretchedness and pain farewell ancient cities we are setting sail for the bright shining islands for the green islands of Cythera for the isles of Lesbos all black and gold.[32]

Notes

1. 'Ma vérité, celle dont je ne savais rien, mais que je reconnaissais à mesure que l'histoire se nouait, se resserrait, me traquait, me poussait à travers les peuples et les siècles, m'empêchait de m'installer, de m'apaiser, de me goûter . . . m'obligeait . . . à m'échapper d'un piège pour me jeter dans une cage . . .'; Hélène Cixous, *Angst*, Paris, 1977, p. 129. All translations in this essay are my own, unless otherwise indicated. All page references given in the text to works analysed are to the French originals. The fictions by Monique Wittig cited have appeared in translation as follows: (*L'Opoponax*) *The Opoponax*, trans. Helen Weaver, London, Peter Owen, 1966/ New York, Simon and Schuster, 1976; (*Les Guérillères*) *Les Guérillères*, trans. David Le Vay, London, Peter Owen, 1971/ New York, Avon, 1973; (*Le Corps lesbien*) *The Lesbian Body*, trans. David Le Vay, London, Peter Owen, 1975/ New York, Avon, 1976; (*Virgile,non*) *Across the Acheron*, trans. David Le Vay, London, Peter Owen, 1987/London, The Women's Press, 1989.

2. 'C'était une voix qui m'arrêtait, qui m'effrayait; me donnait envie
   de fuir, m'en empêchait, me rivait à mon gré au lit que je ne
   pouvais plus quitter, dans lequel je me terrais, je m'enfonçais, je
   rapetissais . . .'; *Angst*, p. 155.
3. Hélène Cixous, *Le Livre de Promethea*, Paris, Editions Gallimard,
   1983.
4. 'D'une part, le travail de ces deux écrivains a transformé comme
   il se doit pour tout travail important la réalité textuelle de leur
   temps. Mais en tant que minoritaires leurs textes ont aussi à charge
   (et le font) de changer l'angle de catégorisation touchant à la
   réalité sociologique de leur groupe.' Monique Wittig, Preface to
   Djuna Barnes, *La Passion*, Paris, 1982, p. 14. On a similar theme
   see for example Monique Wittig, 'The Trojan Horse', *Feminist
   Issues*, vol. 4, no. 2, 1984.
5. 'Avec "j/e" pour sujet, l'écriture du *Corps lesbien* fonctionne avant
   tout comme une entreprise de séduction. Mon écriture a toujours
   été liée indissolublement à une pratique sexuelle interdite: le
   lesbianisme. J'ai commencé à écrire vers 12–13 ans, alors que
   j'étais tombée amoureuse d'une petite fille: j'ai eu ainsi accès à
   un double domaine interdit, innommé même autour de moi:
   l'homosexualité féminine et l'écriture. Par ailleurs, mon langage
   était le seul moyen de donner une réalité à cette experience niée,
   impossible. Et puis, pour parler sincèrement, j'écrivais avant tout,
   comme aujour d'hui, dans le but de séduire. . .'; MoniqueWittig,
   Interview with Laurence Louppa, *L'Art vivant*, no. 45, Dec. 1973–
   Jan. 1974, pp. 24–5. I am grateful to the Bibliothèque Marguerite
   Durand, Paris, for access to the Dossier Monique Wittig.
6. Monique Wittig, 'The Mark of Gender', in Nancy K. Miller
   (ed.), *The Poetics of Gender*, New York, 1986, p. 64.
7. Sophia is the Greek figure of Apollonian wisdom; the maenads
   were wild women who worshipped Dionysus in a dance frenzy
   on the mountains of Ancient Greece. See E. R. Dodds, *The
   Greeks and the Irrational*, Berkeley and Los Angeles, 1951,
   Appendix I: 'Maenadism'. Dodds's analysis of the belief-patterns
   of the Archaic Age overlaid by Classical rationalism was originally
   delivered as a course of lectures at Berkeley in the autumn of
   1949. Its insights into such issues as the social origins of personality
   and the political function of aesthetic and religious experience
   (Dionysian inspiration and Dionysian and Corybantic dance) fed
   into the intellectual atmosphere of the 1960s (see below, on
   Wittig's debt to Herbert Marcuse).
8. Judith Butler, *Gender Trouble: Feminism and the Subversion of
   Identity*, New York and London, 1990.

9. Herbert Marcuse, *One-Dimensional Man: Studies in the Ideology of Advanced Industrial Society*, Boston, 1964 (trans. Monique Wittig and the author, *L'Homme unidimensionnel: Essai sur l'idéologie de la societé industrielle avancée*, Paris, 1968); *Eros and Civilization. A Philosophical Inquiry into Freud*, Boston, 1955 (trans. J.-G. Nény and B. Fraenkel, *Eros et Civilisation. Contribution à Freud*, Paris, 1963). For a note on Marcuse in France, see Elisabeth Roudinesco, *Jacques Lacan & Co. A History of Psychoanalysis in France, 1925–1985*, trans. Jeffrey Mehlman, London, 1990, pp. 481–2. For a useful introduction to Marcuse's work, see Phil Slater, *Origin and Significance of the Frankfurt School: A Marxist Perspective*, London, 1977.

10. Interview with Laurence Louppa (see n. 5).

11. In Julia Kristeva, *La Révolution du langage poétique: L'Avant-garde à la fin du XIXe siècle: Lautréamont et Mallarmé*, Paris, 1974. See Jean Wyatt, *Reconstructing Desire: The Role of the Unconscious in Women's Reading and Writing*, Chapel Hill and London, 1990, for a useful elucidation of Kristeva's exposition of how meaning is produced in poetic language 'through a dialectic between "semiotic" processes, with their origins in pre-verbal times, and "symbolic" processes operated by the speaking subject inscribed in social and linguistic systems' (p. 5) and a stimulating account of the characteristic features of such language (mobile dream scenarios of desire, rhythm foregrounded at the expense of syntax, collapse of subject/object boundaries, etc.).

12. 'Elle crie fort de façon à ce que tout le monde l'entende, mais Robert Payen ne répond pas, ce qui fait qu'on continue d'entendre la voix qui appelle Robert' (p. 7).

13. 'Tant je l'aimais qu'en elle encore je vis' (p. 281).

14. 'Le "on" de l'enfance étouffée et silencieuse' (Interview with Laurence Louppa). This statement is untranslatable. What Wittig seeks to convey is the absence of the marker of a distinctive individual identity in the child's use of the subject pronoun. Unfortunately, where a French child naturally uses the impersonal 'one', an English child doing so signals a precocious and particular upper-class discourse. 'You' is the generalizing term.

15. 'On court à la rencontre de Valerie Borge' (p. 256).

16. 'On les voit rouler dans la poussière l'une sur l'autre, se tirailler se pousser se frapper essayer de se dégager, Valerie Borge et Catherine Legrand sont corps à corps' (p. 256).

17. 'Sa tête est inclinée, ses cheveux sont étalés autour d'elle, on voit que sa bouche s'entr'ouvre, on voit les lèvres sur les dents' (p. 278).

18. '[U]n langage suranné' (p. 94).
19. Gérard Zwang, *Le Sexe de la femme*, Paris, 1967, revised edn. 1974.
20. 'Et d'avantage je vous dirai le secret des secrets: CE LIVRE EST LE CENTRE DE TOUS LES LIVRES.'
21. '[L]a langue de Ronsard et de Rabelais l'ignore' (p. 12).
22. 'Je deviens brusquement le lieu des plus sombres mystères' (p. 8).
23. '[J]e sens m/on sang devenir plus chaud dans m/es artères, j/e perçois tout d'un coup les circuits qu'il irrigue, un cri m/e vient du fond des poumons à m/e faire éclater' (p. 8).
24. 'Il faut en finir avec ce mythe de l'homosexualité féminine mièvre et décorative, sans danger pour l'hétérosexualité, voire récupérable par elle.' Interview with Laurence Louppa.
25. See for example Judy Butler, 'Lesbian S & M: The Politics of Dis-Illusion' in the useful essay collection *Against Sado-Masochism: A Radical Feminist Analysis*, eds Robin Ruth Linden, Darlene R. Pagano, Diana E. H. Russell and Susan Leigh Starr, East Palo Alto, California, 1982, pp. 169–75. See also the special number on *Jouir, Les Cahiers du Grif*, no. 26, March 1983, especially Rosi Braidotti, '"Vanilla Sex" et sadomasochisme', pp. 61–75. Interesting comparisons and comments are to be found in Claude Rawson, 'Cannibalism and Fiction. Part II: Love and Eating in Fielding, Mailer, Genet and Wittig', *Genre*, no. 11, Summer 1978, pp. 227–313, which highlight the issue of the acceptability of violent discourses presented by voices from different points on the spectrum of gender.
26. In her preface to Djuna Barnes, *La Passion*, Wittig describes the writer's job as working on the form of language to make it visible and to liberate, rather than circumscribe, meaning: 'Meaning hides language from sight. Language is constantly, like the stolen letter in Poe's story, clearly there and totally invisible. . . . Working down at the level of the words in the letter re-energises the organisation of the words and in turn gives full meaning to meaning: in practice, at its best, such labour produces in place of meaning a proliferation of significance.' ('Le sens dérobe le langage à la vue. Et en effet le langage est constamment comme la lettre volée du conte de Poe, là à l'évidence mais totalement invisible. . . . Ce travail à ras des mots de la lettre réactive les mots dans leur disposition et à son tour confère au sens son plein sens: dans la pratique et dans le meilleur des cas ce travail fait apparaitre plutôt qu'un sens une polysémie.')
27. Félix Jayle, *La Gynécologie: l'Anatomie morphologique de la femme*, Paris, 1918. Stylistically, in its energetic account of its observations and operations, there are also strong similarities between Jayle's

writing and that of Wittig.

28. '[T]ous cris bloquées dans ta gorge tes dernières pensées derrière tes yeux arrêtées dans mes mains' (p. 9).

29. '[T]es yeux ne sont pas visibles là ou tu me suis moi de même je ne suis pas vue par toi' (p. 10).

30. '[O]n dit, j/e tremble, j/ai le vertige, cela résonne sur m/oi au-dedans' (p. 10).

31. 'Ton poil est tout noir et brillant' (p. 14).

32. '[I]mmergée jusqu'à m/es orifices faciaux j/e vois que la masse liquide ne cesse de s'accroître avec des mucus en suspension des filaments élastiques nacrés, les ors les roux ont à présent même couleur et même consistance que les nuages, le flot montant débouche dans le ciel, adieu continent noir de misère et de peine adieu villes anciennes nous nous embarquons pour les îles brillantes et radieuses pour les vertes Cythères pour les Lesbos noires et dorées' (p. 20).

– 5 –

Hélène Cixous: An Erotics of the Feminine

Emma Wilson

I felt only the caress of moving – moving into the body of another – absorbed and lost within the flesh of another, lulled by the rhythm of water, the slow palpitation of the senses, the movement of silk

Anaïs Nin

Ecriture féminine therefore should be a writing shot through (like shot silk) with otherness

Judith Still

I

'I have some fears for this book. Because it is a book of love'.[1] With these lines Hélène Cixous draws her reader into *Le Livre de Promethea*. This will be a tale of love between women; it is, as the narrator tells us, 'the book that Promethea has lit like a fire in H's soul'.[2] In this reading of *Le Livre de Promethea*, and its sister text, *La Bataille d'Arcachon*, my aim will be to argue that Cixous creates a poetics of the feminine which is intimately dependent on an elusive voicing of lesbian eroticism. This will necessitate an analysis of the specificity of Cixous's engagement in and subversion of a politics of representation. Where erotic relations between women slip seamlessly into her texts, ever implicitly undoing the hegemonic relations of male self to female other, ever inscribing a newly born relation of sexual difference, Cixous has, seemingly without trouble, slipped out of any attempts to define her texts with relation to a particular identity category.

What I want to question here is, firstly, why Cixous's texts are not framed as fantasies and performances of lesbian identity. Critics appear indeed to have espoused Cixous's own notable caution over the employment of the signifier 'lesbian' to designate the sexual acts (between women) performed in her texts.[3] In a reading of analyses of *Le Livre de Promethea* below, I will discuss ways in which the possibly all too easy resolution of relations between female lovers into a model of relations between self and other works to neutralize the politics of Cixous's representation. It might be argued, of course, that the desire to avoid the overt naming of identity categories and the apparent 'outing' of Cixous's fictional personae reflects an all too necessary wariness on the part of critics of the problems of essentializing identity and inappropriately enclosing the text. But this problem leads precisely to what I want to question here secondly, which is how Cixous's texts might be seen to intersect with, and be re-read in the context of, contemporary queer theory. I will draw on the now phenomenally influential work of both Eve Kosofsky Sedgwick and Judith Butler in order to show how these theorists offer models for rethinking sexuality which work neither to deny the radical specificity of (the representation of) lesbian sex acts, nor to delimit and delineate identity categories within fixed and unimpeachable parameters. Drawing on notions of knowledge and transgression, in her creation of an erotics of the feminine, Cixous lavishly explores the tense pleasures of scenarios of secrecy and disclosure. In this way she allows her reader to rethink the all too frequent tender angelizing of lesbian relations seen to reflect a non-antagonistic maternal/filial model, or one of mirroring others. In this sense it is important to maintain that Cixous contends with the politics of the representation of relations between women. This will lead me to argue, indeed, that it is through the textual performance of lesbian sex acts, through the performance of a sexuality which challenges the regulatory practice of heterosexuality, that Cixous pursues a multi-faceted project to destabilize identity in both desire and writing.

II

Le Livre de Promethea was published in 1983 and it can be seen in some senses to mark a transition in Cixous's work. Morag Shiach suggests that it is not until the writing of this text that Cixous realizes 'the possibility of a politicized feminine identity, which both recognizes the complexities of subjectivity and exploits the potential of mythic narrative for a re-conceptualization of social and subjective relations'.[4] Promethea changes Cixous's writing: she comes to embody the power of transgression and she comes to do this through her transformation of desire in writing. In this sense, it might be seen that one of the most definitive departures of *Le Livre de Promethea* is in its relinquishing of the masculine. Where a text such as *LA* opens up the pleasures of feminine eroticism, it inscribes these emphatically within a libidinal economy also open to relations with men. *Le Livre de Promethea* is (more radically?) a text which opens itself exclusively to the female lover, and which seeks, in so doing, not only to rewrite relations between women, but also, as Shiach reminds us so importantly, to rewrite subjectivity.

This has in part been recognized in criticism on Cixous: the text has been privileged as one which transforms notions of subjectivity. As Shiach comments, *Le Livre de Promethea* 'dramatizes the possibility of a relationship of intersubjective identification that is not a relationship of negation and death'.[5] Shiach comments further: 'Promethea is the narrator's lover and her Other'.[6] This statement may itself be seen to touch on a point that is still problematic even in the best criticism on Cixous. In her reading of *Le Livre de Promethea* Shiach states that the narrator and Promethea are lovers and thus draws attention to the love between women which necessarily underpins the exploration of relations between self and other in the novel. Yet where Shiach then proceeds to locate Promethea as the narrator's Other she appears to draw away from a discussion of the specificity of (like) gendered relations between self and other, allowing for an effectively neutralized discussion of language, love and violence.

This reading of the text as a drama of self and other, severed from, or surpassing, its status as a lesbian love story, recurs in the work of other critics. Sarah Cornell suggests that '*Le Livre de Promethea* explores the question of "managing to live the present" through the newly found "paradise" of a love relationship'.[7] She writes of the text as a book of love, without appearing to question the importance of the specificity of that love. Verena Andermatt Conley goes further in her denial of the necessarily female other in *Le Livre de Promethea* where she writes: 'The text is written in the quick of life in transference with and not "on" the other so as not to reduce her *or him* to the status of an object' (my emphasis).[8] This notion of writing not on but in transference with the other is, of course, very illuminating and underlines Conley's sensitivity to the strategies by which Cixous subverts the conventions of discourse. Yet one such strategy, which is perpetually and unquestioningly celebrated in *Le Livre de Promethea*, is the revoicing of desire in the inalienable presence of a female lover.

Amongst Cixous's readers it is perhaps Béatrice Slama who addresses the issue of Promethea's gender most openly. She speaks of the novel as a journal of 'the meeting with the other-woman'[9] and she shows how difference is reinscribed in the relation between two women. Yet Slama too works to generalize the implications of the text, describing it as 'the drama of the self caught in amorous relations. In the wavering of identity.'[10] Indeed, in questioning the representation of love between women in the text Slama writes: 'Masculine? Feminine? Love overcomes boundaries, troubles dual opposition. *Le Livre de Promethea* – together with other texts by Hélène Cixous – uncovers the dazzling and unbearable plurality of being.'[11] And this notion of transgressive plurality recurs in another form in Martine Motard-Noar's reading of *Le Livre de Promethea*. Motard-Noar, like Shiach, acknowledges the difference of the text and its significant place in the context of Cixous's (relatively) later fictions; as she says: 'The feminization of the text is even more clearly marked in the later texts, such as *Le Livre de Promethea*.'[12] Yet Motard-Noar again aligns this drift towards the feminine in both writing and desire with an increased opening and openness of the text. In her analysis of what she describes as 'une autre langue de femme' in the fictions of Cixous, Motard-Noar appears perversely to allow the textual always to elide the sexual. *Le Livre de Promethea* is read as a text which escapes limitations: 'Thus the Cixousian text opens itself even more than it declares itself open. Every restriction, which is thus a repression of her writing is in this way intended to be subverted.'[13] What Motard-Noar leaves relatively uncharted is the relation between this textual subversion and the sexual transgression afforded in the love of Promethea. In a reading of a text which so overtly celebrates oral eroticism, it seems somewhat limiting that for Motard-Noar *langue* appears to mean nothing other than language.

Thus, whilst the language of Cixous's texts has been analysed with subtlety and sensitivity, whilst Cixous's challenge to notions of subjectivity has been admirably addressed by such a searching critic as Morag Shiach, I would argue that this challenge to unified identity (both sexual and textual) should be examined specifically within the context of the writing of erotic relations between women.

III

It is indeed evident to the reader that *Le Livre de Promethea* is a novel which disperses and displaces notions of identity and subjectivity. The questioning of the I who writes, prolonged and shifting throughout Cixous's works, dictates the narrative strategies adopted in *Le Livre de Promethea*, effectively unsettling the reader's confidence in the apparently intradiegetic narrator who gives her voice to the text. *Le Livre de Promethea* is a novel divided between 'Je' and 'H': the language of the text is itself produced between two women. Their relation is at times tenuous, at times so intimate the reader becomes convinced that these are the two named identities of a single individual.

The novel begins with the voice of 'Je' who tells her reader: 'So be it. I am going to try to make an introduction.'[14] We become aware very quickly that 'Je' has assumed the voice of the narrative, where 'H' has failed; as 'Je' tells us: 'For a week H has been trying in vain.'[15] Yet any greater security in 'Je's' ability to express the disarming, all-encompassing passion that is the subject of the text is itself also quickly undone. Indeed 'Je' and 'H' are seemingly at one in their fear of voicing the text; as 'Je' explains: 'Because it is a book which has no fear. Moreover this is why H could not have written it alone. And nor could I '[16] At times 'H' appears an individual, evoked by 'Je', and sharing a more than coincidental number of features with Hélène Cixous herself, yet Cixous seeks to undo this ready identifying of herself with the narrative. We learn from 'Je' that 'there are moments when I am H'.[17] Yet this in itself becomes no clearer a guide to a fixed identity since, following Rimbaud, Cixous appears to attempt to disrupt any stable relation between the self who speaks and her chosen pronoun. The reader discovers that: 'I abandons herself. I abandon myself. I gives herself up, loses herself, does not understand herself.'[18] Not only does Cixous disrupt notions of the autobiographical in her novel, she goes further in developing a strategy to create conscious textual trouble and to focus on the instability of identity.

Morag Shiach argues that the action of *Le Livre de Promethea* is divided 'between three characters'.[19] Martine Motard-Noar finds in the text 'triple tension between three narrators'.[20] This is more closely the case in the later fiction *La Bataille d'Arcachon*, again a drama of 'Je', 'H' and Promethea, where 'Je' is more fully realized as an individual subject position and where her autonomy from 'H' is deliberately and readily inscribed. In *Le Livre de Promethea*, however, it seems that the eventual inextricability of 'Je' and 'H' is necessary to the narrative effects of the text, to its questioning of sexuality and its enactment of eroticism. It is, after all, the passion between Promethea and 'H' which is the premise for the telling of the tale and the subject of the text. Yet in the text's prolonged scene of lovemaking narrated in the 'Premier Cahier – Fin Printemps' (a scene to which we shall return below) it is 'Je' who speaks to 'Tu', uncovers her and enters her. The names of 'H' and even of Promethea are lost in their coming together.

Early in the text 'Je' has told us: 'For the moment I cannot do without H. I do not have the mental courage to be only I.'[21] It is this courage that is born in the text as, in its escalating scenarios of eroticism, 'Je' comes in part to dispense with 'H' and to find her own voice as Promethea's lover. I intend to argue indeed that *Le Livre de Promethea* is a text which explores the finding of a voice and the assumption of an identity. 'H' becomes a signifier and a third person identity which has the potential to conceal or protect 'Je' from her vulnerable position of lone responsibility for her own desires. The text will thus be mediated between 'Je' and 'H' who each displace and replace each other, effectively denying a singular narrative position.

Verena Andermatt Conley describes *Le Livre de Promethea* as a '"braiding" of voices'[22] and she suggests that the author herself is asserted to be plural, existing as writer, narrator and as letter 'H'. Cixous comments, in her paper 'Difficult Joys' given at a conference in Liverpool in 1989, that although she is a writer who very often says 'I' and writes in the first person, she admits: 'Of course I don't know who "I" am/is/are. The scope between the writer and truth, that opening, is probably where the writing slides by.'[23] In *Le Livre de Promethea* it seems that the writing slides by between 'Je' and 'H': the reader comes at once to associate these identities with Cixous herself, and yet also to dispossess her of them. And this can be illustrated specifically with relation to the choice of the signifier 'H'.

Verena Andermatt Conley makes an open reading of the possible echoes which emanate from the signifier 'H' in Cixous's texts. She suggests that 'H' holds familiar associations of Cixous's own name Hélène, that it is 'a mute letter . . ., an axe that fractures, kills, or blazes a trail (la hache); the monogram of goddesses of good (Hélène) and evil (Hécate) and the sign of life itself, inspiration and breath (Haleine)'.[24] I want to suggest that a further way of reading the signifier 'H' might relate particularly to Rimbaud's poem of the same title in *Illuminations*, or indeed to the extract entitled 'The goddess H' in *Roland Barthes by Roland Barthes*. Rimbaud has of course been called forth by Cixous in her questioning of subjectivity and her dislocation of subject and verb. That his 'H' with its supposed connotations of both homosexuality and hashish should also appear as a palimpsest behind *Le Livre de Promethea* adds a further possible layer to the text. 'H' functions as a signifier for a desire unnamed, which retains its power from the lack of naming. Homosexuality is designated yet not disclosed. For Barthes, 'the goddess H' intensifies sensation; as he says: 'I am more sensitive, more perceptive, more loquacious, more amused.'[25] He describes 'H' as 'a goddess, a figure that can be invoked, a means of intercession'.[26] And it is precisely as a 'means of intercession' that 'H' is used in *Le Livre de Promethea* where her presence intercedes between 'Je' and Promethea.

IV

In suggesting that the choice of 'H' as signifier is motivated also by a concern to indicate an intertextual relation to veiled enactments of homosexuality, it is my aim not only to relate Cixous's novel to other textual performances, but to argue that the exploration of eroticism in *Le Livre de Promethea* is inextricably linked to the question of closeted desire. In this text 'Je' addresses Promethea, saying: 'Promethea, I love you, my beautiful chance. I don't want to justify myself. I don't want to disguise myself. I don't want to explain love. There is chance. I want to sing about it.'[27] Cixous would appear to locate novels which enact lesbian desire as existing between justification and disguise; her own strategy differs in denying justification and undoing disguise. The song of Promethea the text becomes is itself a hybrid, metamorphosing fiction which depends on the troubling of knowledge and of identity categories. These are issues which inhabit current queer theory, and to pursue this reading of the relations between secrecy and celebration in *Le Livre de Promethea* I will refer specifically to Eve Kosofsky Sedgwick's groundbreaking work in *Epistemology of the Closet*.[28]

In *Epistemology of the Closet* Sedgwick makes a powerful analysis of images of the closet and of coming out. Her work proceeds on the one hand both to reflect and to reflect on the experiences of gay people. As Sedgwick puts it, most persuasively: 'there can be few gay people, however courageous and forthright by habit, however fortunate in the support of their immediate communities, in whose lives the closet is not still a shaping presence'.[29] In her analyses of real cases of discrimination, and of the encounter with issues of secrecy and disclosure in the legal system, Sedgwick locates her study in the specificity of lived experience. Yet her work takes as its real impetus the desire to prove that the epistemology of the closet has been 'inexhaustibly productive of modern Western culture and history at large'.[30] Following Foucault, Sedgwick works to posit the perceived relation between sex and knowledge; as she suggests: 'cognition itself, sexuality itself, and transgression itself have always been ready in Western culture to be magnetized into an unyielding though not unfissured alignment with one another'.[31] Sedgwick suggests indeed that we might recognize or acknowledge the relation of issues of homosexuality to wider mappings of secrecy and disclosure, and of the private and the public. And by way of example she draws attention to the way in which 'the closet' and 'coming out' are now verging on standing as 'all-purpose phrases for the potent crossing and recrossing of almost any politically charged lines of representation'.[32]

Epistemology of the Closet works further to define two different views of sexual definition, one which is designated as 'minoritizing' and a second designated as 'universalizing'. In Sedgwick's terms the 'minoritizing' view of sexual definition posits a separate (and even separatist) gay identity, dependent on bonding on the axis of sexual desire. In opposition to this is placed the 'universalizing' view of sexual definition which may be seen as integrative, as dependent on a recognition of a bisexual potential and on the tropes of liminality and transitivity. Sedgwick suggests that this dynamic impasse between minoritizing and universalizing views of homosexual definition, and between transitive and separatist tropes of homosexual gender, has its own complicated history. What I shall go on to analyse below is how Cixous's writings may be seen to intersect with these opposing models, and how the enactment of relations between sexuality and knowledge in *Le Livre de Promethea* may be re-read with relation to Sedgwick's magnetic image of the closet.

In no sense is this study intended as an attempt to out Cixous's 'Je' from the closet of her text; rather I intend to demonstrate how far the closet and its implied relations of interior and exterior, secrecy and disclosure, are themselves inescapably compelling features of Cixous's writing on desire between women.

In *La Bataille d'Arcachon* literal encounters with the closet, and with secrecy, enter the text. Cixous stages a scene of parting at the station at Arcachon, where Promethea leaves 'H' to return to Paris. In this moment they speak to one another in English: 'H cries: You are my life. Because of the station master. Promethea cries: You too!'[33] It is left to 'Je' to question: 'And what if the station master understands English?'[34] After the train has left 'Je' tells her reader that 'H' has left with Promethea, that Promethea has remained on the platform with 'H', that even after separation they are in their love inseparable, yet again her mind wanders back to the outside observer as she questions: 'I wonder what the station master was thinking there on the platform.'[35]

Cixous's texts of lesbian desire do not ignore the specificities of literal lesbian existence. *La Bataille d'Arcachon* in particular deals in part with the question of visibility.[36] When 'H' meets Promethea at the airport, for example, their refinding of each other is viewed by a little girl: 'And it was then, while they were kissing and going so far towards the heart, that they were seen by a little girl.'[37] They do not notice the child, instead 'Je' intercedes: 'I saw the little girl; but I said nothing. I thought that nothing so gentle could harm a little girl.'[38] Later 'H' and Promethea are eating a meal together in a Vietnamese restaurant, next to a Vietnamese couple. 'Je' notes: 'Then the young man leaned towards Promethea and he said to her: either you're her mother or you must be very close friends.'[39] Cixous concentrates on the visibility of the love between 'H' and Promethea; like 'Je' her tactic is neither precisely to justify or disguise but, rather, to perform and to celebrate.

In *La Bataille d'Arcachon*, in entirely literal terms, 'H' and Promethea occupy a liminal position, neither entirely in or out of the closet. Their relationship is viewed by others both for what it is and also for what it is not. And it is in the way in which she shows that their love might be mistaken for that between close friends, between a mother and daughter, that Cixous underlines her own commitment to a sense of continuum between the female homosocial and the female homosexual. Her work enacts this very continuum where she invites the reader to re-view lesbian relations and to question the minoritizing closet constructed by society.[40]

V

Le Livre de Promethea differs in part from *La Bataille d'Arcachon* in the way in which it almost exclusively narrates and creates a text of the interior and of metaphor, only loosely related to social reality. Indeed Cixous creates in this novel, as in many others, an interior realm of consciousness, perception and imaginary scenarios. Verena Andermatt Conley suggests, with relation to a different novel, that reading Cixous is like 'watching home movies with their repetitions, their hidden affect, their unedited totalising of rushes or dailies, their over and under exposure, their blurry moments as well as their moments of genuine psychic intensity'.[41] The comparison appears extremely apt and it is one which might be drawn out further to emphasize the specificity of the cinematic quality of Cixous's texts. Cixous may be seen to focus in *Le Livre de Promethea* on the visualizing of desire for Promethea in an interior cinema of the mind. It is a cinema whose images are subjective, tenuous, dispossessed and born out of absence. Indeed 'Je' draws attention to this when she tells the reader that when Promethea is no longer with her, she still sees her; as she says: 'in my mind I watch long, slow imaginary films, imposing and magnifying images which let me see her in the closest detail'.[42] The text itself becomes a series of these 'films imaginaires'. If these are home movies, they exist between fantasy and loss, interspersed with moments of amnesia, like the recurring memories and translucent images projected in the cinema of Tarkovsky.

Rather than representing an identifiable social reality *Le Livre de Promethea* attempts to give voice to sensation, to recreate erotic obsession from a body of metaphor. It is a text which repeatedly, perpetually contends with interiority, and questions what might be seen as the paradoxical necessity to come out in order to come into writing. I have tried to illustrate how far the literal dynamics of the closet infiltrate a text such as *La Bataille d'Arcachon*. This text comes closest in Cixous's works thus far to addressing the question of the representation of lesbian existence. Yet it will be seen in the discussion that follows that the trope of the closet and of coming out subtends much of Cixous's textual practice and her theorizing of relations of knowledge and desire. Indeed the questioning of issues of openness and (dis)closure surrounding the erotics of relations between women will be seen to have an entirely central place in Cixous's theories of reading and writing, and in her writings on desire in the feminine.

Le Livre de Promethea is a novel of explicit and exquisite eroticism. Cixous explores a language and images of lush sensuality, of lyricism and intoxication. It is a novel which seeks to enact the birth of a new eroticism which is at once freed from heterosexual assumption and binary gender oppositions, yet also explores conflict and difference within identity. In the text, appropriately in the context of this birth of a new eroticism, the metaphor of birth recurs compulsively in erotic scenarios. 'Je' perpetuates images of awakening and initiation as she says: 'it was as if Promethea had brought me living, as an adult to attend my own birth, my own awakening, and my own contemplation'.[43] Equally, Promethea's body, as they awaken in the morning, is new-born for 'Je': 'Promethea's body leaving my belly in the morning is moist, coated in golden, velvety membrane. I lick her all over.'[44] Cixous effectively elides difference between oral eroticism and the sensory signifiers of the birth scenario.

The image of birth is one which evidently privileges the metaphor of coming out: the notion of awakening into a new identity is strongly emphasized in Cixous's texts. She appears, however, to wish to perpetuate this process of awakening rather than its culminating moment of enlightenment. In *Le Livre de Promethea* one lover asks the other if she will still desire her next year and her lover replies: 'I want you every day and I want you every night. Forget what I have just told you.'[45] And when asked why she must forget, her lover replies: 'Forget. So that one day I can tell you for the first time again: "I want you every night and every day I want you".'[46] *Le Livre de Promethea* becomes a song with an insistent refrain: its awakenings are dependent on amnesia as Cixous seeks to bear witness, again and again, to the birth of desire and its fracturing eroticism. Cixous's privileging of awakening and coming out into writing is, however, necessarily, even viscerally, dependent on the interior and on the perceived relations between femininity and interiority.

These ideas she elaborates in most detail in the texts collected in the volume *L'Heure de Clarice Lispector*. In her essay 'L'Auteur en vérité', Cixous writes that Eve has no fear of the interior, of her own interior or of that of others. Her relation to the interior, to penetration, 'to touching within',[47] is positive. She continues: 'for, potentially or really mothers, all women have an experience of the interior, an experience of being able to hold the other, a positive experience of being changed by the other, an experience of good receptivity'.[48] This theory appears integral to Cixous's writing, underpinning her theories of reading and receptivity as expounded in her seminars at the Collège International de Philosophie, and elaborated in her re-enactments of the reading scenario in her writings on Clarice Lispector. Repeatedly Cixous returns to the tropes of maternity, reciprocity and symbiosis. She attempts indeed not to justify or disguise her theories but to transform her texts into celebrations of them. The libidinal economy she draws out is one of possession and dispossession; at its centre is a nexus of desire dependent on, yet perpetually questioning, the openness and permeability of the other.

In this reading of eroticism within *Le Livre de Promethea* I will argue, indeed, that Cixous's investment in interiority is in some senses more troubled than she herself appears to suggest. In her performance of desire, with her 'lyric tongue',[49] 'Je' creates a love song to Promethea which metamorphoses into love-making with Promethea. Both the song and the sex act move between inside and out, between surface and interiority, between secrecy and disclosure, between voice and silence. Paradoxically, as will be seen, it will be in her entering of Promethea that 'Je' comes out into writing.

VI

At the end of the 'Premier Cahier – Fin Printemps' comes a privileged passage, an instant of interiority, a scenario of love-making. 'Je' describes the passage as 'a small fragment of depth which with my own hands I am going to fish from the flowing river of love, and I can do nothing other with it than set it down all wet and quivering on the paper'.[50] The text comes into life, newly born, quivering on the paper. Cixous implicitly isolates her aim to elide difference between sensation and its expression. In her language of eroticism she seeks an immediacy of feeling, a performance of desire which destroys divisions between text and sex act, entirely involving the reader in a scenario which s/he must enter, denying any possible position of voyeurism or exteriority.

The scene opens with the imperative, 'I must enter'.[51] 'Je' speaks to Promethea who is described as so naked before her. Yet she also speaks to the reader, designating her desire, drawing us into the drama of interior and exterior this scene will become. Cixous begins in repetition, reiterating the imperative, allowing the scene to take form little by little, allowing Promethea's body and the desire it arouses in 'Je' to encompass the text completely. The evocation of her body is such that it dissolves surface and substance, and denies stasis and reification. 'Je' images the unveiling of Promethea, shows her as 'so unveiled'[52] yet avoids lingering literally over the parts of her body. It is the disclosure of Promethea, her openness, that is so erotic for 'Je', but it is Cixous's own avoidance of intrusive images which is itself erotic for the reader. 'Je' shows Promethea's skin to be so luminous that her face seems shaped in light. And it is in imagery of light, of liquid, of honey and of silk that Cixous creates an erotics of the feminine.

This drawing on sensory and sensual metaphors serves to allude not to the body itself but to the sensations it arouses. Cixous seeks in her text to trace these transient feelings and to do so she shows the body in movement and metamorphosis. As 'Je' watches Promethea she observes: 'Your lips move forward, your lips come softly from the soul-light, your lips are flowers growing on the surface of the pools of tears.'[53] The text is left apparently ambiguous, the reader's uncertainty endorsed as 'Je's' image hovers between Promethea's lips and her vulva. These lips are themselves in transition, transformed into flowers as the text shifts away from flesh into metaphor. And it is this metamorphosis which draws 'Je's' desire, as she voices her response to the open, moving body before her: 'I cannot not enter.'[54]

Yet this desire to enter and to exist within Promethea is itself withheld where 'Je' relates: 'But I do not enter, I do not enter.'[55] Cixous allows for no easy fusing between self and other; she seeks instead to undo divisions between exterior and interior, to locate her texts in a position of liminality, and to explore a tantalizing eroticism which desires yet dissolves the possibility of entering or possessing the metamorphosing body of a female lover.

VII

In this scenario of eroticism Cixous may be seen to draw on the image of the closet and its implied relations of inside and out. Eroticism is encoded in a dynamics of entrance and exclusion. The very opening of the passage envisages the possibility of entering, yet here, as 'Je' tells us, there is no door. She finds she cannot not enter Promethea, yet equally also she cannot enter her lover. She does not enter her, yet finds herself already within her: 'I am already up to my waist in your eyes, I am already up to my breasts in your heart.'[56] The literal image of entering is replaced by an allusion to 'Je's' dependence on Promethea, and her involvement with her, which is itself expressed resolutely in terms of the body. In 'Je's' involvement with Promethea there is no longer room for exteriority; Promethea is so open, so vast, that 'Je' fears falling inside her. The relation between the lovers is such that, paradoxically, 'Je' exists always already within Promethea, yet also always outside her. And this ambiguity, this liminality, is itself seemingly a deliberate ploy within the text.

Throughout this representation of love-making, the desire to enter the body of the lover is all but indistinguishable from the cognitive quest to know the other, her silence and her secret life. And this desire for knowledge is enacted in a performance of opening and disclosure. 'Je' reveals: 'What interests me is the door, the door of this moment: I must find the door to the soul which leads suddenly to a secret life.'[57] Cixous invests the door with the power to disclose, but she suggests that once opened the door loses its power, that another door must be found and must be opened. 'Je' claims indeed that this will become 'a book of doors'.[58]

Cixous's text allows for a perpetually reiterated scenario of transgression and disclosure. In Sedgwick's terms, what she describes so aptly as 'the deadly elasticity of heterosexist presumption'[59] means that gay people can find that every encounter with a new class of students, a landlord, a doctor, erects new closets which themselves necessitate new surveys, calculations and requisitions of secrecy and disclosure. For Cixous this re-viewing and recharting is revealed to define even the most intimate relationship. Cixous shows implicitly that the fraught possibilities of disclosure define and refine the eroticism of her texts. 'Je' seeks to relive and Cixous seeks to re-enact the moment when the door will be opened. The possibility of re-enactment depends on amnesia and the cautious enclosing of memories in a closet of the mind.

'Je' undermines and denies any knowledge of her love-making with Promethea. The fragments of pleasure which remain in the text are circumscribed in a narrative of transience, ephemerality and unknowability, as 'Je' assures us: 'but I know that we will never live here again, in this light, with this innocence, never again will we breathe in the perfumes of this night'.[60] As narrator 'Je' works to bear witness to the erosion of sensation in writing, to the uncertainties of memory and desire. 'Je' does not remember and will not look back, rather she looks forward into new openings, into new writing. For 'Je' and Promethea, indeed, 'the new unknowing unfolds softly in the depths of the sky'.[61]

Le Livre de Promethea is, seemingly, motivated by a double strategy. Throughout her work Cixous foregrounds and troubles notions of interior and exterior. One of the first in her long line of texts is itself named *Dedans*, yet where it is a text of interiority, incorporation and melancholia, its motive force is outwards, its apparent aim expiation. Cixous allows no easy mapping of interior and exterior; the tenuous, ever inverting relations between the two are illustrated in *Le Livre de Promethea* through a scenario of eroticism where metaphor inhabits reality, where surfaces dissolve and bodies mingle. Yet where this performance of desire serves to disrupt any fixed notions of inside and out, inversely, in Cixous's text, questions of secrecy and disclosure serve to focus and intensify eroticism.

VIII

Cixous's texts are marked out by their inscription of painful pleasures. In her reading of Clarice Lispector in *Vivre l'orange* Cixous writes of the fear implicit in her adoration. She evokes her sensations painstakingly in the following terms: 'Fear? Perhaps: an exalting fear, like a joy. Fear in the Joy. A fear without fright, only the trembling of the Joy.'[62] Cixous reveals that her task in *Vivre l'orange* is to give a voice to this melting of joy and fear, to this joy within fear. Her text is one which describes a reading encounter in visceral and erotic terms. Cixous's first reading of Lispector is re-read as an annunciation and as the coming of another woman into her life. The cluster of metaphors which embellish and encircle the encounter are close to signifiers of eroticism. Cixous images Lispector's voice entering her veins and her words entering her bloodstream and stresses: 'nothing is more powerful than the intimate touch of a veiled voice, profound but reserved coming to awaken my blood'.[63]

The relevance of this reading encounter to *Le Livre de Promethea* is made clear in the later text. The encounter with Lispector is circumscribed by its impossibility. It exists only in metaphor, only as a performance of the necessary sensuality of *lecture féminine*. Yet the encounter is itself re-read in *Le Livre de Promethea*. 'Je' tells the reader that she knows a woman for whom 'H' has a fantastical passion, and this woman is Clarice. Cixous frames the narration of her obsession with Lispector in a narrative of desire between women, coming thus apparently to disclose the emotive and erotic investment behind her championing of the feminine in the writings of Lispector. She also makes a glancing reading in *Le Livre de Promethea* of Lispector's text *The Hour of the Star* which becomes, in Cixous's terms, an attempt in narrative to draw close to another woman. Cixous explains Lispector's choice of Macabea as heroine saying: 'She wanted to love a woman who wouldn't let herself be seduced by her.'[64] Yet Cixous shows how Lispector has chosen a male narrative voice since 'otherwise she wouldn't have had the courage to approach her so closely, and even, if necessary, to go right into her, entering her very entrails'.[65] Cixous shows Lispector, like Duras in *Le Ravissement de Lol V. Stein*, exploring desire for a woman through the mediation of the male gaze and a male narrative voice. These strategies Cixous herself eschews. Her reference to *The Hour of the Star* serves to draw attention, indeed, to the distance of this text from *Le Livre de Promethea* and to the way in which 'Je' will herself come close to Promethea, that her text will reinvent the possibilities of entering a woman's body. Yet these possibilities are themselves revealed to be a source of pain as much as pleasure.

In her writing on Lispector Cixous disturbs borders between the homosocial and the homosexual. Her account of the reading encounter as a sensual and sexual scenario disrupts notions of any fixed division between the erotic and the metaphoric. In these terms Cixous might be seen to favour a continuum model which posits no essential division or difference between lesbian desire and other strong affective bonds between women. Yet it should be noted too that the encounters performed in Cixous's texts all depend to some extent on difficulty and difference, and it is from this that they are seen in part to draw their allure. As regards Lispector, it is perhaps significant that the relation between Cixous and Clarice should be marked by a difference in language, a distance between continents and of course the irrevocable division between the dead author and the living critic. In *Vivre l'orange* Cixous creates a love song to a woman she cannot seduce. Despite the overt, seductive physicality of the text, its sexual relations are only ever metaphoric, no more than textual.

IX

What I want to argue is that this privileging of troubled relations is pervasive in Cixous's works and that it marks even the relations evoked between 'Je' and Promethea. Like *La Bataille d'Arcachon*, this is a text of contest and conflict. Near its end 'Je' reveals, apparently to Promethea: 'How happy I am to have been sad sometimes, and now I find joy in the sorrows you return to me parcelled in transparent wrappings, I see them gleam through the silks.'[66] *Le Livre de Promethea* itself commemorates fear and pain within pleasure. In the 'Portrait de Promethea en H', 'Je' charts Promethea's cruelties as much as her divinities. Yet the novel also surpasses the familiar reckoning with stresses within a relationship. It deals certainly with imagined infidelities, with the fear of the loss of the lover and with the psychic landscape of jealousy and its vicissitudes. The reckoning with pain, however, reaches far deeper into the text and is inextricably linked with its enactment of eroticism. The desire 'Je' feels tortures her; it is 'the deepest, slowest and most certain grief . . . which pressed and penetrated unceasingly straight to the heart, it was a grief named in gold'.[67] 'Je' shows her body entered by a voluptuous pain; it is a pain which runs throughout the text and which is associated, it seems, with the capacity to be entered by Promethea, and to feel from within. Equally 'Je' fears her own ability to enter Promethea; she avows: 'I am afraid of going towards you to the very limits of myself.'[68]

Cixous explores the coexistence of pain and pleasure, stressing that her aim is to analyse the extremities of love, its very borderlines. Her work can be seen then, as I have suggested earlier, to engage in an implicit questioning of representations of sex between women and to challenge some underlying assumptions about lesbian sex acts. The filmmaker Sheila McLaughlin says of the representation of eroticism in her film *She Must Be Seeing Things*: 'I wanted to undermine the idea of women as narcissistic extensions of each other . . . I wanted to bring out the eroticism between them, particularly in the seduction scene, and the aggression in their sex.'[69] And this desire might also be ascribed to Cixous in *Le Livre de Promethea*.

Cixous's representations of passion between women transgress the limits imposed on lesbian eroticism by theorists such as Julia Kristeva. In her essay 'The Malady of Grief: Duras', Kristeva writes: 'As an echo to death-bearing symbiosis with the mothers, passion between two women represents one of the most intense images of doubling.'[70] Despite the psychoanalytic framework which constructs Kristeva's theory, in effect her work has hardly moved on from Beauvoir who makes mention of doubling, or mirroring between women, in *The Second Sex*, saying: 'this mirroring may assume a maternal cast; the mother who sees herself and projects herself in her daughter often has a sexual attachment for her; she has in common with the lesbian the longing to protect and cradle a soft carnal object in her arms'.[71] Cixous's textual inscriptions of lesbian desire in *Le Livre de Promethea* work indeed to undermine this view of female/female relations depending necessarily on a libidinal economy of narcissism and doubling. While 'Je' may voice the fear of losing herself within

Promethea, there is no sense in which the two women are seen as one and the same: at times 'Je' is harrowed, indeed, by the very difference of Promethea. Any possible doubling relation is emphatically disrupted between the two women. Equally, in her deployment of images of birth and maternity, Cixous allows no easy designation of the relation between Promethea and her lover as one between mother and daughter. She explores the implied imagery of interiority afforded by maternal metaphors, but she inverts and dissolves any fixed roles either of her protagonists might be seen to adopt. If the mother/daughter couple has its place in the text, it is due to the exploration of proximities between the female homosocial and the female homosexual, rather than to any privileged role chosen for this dyad in the analysis of a feminine libidinal economy. In the politics of her representation, Cixous seeks a rewriting of lesbian eroticism, a re-encoding of violence within desire and a recognition of patterns of difference inherent (even) in same-sex relations.

X

This recognition of difference is resurgent in Cixous's texts and it is readily linked with her theorizing of bisexuality. This is an issue which is raised in *Le Livre de Promethea* where 'Je' alludes to 'all my fine theories more and more perfected'[72] and lists amongst them 'the theory of bisexuality which always gave me some trouble'.[73] Cixous speaks of her theory of bisexuality in the essay 'The Laugh of the Medusa' where in her writing (on) *écriture féminine* she pluralizes the notion of feminine sexuality, saying, 'you can't talk about a female sexuality, uniform, homogenous'.[74] This theory of multiple and non-identical sexualities is developed as the text continues and Cixous describes this as the other bisexuality which depends not on sex acts with individuals of either gender but which is described rather as 'each one's location in self [repérage en soi] of the presence – variously manifest and insistent according to each person, male or female – of both sexes'[75] and which allows for the 'multiplication of the effects of the inscription of desire'.[76] In this sense where a text like *LA* (and many others by Cixous) voices relations between 'Je' and lovers of either gender and may be seen in this sense to enact a bisexual identification, in *Le Livre de Promethea*, through the exclusive representation of relations between women Cixous enacts representations of the other bisexuality revealing the differences and multiple desires which inhabit relations of apparent proximity and similarity.

This theorizing of bisexuality, of a sexuality which, in Cixous's terms, 'doesn't annul differences but stirs them up',[77] locates Cixous's work specifically within the universalizing model constructed in *Epistemology of the Closet*. It seems also that Cixous's work draws surprisingly close to that of Judith Butler, whose *Gender Trouble: Feminism and the Subversion of Identity* has done so much to destabilize fixed gender categories, and to disclose the performative nature of both sexuality and gender.

Butler makes scant mention of Cixous in *Gender Trouble*; her one reference is, however, to 'The Laugh of the Medusa' and to how this essay exposes the dialectic of same and other as taking place through the axis of sexual difference. And it is in the questioning of difference and the inversion of roles in gay relationships that the work of Butler and Cixous might readily be compared. In her essay 'Imitation and Gender Insubordination',[78] Judith Butler analyses what it is to be a lesbian. She suggests here that it is precisely through the repeated play of this sexuality that her 'I' is insistently reconstituted as a lesbian 'I'. She concludes, indeed, that there is no 'I' who precedes the gender or sexuality that it is said to perform. Now I want to suggest that this theory of performativity offers a valuable insight into the construction of 'Je' in *Le Livre de Promethea*. Cixous avoids names or labels in her text, never using or mentioning the word 'lesbian' or 'homosexual' in a novel emphatically, overtly, about desire between women. This stance might, in Butler's terms, be seen to suggest precisely that no identity precedes performance. Cixous presents her reader with the enactment of desire: the ever tenuous identity of her protagonist 'Je' is entirely dependent on the repetition of sex acts and the voicing of speech acts which themselves form the narrative we read.

Butler suggests, further, that 'If I claim to be a lesbian, I "come out" only to produce a new and different "closet".'[79] It is this closetting that Cixous avoids in *Le Livre de Promethea*. Butler suggests that it is always finally unclear what is meant by evoking the lesbian-signifier, since its signification is always to some degree out of one's control. And indeed this is recognized also by Cixous in 'The Laugh of the Medusa' with reference to a different signifier, where she says that it should be impossible to define *écriture féminine*, that this practice can never be 'theorized, enclosed, coded'[80] but that this does not mean that it does not exist. *Ecriture féminine* exists not in theory, but in practice.

Feminine writing is performed, but not defined in Cixous's texts where she works to cross borders between fiction and theory, fantasy and criticism. In the feminine writing of her fictions Cixous gives voice to an erotics of the feminine which itself troubles accepted identity categories and which is enacted in an ever-unfolding drama of secrecy and unveiling. And indeed the presence of this perpetuated series of liminal encounters bears witness to Cixous's apparent commitment to the view that sexuality depends in part on the denial of transparency and disclosure, and the instability of knowledge.

Butler makes one of her most revelatory statements about sexuality and identity categories when she writes: 'if the category were to offer no trouble, it would cease to be interesting to me: it is precisely the pleasure produced by the instability of those categories that makes me a candidate for the category to begin with'.[81] Cixous herself also seeks this pleasure in instability in *Le Livre de Promethea*. Her strategies work in every way to cause trouble: her narrative voice is fractured and non-self-identical, her text hovers between memory and metaphor, the sex acts it describes are permeable, metamorphosing, the pleasures she evokes are inhabited by pain and fear.

In a paper given at a conference in Queen's University in Ontario in 1991, Cixous said: 'And love of women? A troubling, troubled subject. I rush to say; we don't know much. That's what experience has whispered to me. The extent to which we haven't yet thought out – we have lived but not thought or written – the difference inside women, or inside a woman.'[82] Cixous discloses the trouble inherent in the identity category. In her terms, the performance of desire, her experience, offers no more than a revelation of the uncertainty of the category to which her acts give her access. Judith Butler speaks of letting 'that which cannot fully appear in any performance persist in its disruptive promise'.[83] And this, or perhaps something still further, is what Cixous appears to achieve in her writing of an erotics of the feminine. In *Le Livre de Promethea* she creates a textual entrance into the difference in the interior, as her heroine 'Je' attempts to enter into her lover, Promethea. The performance of desire within the text is ever partial, 'Je' is never fully within yet never fully without Promethea. Cixous nevertheless retains the promise of further engagement with the writing out of love between women. Her privileging of unknowability and instability is itself liminal where her text remains poised between the transient hope of knowledge and the opacity of amnesia. Her text is, tentatively, prospective, opening new vistas for its reader, exploring the pleasures of instability with a clear, unwavering vision.

Le Livre de Promethea emphatically exceeds any minoritizing classification. Whilst never denying the specificity of her exploration of sexuality, Cixous works effectively to disrupt discrete identity categories. For her, the act of coming out would merely serve to enclose her work, the text and its inhabitants, within new boundaries. Her novel seeks to cross borders, – to deny the fixity of inside and out, whilst simultaneously exploring the erotics of liminality. *Le Livre de Promethea* allows a rethinking of sexual difference within a lavish and luxuriating enactment of eroticism. It is a text with which Cixous appears to have taken risks, and these risks entirely enhance the intensity of her inscription of desire; as 'Je' reminds us in her opening lines: 'Once in the fire, one is flooded with sweetness.'[84]

Notes

1. Hélène Cixous, *Le Livre de Promethea*, Paris, Gallimard, 1983, p. 9. Translations are my own, unless reference is made to an English edition. ('J'ai un peu peur pour ce livre. Parce que c'est un livre d'amour.')
2. Ibid., p. 21 ('le livre que Promethea a allumé comme un incendie dans l'âme de H').
3. Cixous herself comments on the term 'lesbian' in the interview 'Rethinking Differences'. Here she makes a specific distinction between lesbianism and female homosexuality, saying: 'Lesbianism gives way to the latent "man-within," a man who is reproduced, who reappears in a power situation. Phallocracy still exists, the phallus is still present in lesbianism. What it reveals is a woman who "makes like" [fait], "counterfeits" [contrefait] a man. On the other hand, there is a homosexual side of feminism. It is a dream of femininity . . .', 'Rethinking Differences', in George Stambolian and Elaine Marks (eds), *Homosexualities and French Literature, Critical Texts*, Ithaca and London, 1979, pp. 70–86, pp. 74–5. In her own terms, Cixous would appear to represent female homosexuality, and not this peculiarly 'false' and 'phallic' construction of lesbianism, in *Le Livre de Promethea*. In the course of this essay, however, I have chosen to use the term 'lesbian' to connote relations between women since the distinctions Cixous makes in this interview no longer reflect current thinking and deployment of terminology to designate sexual identity categories. It should be noted, too, that the interview in *Homosexualities and French Literature* is prefaced by the comment that Cixous's beliefs about women have undergone great changes since she granted the interview. Indeed *Le Livre de Promethea*, coming seven years later, might possibly be seen as one of the texts in whose performance Cixous has come to rethink her ideas about relations between women.
4. Morag Shiach, *Hélène Cixous: A Politics of Writing*, London, 1991, pp. 95–6. Sarah Cornell also notes that *Le Livre de Promethea* is 'situated at an important pivotal period', 'Hélène Cixous's *Le Livre*

de Promethea:Paradise Refound', in Susan Sellers (ed.), *Writing Differences: Readings from the Seminar of Hélène Cixous*, Milton Keynes, 1988, pp. 127–40, p. 130.

5. Shiach, *Hélène Cixous: A Politics of Writing*, p. 96.
6. Ibid., p. 97.
7. Cornell, 'Hélène Cixous's *Le Livre de Promethea*: Paradise Refound', p. 131.
8. Verena Andermatt Conley, *Hélène Cixous*, London, 1992, p. 120.
9. Béatrice Slama, 'Entre amour et écriture: *Le Livre de Promethea*', in Françoise van Rossum-Guyon and Myriam Diaz-Diocaretz (eds), *Hélène Cixous, chemins d'une écriture*, Amsterdam, 1990, pp. 127–48, p. 128 ('la rencontre avec l'autre-femme').
10. Ibid., p. 131 ('le drame de l'être pris dans le rapport amoureux. Dans le vacillement d'identité').
11. Ibid., p. 133 ('Masculin? Féminin? L'amour renverse les frontières, bouscule l'opposition duelle. *Le Livre de Promethea* – avec d'autres textes d'Hélène Cixous – découvre l'éblouissante et insoutenable pluralité de l'être').
12. Martine Motard-Noar, *Les Fictions d'Hélène Cixous: Une autre langue de femme*, Kentucky, 1991, p. 63 ('La féminisation du texte est encore plus clairement marquée dans les textes plus tardifs, tels *Le Livre de Promethea*').
13. Ibid., pp. 37–8 ('Aussi le texte cixousien s'ouvre-t-il d'autant plus qu'il se déclare ouverte. Toute limitation, donc répression de son écriture se veut par là subvertie').
14. Cixous, *Le Livre de Promethea*, p. 11 ('Soit. Je vais essayer de faire l'introduction').
15. Ibid., p. 11 ('Depuis une semaine H s'efforce en vain').
16. Ibid., p. 21 ('Parce que c'est un livre qui n'a pas peur. D'ailleurs c'est ce qui fait que H n'aurait pas pu l'écrire seule. Et moi non plus').
17. Ibid., p. 21 ('il y a des moments où je suis H').
18. Ibid., p. 28 ('Je s'abandonne. Je m'abandonne. Je se rend, se perd, ne se comprend pas').
19. Shiach, *Hélène Cixous: A Politics of Writing*, p. 96.
20. Motard-Noar, *Les Fictions d'Hélène Cixous: Une autre langue de femme*, p. 21 ('la triple tension entre trois narratrices').
21. Cixous, *Le Livre de Promethea*, p. 27 ('Pour l'instant je ne peux pas me dispenser de H. Je n'ai pas le courage mental de n'être que Je').
22. Andermatt Conley, *Hélène Cixous*, p. 120.
23. Hélène Cixous, 'Difficult Joys', in Helen Wilcox, Keith McWatters, Ann Thompson and Linda R. Williams (eds), *The*

Body and the Text: Hélène Cixous, Reading and Teaching, London, 1990, pp. 5–30, p. 9.

24. Andermatt Conley, *Hélène Cixous*, p. 120.

25. Roland Barthes, *Roland Barthes by Roland Barthes*, trans. Richard Howard, London, 1977, p. 64; *Roland Barthes par Roland Barthes*, Sevil, 1975, p. 68 ('je suis plus sensible, plus perceptif, plus loquace, mieux distrait').

26. Ibid., p. 64; ibid., p. 68 ('une déesse, une figure invocable, une voie d'intercession').

27. Cixous, *Le Livre de Promethea*, p. 49 ('Promethea, je t'aime, ma belle chance. Je ne veux pas me justifier. Je ne veux pas me déguiser. Je ne veux pas expliquer l'amour. Il y a la chance. Je veux la chanter').

28. Eve Kosofsky Sedgwick, *Epistemology of the Closet*, London, 1991.

29. Ibid., p. 68.

30. Ibid., p. 68.

31. Ibid., p. 73.

32. Ibid., p. 71.

33. Hélène Cixous, *La Bataille d'Arcachon*, Laval, Québec, 1986, p. 111 ('H crie: You are my life. A cause du chef de gare. Promethea crie: You too!').

34. Ibid., p. 111 ('Et si le chef de gare comprend l'anglais?').

35. Ibid., p. 112 ('Je me demande ce que pensait le chef de gare sur le quai').

36. For a consideration of lesbianism and visibility, see Teresa de Lauretis, 'Film and the Visible' in Bad Object-Choices (ed.), *How Do I Look: Queer Film and Video*, Seattle, 1991, pp. 223–64.

37. Cixous, *La Bataille d'Arcachon*, p. 36 ('C'est alors, pendant qu'elles s'embrassaient et s'avançaient si loin vers le coeur, qu'elles ont été vues par une petite fille').

38. Ibid., p. 36 ('Moi je voyais la petite fille; mais je n'ai rien dit. J'ai pensé que rien de si doux ne pourrait faire de mal à une petite fille').

39. Ibid., p. 154 ('Ensuite le jeune homme s'est penché vers Promethea et il lui a dit: ou bien vous êtes sa mère ou bien c'est que vous êtes de très grandes amies').

40. In this sense Cixous's representations of relations between women might find their place in what Marianne Hirsch describes as: '[t]he space of "otherness" located in the feminine [which] is the pre-oedipal space of mother–daughter mirroring'; *The Mother/Daughter Plot: Narrative, Psychoanalysis, Feminism*, Bloomington and Indianapolis, 1989, p. 135. This desire or inclination to relate the mother–daughter relation to sexual relations between women

is of course resurgent in feminist criticism and can be seen in part as a product of the attempt to relate the homosocial and the homosexual. This Eve Kosofsky Sedgwick does in one of her most notorious sweeping statements, where she says: 'At this particular historical moment, an intelligible continuum of aims, emotions, and valuations links lesbianism with the other forms of women's attention to women: the bond of mother and daughter, for instance, the bond of sister and sister, women's friendship, "networking," and the active struggles of feminism'; *Between Men: English Literature and Male Homosocial Desire*, New York, 1985, p. 2. It is important to my argument about Cixous that this relation between the homosocial and the homosexual should be perceived to exist, but that it should in no way deny or domesticate the erotic charge or transgressive force of lesbian relations.

41. Andermatt Conley, *Hélène Cixous*, p. 70.
42. Cixous, *Le Livre de Promethea*, p. 62 ('je me passe de longs et lents films imaginaires grandioses et grossissants qui me permettent de l'observer de très très près').
43. Ibid., p. 41 ('ce fut comme si Promethea m'avait amenée adulte vivante assisterà ma propre naissance, à mon propre éveil, et à mon recueillement').
44. Ibid., p. 51 ('le corps de Promethea au sortir de mon ventre le matin, est enduit d'une couche de moite velours doré. Je la lèche entièrement').
45. Ibid., p. 91 ('Je te veux tous les jours et je te veux toutes les nuits. Oublie ce que je viens de te dire').
46. Ibid., p. 91 ('Oublie. Afin qu'un jour je puisse te dire à nouveau pour la première fois: "Je te veux toutes les nuits et tous les jours je te veux"').
47. Hélène Cixous, 'L'Auteur en vérité', *L'Heure de Clarice Lispector*, Paris, 1989, pp. 121–68, p. 139 ('au toucher du dedans').
48. Ibid., p. 142 ('car, virtuellement ou réellement mères, toutes les femmes ont quand même une expérience de l'intérieur, une expérience de la capacité d'autre, une expérience de l'altération non négative par de l'autre, de la bonne réceptivité').
49. Cixous, *Le Livre de Promethea*, p. 127 ('langue lyrique').
50. Ibid., p. 134 ('un petit fragment de profondeur que je vais pêcher avec mes mains dans le cours du fleuve Amour, et je ne peux rien en faire d'autre que le déposer tout mouillé et palpitant sur le papier').
51. Ibid., p. 134 ('Il faut que j'entre').
52. Ibid., p. 135 ('si dévoilée').
53. Ibid., p. 135 ('Tes lèvres poussent, tes lèvres sortent doucement

de la lumière d'âme, tes lèvres, des fleurs qui poussent à la surface des puits de larmes').

54. Ibid., p. 135 ('Je ne peux pas ne pas entrer').

55. Ibid., p. 135 ('Mais je n'entre pas, je n'entre pas').

56. Ibid., p. 135 ('je suis déjà jusqu'aux hanches dans tes yeux, je suis déjà jusqu'aux seins dans ton âme').

57. Ibid., p. 137 ('Ce qui m'intéresse c'est la porte, la porte de cet instant: il faut trouver la porte dans l'âme qui mène soudain à une vie secrète').

58. Ibid., p. 137 ('un livre des portes').

59. Kosofsky Sedgwick, *Epistemology of the Closet*, p. 68.

60. Cixous, *Le Livre de Promethea*, p. 137 ('mais plus jamais je le sais nous ne vivrons ici, à cette lumière, avec cette innocence, plus jamais nous ne humerons les parfums de cette nuit').

61. Ibid., p. 138 ('la nouvelle ignorance se déroule doucement au fond du ciel').

62. Hélène Cixous, *Vivre l'orange* (bilingual edition) in *L'Heure de Clarice Lispector*, pp. 7–113, pp. 60–1 ('Peur? Peut-être: une peur exaltante, comme une joie. Peur dans la Joie. Une peur sans crainte. Seulement le tremblement de la Joie').

63. Ibid., pp. 8–9 ('rien n'est plus puissant que l'intime toucher d'une voix voilée, profonde mais réservée venant me réveiller le sang').

64. Hélène Cixous, *Le Livre de Promethea*, p. 47 ('Elle a voulu aimer une femme qui ne se laisserait pas séduire par elle').

65. Ibid., p. 48 ('autrement elle-même n'aurait pas eu le courage d'aller aussi près d'elle, et même s'il le fallait, d'aller jusqu'en elle, jusque dans ses viscères').

66. Ibid., p. 230 ('Comme je suis heureuse d'avoir été quelquefois si triste, comme j'ai maintenant de joies à ces tristesses que tu me rends enveloppées dans des papiers souvenirs transparents, je les vois briller à travers les soies').

67. Ibid., p. 84 ('la plus profonde et lente et sûre des douleurs . . . qui appuyait et s'avançait inéluctablement jusqu'au coeur, c'était une douleur s'appelant dor').

68. Ibid., p. 175 ('j'ai peur de m'avancer vers toi jusqu'à l'extrémité de moi').

69. 'She Must Be Seeing Things', an interview with Sheila McLaughlin by Alison Butler, *Screen*, vol. 28, no. 4, Autumn 1987, pp. 20–8.

70. Julia Kristeva, 'The Malady of Grief: Duras', in *Black Sun: Depression and Melancholia*, trans. Leon S. Roudiez, New York, 1989, pp. 219–59, p. 250; 'La Maladie de la douleur: Duras' in *Soleil noir*, Paris, 1987, pp. 227–65, p. 257 ('En écho à la symbiose

mortifère avec les mères, la passion entre deux femmes est une des figures les plus intenses du dédoublement').

71. Simone de Beauvoir, *The Second Sex*, trans. H. M. Parshley, London, 1953, pp. 406–7; *Le Deuxième Sexe*, Paris, 1949, p. 500 ('Ce dédoublement peut prendre une figure maternelle; la mère qui se reconnaît et s'aliène dans sa fille a souvent pour elle un attachement sexuel; le goût de protéger et de bercer dans ses bras un tendre objet de chair lui est commun avec la lesbienne').

72. Cixous, *Le Livre de Promethea*, p. 13 ('toutes mes belles théories de plus en plus perfectionnées').

73. Ibid., p. 13 ('celle de la bisexualité qui me donna toujours un peu de mal').

74. Hélène Cixous, 'The Laugh of the Medusa', in Elaine Marks and Isabelle de Courtivron (eds), *New French Feminisms*, Brighton, 1981, pp. 245–62, p. 246; 'Le Rire de la méduse', *L'Arc*, no. 61, 1975, pp. 39–54, p. 39 ('on ne peut parler d'une sexualité féminine, uniforme, homogène').

75. Ibid., p. 254; ibid., p. 46 ('repérage en soi, individuellement, de la présence, diversement manifeste et insistante selon chaque un ou une, des deux sexes').

76. Ibid., p. 254; ibid., p. 46 ('multiplication des effets d'inscription du désir').

77. Ibid., p. 254; ibid., p. 46 ('n'annule pas les différences, mais les anime').

78. Judith Butler, 'Imitation and Gender Insubordination', in Diana Fuss (ed.), *Inside/Out: Lesbian Theories, Gay Theories*, New York and London, 1991, pp. 13–31.

79. Ibid., p. 15.

80. Cixous, 'The Laugh of the Medusa', p. 253; 'Le Rire de la méduse', p. 45 ('théoriser cette pratique, l'enfermer, la coder').

81. Butler, 'Imitation and Gender Insubordination', p. 14.

82. Hélène Cixous, 'En Octobre 1991 . . .', in Mireille Calle (ed.), *Du Féminin*, Sainte-Foy, Québec, 1992, pp. 115–37, p. 127 ('Et l'amour des femmes? Sujet inquiétant, inquiet. Je me précipite pour dire; nous ne savons pas grand-chose. Ce que l'expérience m'a soufflé, c'est cela. A quel point nous n'avons pas encore pensé – nous avons vécu mais pas pensé, inscrit – la différence à l'intérieur des femmes, ou à l'intérieur d'une femme').

83. Butler, 'Imitation and Gender Insubordination', p. 29.

84. Cixous, *Le Livre de Promethea*, p. 9 ('une fois dans le feu, on est inondé de douceur').

– 6 –

L'Amour la Mort: The Eroticism of Marguerite Duras

Kate Ince

I don't know how to write about love. I just don't know.[1]

In spite of this denial that her writing constitutes any deliberate exploration of the theme of love, issued in the early 1980s, it is difficult to think of any living author whose texts have reworked the myriad possibilities of erotic love more obsessively than those of Marguerite Duras. In a career which spans over fifty years, relationships between the sexes and within the family have always been the main focus of her numerous novels, films, plays, *récits* and film-scripts. Frustration, unsatisfied longing, the difficulty of communication and painful separation dominate most of the texts published up to the mid-1960s. Duras's 'Indian Cycle', which opened with *Le Ravissement de Lol V. Stein* in 1964 and closed with the film *Son nom de Venise dans Calcutta désert* in 1976, exploited the oppressive atmosphere of the colonial French Indochina of Duras's youth to add languor and despair to stories of desire already heavy with the weight of traumas recent or long past. Since then the characteristics of human love most frequently singled out for re-enactment are its precariousness, fragility, darkness and violence, aspects which have been treated in an increasingly direct and explicit manner. In the 1980s Duras published several texts which were more overtly and explicitly erotic than anything she had previously written, texts which focus with unflinching cinematic concentration on an encounter between one man and one woman. *L'homme assis dans le couloir*, *La Maladie de la mort* and *Les yeux bleus cheveux noirs* indubitably establish Duras as an author of erotic fiction.

The route followed by Duras to the style of erotics she so forcefully stamps as her own in these texts is one of intensification and minimalization. Their tenor is anonymous and pronominal, quite distinct from the verbal virtuosity characteristic of much erotic writing or writing which treats sexuality and gender identity in a complex fashion.[2] For it is a particularity of Duras's fiction, and especially of the texts I shall be discussing here, that it reveals the exploration of the mobile patternings of desire and the shattering of conventional gender representations to be inseparable processes. Lexical wealth, and the accumulation of multiple and proliferating images of sexuality, are rejected; instead it is the slight substance of her narratives which exposes both desire in the raw and oblique and enigmatic codings of gender.

One effect of this minimalist style of writing sexuality is to reveal an obvious trait of the French language, which is its incapacity to denote any person or object not sexed masculine or feminine. The dual coding of gender in French might seem to favour binary difference over the freer and more multiple field of differences envisioned by much recent and contemporary theory. In fact, the effect of stripping language bare and reducing it to its most minimal elements of syntax and vocabulary is to generate an abundance of what Susan Suleiman, after Derrida, calls 'incalculable choreographies' – flights of fancy in search of combinations of and variations on gender which are not reducible to a binary structure.[3] In the three texts I shall examine here the relationship between representation and gender is undone and reworked from first principles, producing what may only be described as a deconstructive erotics.

The first of these texts is *L'homme assis dans le couloir*. Eschewing all unessential information about character and the motivation for the encounter it describes, this *récit* draws upon the fundamental dynamic of representation for its construction, making the difference between male and female bodies and masculine and feminine pronouns into its very *mise-en-scène*. In staging so directly the bodily and linguistic modalities of sexual difference, *L'homme assis dans le couloir* concentrates and intensifies the antagonisms between genders to the point where language proves inadequate to contain them, and the correspondence of (sexed) pronoun to (sexed) body breaks down altogether.

Positions, in the *récit*, seem to be quickly established, only to be subverted and destabilized at a number of levels. Written in the conditional perfect, the tense which, when used in alternation with a bluntly assertive present in a number of Duras's shorter texts, maintains an oscillation between 'realistic' description and projection or fantasy, the narrative falls into a triadic structure. Two scenes of male ascendancy frame one extended central episode, which takes the unexpected turn of cruelty and suffering inflicted by the woman, from her situation of submission and subjugation. Beginning in ineffable 'douceur', the woman's act of fellatio becomes unrelenting, causing the man to cry out with increasing shrillness, and eventually with such pain that she is forced to stop. Her violence is no match for his in the variety of forms it takes, but a moment of total masculine passivity and helplessness which directly follows the apogee of her aggression is insisted upon with particular emphasis – 'I see that he does not object, looking on once again with her. That he looks at what she is doing, that he lends himself to her desire as far as he is able. That he offers his manhood to this starving woman' ('Je vois qu'il laisse faire . . . Qu'il la regarde faire, qu'il se prête à son désir autant qu'il est possible. Qu'il tend à cette affamée l'homme qu'il est').[4] The uncertain referentiality of 'l'homme' (manhood) here is typical of the linguistic compression of Duras's writing, which re-emphasizes the violence – suppressed as well as expressed – of the sadomasochistic scene; the word seems to contain all the brutality which the man himself is, momentarily, containing.

During the fellatio episode itself, however, it is a question not so much of ellipsis and uncertain reference as of flagrant pronominal contradiction. Throughout a passage beginning at the exact midpoint of the narrative, when the scene changes from outside to inside, the woman enters the corridor of 'la maison de la plate-forme' and blinding summer light is exchanged for cool shadow, the penis is repeatedly and insistently referred to as 'elle'. Rather than being symbolically associated with power and manipulation, the penis becomes the second – and arguably the dominant – erotic *object* of the narrative.[5] Any noun accounting for this reversal of gender in the pronoun is conspicuously absent from the text, if not difficult to supply (most of the slang words for penis are feminine in French); what could be explained away as an ellipsis typical of erotic writing – and a rhetorical feature characteristic of Duras's erotic narratives – in fact has more marked deconstructive effects. Although it could be matched to the word 'forme', which is used several sentences later to describe the penis's primitive shape, 'a primordial shape, indistinguishable from stones and lichens, immemorial' (p. 272),[6] the pronoun 'elle' precedes any noun it might stand in for. Ambiguity is compounded by the fact that elsewhere in the text 'la forme' refers to the entire human body. As in Lacan's description of sexual relations where the female body is said to *be* the phallus, the body holds out the promise of imaginary wholeness and formal perfection. But in this case that body may be either male or female, an undecidability of sexual difference which disrupts the phallocentrism and gender bias of the Lacanian model.

The penis is not the only part of the male anatomy whose sex is put into question, as shortly afterwards the rest of the male sexual organs are referred to as 'that other femininity' (p. 273, p. 28). As the woman's act of fellatio begins, the femininity of the penis is emphasized by a rhetorical repetition of the object pronoun 'elle', juxtaposed with the subject pronoun describing the woman in a way which reinforces its status as object, whilst simultaneously breaking down the boundaries between subject and object, or masculine and feminine: 'She [elle] has come up beside him, is crouching between his legs looking at it and it alone [la regarde elle, et seulement elle]' (p. 272).[7] Woman and phallus mirror each other in a momentary transfer of sexual power. And as the man's penis and heart are described as sharing the same rhythmic beats, the axis of masculinity in the text is divided and seems to collapse altogether, giving way to a free circulation of sexual signifiers mobilized by the force of erotic pleasure. Far from being identifiably masculine or feminine, *jouissance* threatens to explode gender identity from within: 'It [elle] is full of pleasure, bursting with pleasure, so distended that you would hesitate to lay a hand on it' (p. 272).[8]

Despite the dominance of the feminine pronoun in Duras's text, her cross-currents of gender also work in the opposite direction. The woman's body, to which are attributed at one point the 'feminine' qualities of softness and pliability which will later yield under the impact of the man's blows, is elsewhere described in very masculine terms: 'I see the body [je le vois] at brutally short range. It [il] is running with sweat, it [il] is in the harsh light of the sun's awful rays' (p. 269).[9] Associated with harsh light and heat so intense that it makes her cry out, the woman's situation in the first half of the narrative is an inversion of the homology one might expect between interiority and femininity on the one hand, and masculinity and exteriority on the other. Literal physical situations and poses become another level of signification to be utilized in Duras's disruptive rewriting of gender positionings; when the woman enters the corridor, her erect stance contrasts directly with the reclining one adopted by the man for most of the encounter, and the symbolic potential of her entry is exploited to the full ('Say she remained for a moment with her back leaning against the door-frame before entering the coolness of the passage' (p. 271)).[10] Throughout *L'homme assis dans le couloir*, there is no simple correlation of physical position and sexual power relations; the most extreme episodes in the man's abuse of the woman, including the beating she requests and receives at the end of the narrative, occur when he is sitting in the armchair, hardly an image of dominance. An image of the man sitting in the doorway, in direct contrast to the woman's stance when she is seen there, immediately precedes the beating episode. Although the conventional power relations of a sadomasochistic scene are broadly respected, Duras contorts and reworks the figures one might expect to accompany them.

If an effect of bathos is produced by the linguistically stark, over-stated symbolism of the woman's entry into the corridor, the same could not be said of a parallel moment in the central episode of the text. Here Duras's writing performs a similar but even more improbable (because non-metaphoric) reversal which attributes an act of penetration to the woman whilst maintaining the ambiguity between proximity and distance, and avoiding stereotyped images of devouring femininity: 'Mouth open, eyes shut, she is in the man's depths, hidden away inside him, far away from him, alone in the obscurity of the man's body' (p. 273).[11]

L'homme assis dans le couloir convincingly establishes a link between the violence and *jouissance* of desire and uncertain, oscillating representations of sexual identity in language. But do the lengths to which the kinds of reversals it stages are pursued defend Duras against accusations claiming that authoring such a text was a politically retrograde act which reinforces the violence inherent in patriarchy's oppression of feminine sexuality? In a feminist reading of the text which objects to its pornographic elements and to the identification of woman as masochist, Marcelle Marini views Duras's narrative as 'the killing of any kind of feminine erotic discourse'.[12] For Marini, female masochism is nothing but the eroticization of women's humiliation and suffering, a view in line with feminist critics of pornography who see erotic relationships between men and women as entirely determined by the logic of male domination endemic to patriarchy.[13] Despite acknowledging the avowal Duras has made which connects the events of *L'homme assis dans le couloir* to a violent erotic experience of her own,[14] Marini does not entertain the possibility of analysing feminine submission, or the possible link between women's desire and their participation in relationships of domination.[15] Resentful of Duras's failure to conform to the 'erotics of happiness' she sees as the more proper subject of women's writing, Marini views the inclusion of any cruelty within sexual scenes as essentially masculine, the heritage of the male erotic tradition.[16] Since this leaves her without any real framework to analyse Duras's work, it is perhaps not surprising that she is obliged to modify the accusations with which her polemically entitled critique begins, namely, that if pornography is defined as a narrative, image or film which isolates the sexual act from its social context, then *L'homme assis dans le couloir* is indeed pornographic.[17] Anonymity and vagueness of place are in fact aspects of the text given more emphasis in the 1980 edition of *L'homme assis*

Kate Ince

dans le couloir than in the first (1962) version published, where the female protagonist is identified as Anne-Marie Stretter of Duras's Indian Cycle (her first appearance in print), and the location is more specific than the 'immensité indéfinie du paysage' which surrounds the hotel corridor and vitally extends the intensity and menace of the encounter. Duras herself reveals, in her 1980 collection of occasional writings *Les Yeux verts*, that the idea of setting the narrative in this obfuscatory vastness was the key to being able to rewrite it.[18]

But if these two modifications characterize the apparent movement of Duras's fiction at the beginning of the 1980s towards depsychologized anonymity, a tendency which invites the reader to consider its proximity to pornography, another change counteracts this drift. This is the inclusion, paradoxical though it may seem, of a mutual declaration of love by the two protagonists. In the man's case the form of his words matches the brutal dominance of his actions; as he speaks he is crushing the flesh of the woman's breasts underfoot. For in the rhetoric of his utterance, 'I love you. You' (p. 270),[19] the abrupt caesura and repetition of the isolated object pronoun are heavy with the menace of further violence. These indicators are missing from the woman's reply, which follows after an intensification and involuntary relaxation of the man's brutality, and after she has entered the cool corridor. In turn, he replies to her with a self-assurance which reinforces his dominance and her submission:

'I love you.'
I hear him reply that he knows:
'Yes'
(p. 272)[20]

But in rewriting *L'homme assis dans le couloir* to include love, and considering it and the vastness of the landscape essential features of the *récit*'s definitive form ('First I found the indeterminate vastness of the landscape. Then the love. The love was absent from the first text'[21]), Duras insists on the tense association of eroticism and violence. Rather than adapt her material to the kind of moralistic dictates about the representation of violence that feminism sometimes issues, she poses the relationship of aggression and sexuality – including women as the agents of violence – as a question to her readers, female and male. In so doing she produces a text whose content may only be labelled pornographic if it is abstracted both from intertextual anticipation within her own work (*Moderato Cantabile* and *Le Vice-Consul*[22]) and from the carefully crafted disorientation and dissemination which the *récit* as a whole demonstrates, characteristics which militate against any straightforward identification of female reader with female protagonist.[23] The effect of subtly interweaving complexities of narrative voice and finely balanced symmetries of scene, action and form with blatant violence is certainly aesthetically jarring, but the chief result is to add a new combination or undecidable to the numerous awkward questions Duras's work has consistently posed to problems of literary genre. *L'homme assis dans le couloir* confronts the taboo forbidding women to consider their relationship to heterosexual sadomasochism, places the latter in an erotic context by insisting on the element of love – a sadist who is 'wasted with love and desire'[24] – and, by means of complex and uncertain representations of gender identity, reveals the constant mobility and fluctuation of power relationships between the sexes, and the ethico-political dilemmas that they pose.

In reading *L'homme assis dans le couloir* I have argued that its bleak violence should not be understood to indicate a simple endorsement of feminine masochism or men's violence towards women. The *récit* does, nevertheless, along with *Le Navire Night* of 1979 and the play *Agatha* of 1981, usher in a succession of texts devoted to the unfaltering depiction of painful and hopeless love-relationships. The broaching of the subjects of incestuous love and homosexuality in *Agatha*, *La Maladie de la mort* and *Les yeux bleus cheveux noirs* not only decisively removes them from any literary mainstream, but leaves them suspended in the margins of the genre of erotic writing, by either men or women. It is difficult to find an appropriate heading under which to consider texts whose lexical poverty and graphic immediacy of style halts all the conventions and assumptions of eroticism in their tracks and demands that they be considered afresh. In much of her 1980s work Duras writes in the teeth of the erotic tradition, not even pausing to pay homage to the literary myths which make love out to be an enduring, transcendent, unifying force. Brevity, finitude and deathliness are the recurrent motifs of these more recent writings, which, as one critic has suggested, 'force all the discourses of love, if not of the entire literary tradition of the West, to stop momentarily and meditate on their emptiness'.[25]

No tracing of the development of this apocalyptic mode of eroticism in Duras's earlier work could dilute the impact of a text such as *La Maladie de la mort*, but it is none the less evident that the style is a continuation and exacerbation of concerns and convictions which have always figured in her writing. A disabused attitude to love is already well established in *La Vie tranquille* of 1944, where the female protagonist Françou never sees her relationship with her lover Tiène as anything but provisional. Love and death are already fatally intertwined: 'One day I won't love Tiène any more. Now that I think about it, do I still love him? One day, I'll live without the memory of Tiène . . . One day I'll die.'[26] Throughout Duras's work love is more a harbinger of the pain of difference and distance than the pleasures of unity and mutual understanding, a subject commented on extensively in recent volumes of her journalism and personal prose, where she expresses categorical and derisory opinions about 'conventional' marital love. Happiness experienced in a relationship is not necessarily an indication of love, since the main reasons for cohabiting are practical benefits and the fear of solitude.[27] In all Western societies the cohabiting couple, whether or not joined in law, is a Christian notion which has no connection with 'le couple des amants', whose union is only ever transitory.

Duras's increasingly frequent commentaries on the incompatibility of erotic love and the normative social structures of Western civilization have accompanied ever more condensed explorations of this tension and unease. If the inevitable brevity and failure of love-relationships is a stock literary theme from which early stories of separation and divorce do not clearly distinguish themselves, a clear divergence is marked by *Le Navire Night* and *Agatha*, in which the impossibility of love being actualized or acted upon at all is directly thematized. In *Le Navire Night*, where a love affair is conducted entirely by telephone, and the consummation of the relationship never likely, the struggle between love and death provides the very framework for the narrative, the woman's passion for her faceless lover aggravating and accelerating her terminal illness by weakening her still further. In *Agatha* impossible love takes the form of incestuous love between brother and sister, already a prominent narrative thread in *La Vie tranquille* and *Un barrage contre le Pacifique*, and one which has been continued in *L'Amant*, *La Pluie d'été*, and *L'Amant de la Chine du Nord*.

Together *Le Navire Night* and *Agatha* establish the taut and fluctuating dynamic between love and death as fundamental to Duras's more recent work. Eschewing progressive narrative in favour of a style of writing which proceeds by explorations of and retreats from newly discovered intensities of feeling, and by allowing these to resonate in repeated silences, they prefigure the exclusive concentration on the same dynamic in two subsequent texts which in many ways belong together, *La Maladie de la mort* and *Les yeux bleus cheveux noirs*. Duras has spoken disparagingly of the obvious parallels between these two books, saying that only those inclined to generalities will want to read *La Maladie de la mort* as an early version of *Les yeux bleus cheveux noirs*.[28] It would seem, however, that a comparative reading which is attentive to Duras's particular brand of intratextual rewriting, and does not aim to set up a hierarchy between primary and secondary versions, can give due attention to both the similarities and the differences between them, the latter being what is particularly significant for the thematic and formal exploration of the economy of love and death.

Several parallels between the two texts seem particularly important, the most obvious of which are the situation of the protagonists, a man and a woman brought together by 'un contrat des nuits payées', and the motivation behind the shared isolation the contract imposes, which is the creation or activation of 'impossible' desire. In neither text is the woman a prostitute, despite accepting remuneration for her time. A number of differences also stand out; whereas the woman's arrival in *La Maladie de la mort* is as unexplained as her disappearance, the female protagonist of *Les yeux bleus cheveux noirs* falls in love with the man at the beach-café where she first catches sight of him, thereby becoming the third member of an uncertain love-triangle involving at least one other young man with blue eyes and black hair. In *Les yeux bleus cheveux noirs* homosexuality is named as one of the man's reasons for paying the woman to stay with him; he admits to her that he has never been able to love a woman. (His second reason for taking out a contract on a woman's body, linked to the first, is to overcome his intense obsession with a young man sighted in a hotel lobby at the opening of the novel.) In *La Maladie de la mort* this limitation on love remains unspecified and unspecific, reserving the possibility that what the man is actually suffering from is a general infirmity of desire, a total incapacity for physical love. Impossible love, and a maddening concentration of effort on resolving the suffering it causes, is, as in *Agatha*, the mainstay of the narrative.

The woman of *La Maladie de la mort* observes how the man's disease of death, 'this insipidity . . . this immobility of feeling',[29] is gradually worsening, contaminating him physically. An absolute failure to recognize his disease, to have knowledge of his deathliness, both partly constitutes and reinforces the man's dilemma (p. 19, p. 45/p. 24, p. 47). The woman asserts this kind of knowledge by naming his illness (her recognition of his infirmity was instantaneous, and was her reason for accepting the contract), but it remains inaccessible to the man, even more impenetrable than her body, confined within the reaches of the unsayable – 'She couldn't tell you. You couldn't find out anything about it from her . . . She is incapable of knowing' (pp. 14–15).[30] Between the man and the woman, as between the woman and her knowledge, there is a gulf which no communication can bridge. Their relationship shows no trace of the clandestinity and intimacy typically associated with the togetherness of lovers, the dominant metaphysical model of romantic love which Jean-Luc Nancy observes still to be at work in Bataille's representation of lovers' community and suggests may be traced back to the roots of Western thought.[31] In this conception of love, fundamentally indebted to Plato's *Symposium*, Eros always desires unity, and lovers' relationships therefore aspire to a complementary fusion in which a pair equals a totality, bound together by a spiritual force which transcends death.[32]

The unrelenting tug of death exerted on the forces of desire between Duras's lovers means that erotic communication and fusion are never even envisaged. Man and woman, here, rather than constituting a pair of complementary terms, are in an asymmetrical and non-reciprocal relation resembling that described by Emmanuel Levinas in his 'Phénoménologie de l'Eros'.[33] Non-reciprocity thwarts any totalizing relation; the man's attempts to wish the woman dead in *La Maladie de la mort* – to reflect death upon her by containing her in a specular, symmetrical relation which would override their unequal relations of knowledge and desire – come to nothing. She is impervious to them, and the man recognizes them for the ultimately self-directed palliatives they are, although not before completing an elaborate fantasy of disposing of her body in the turbulent black sea. (The sea, as so often in Duras's writing, here symbolizes the infinite; it is significant that the one thing the woman accuses him of misrepresenting to her is the colour of the sea. This 'lie', born out of a total lack of understanding of its elemental significance, is seen by the woman as an integral part of his illness.) The woman twice restates her diagnosis of the man's malady, with knowing superiority; 'A dead man's a strange thing' (p. 31, p. 42).[34]

No amount of sexual intimacy can generate love which does not occur fortuitously, 'a sudden lapse in the logic of the universe' (p. 50).[35] Although it appears to be an opportunity to learn, or change, the contract is too premeditated to represent a chance; the man desires desire, understanding its importance, but never descends from this metaphysical level. *La Maladie de la mort* is a static or ec-static non-narrative in which desire never begins: 'She says: It's day, everything is about to begin, except you, you never begin' (p. 48).[36] The woman understands both the necessity of this access to infinite rebeginning and the resistance it affords to death, and demonstrates it in the pleasure the man is uncomprehendingly able to give her. Whereas his body is a closed circuit, insensitive to the intimacy he determines hopelessly to indulge in, hers is amorphous, fluid and shifting, a site of the multiple and diversified feminine pleasure Luce Irigaray finds as the repressed underside of Western metaphysics.[37] As he watches her sleep, its orifices open up before his gaze:

First you see slight tremors showing on the skin, just like those of suffering. And then you see the eyelids flicker as if the eyes wanted to see. And then you see the mouth open as if it wanted to say something. And then you notice that under your caresses the lips of her sex are swelling up, and that from their smoothness comes a hot sticky liquid, as it might be blood. (p. 36)[38]

An imperturbable witness to the orgasm he unwittingly provokes, the man then watches as the woman's body again becomes still, and her eyes close, returning her to her separated, inscrutable realm of pleasure. He has watched everything ('You've looked at everything' (p. 38)[39]) but 'seen' nothing. Although he previously silenced her pleasure by forbidding her to make any noise, an attempt to transform *jouissance* into pure spectacle, it remains obstinately foreign to vision, to the economy of the gaze.

La Maladie de la mort appears, then, to figure an unbridgeable difference between man and woman, the identification of the feminine term with life and 'the understanding of love',[40] and of the masculine with death and irremediable ignorance of the body. But although the woman appears to occupy a position immune to infection by his mortal disease, the man also finds death on her body without looking for it or imposing it on her: 'You look at the malady of your life, the malady of death. It's on her, on her sleeping body, that you look at it' (pp. 32–3).[41] This unexpected transference undermines the conception of Eros as infinite suggested by her body, 'made in a single sweep . . . as if by God Himself' (pp. 15–16),[42] and displaces any simple equivalence of feminine sexuality with life. Death names his difference from her ('You shut your eyes so as to get back into your difference, your death' (p. 32)[43]), but she is not immune to it. Similarly, the room she occupies for the duration of the contract is not enlivened by her sexuality, but 'emptied of life, without either you or your like' (p. 30).[44] Any equation of the malady of death with masculinity is contradicted again, and more decisively, shortly after the 'sighting' of death on the surface of her sleeping body, in a moment comparable to the complete reversal of polarities in *L'homme assis dans le couloir*: 'You realize it's here, in her, that the malady of death is fomenting, that it's this shape stretched out before you that decrees the malady of death' (p. 34).[45] The unequivocality of this moment upturns the dominant identificatory tendencies of Eros and Thanatos in *La Maladie de la mort*, transforming what appears to be a regular, containable economy into an utterly unpredictable one.

For the male protagonist of *La Maladie de la mort*, desire is so long forgotten that he no longer even mourns it; the woman tells him that his weeping is due only to the frustration of not being able to impose death on others. The man withdraws further and further into libidinal sterility, as the futility of his abstract determination to conduct a neutral, objective 'experiment' into love becomes apparent. His desire for solitude, self-determination and closure reawakens. Their last union is purely symbolic, an impassive observance of the contract which changes nothing: 'She says: Take me, so it may have been done' (p. 51).[46] After the woman's departure, the man does not mourn her for a moment, proof of the egocentricity of his weeping. The only effect of her absence is to confirm his 'complete difference' (p. 39)[47] from her, and the experiment represented by the contract slips quickly into an oblivion where its status hovers uncertainly between reality and fantasy. Attempts to narrate it fail.[48] The overseeing narrative voice considers it unlikely that the woman will ever be missed; if she is remembered it is only for the otherness which kept her removed from him in their sterile, enforced intimacy – 'the marvelous impossibility of reaching her through the difference that separates you' (p. 54).[49] The uncertain difference and knowledge of difference witnessed during the contract imperceptibly repolarizes itself, regathering around absolute terms. All the man retains from his days and nights with the woman is the name of his dilemma, words uttered in her sleep which also name the total failure of the experiment and his non-progression in the knowledge of his disease.

Seeming to end by confirming what it initially set out to explore, the impossibility of love, or desire, *La Maladie de la mort* is steeped in an ethical and political pessimism which shows an irremediable ignorance of pleasure on the part of man. The reader's attention is divided between this apparently metaphysical dimension of impossibility and an inverted eroticism which graphically conveys the failure of desire to unite two 'lovers'. The intense concentration on both these dimensions makes it uncertain whether what is envisaged is a general impossibility of erotic love affecting all relationships, or a failure of desire determined by the specific nature of the relationship in question. An oblique comparison of sexual experiences by the male protagonist provides the only significant hint as to what this specificity might be: 'You say: Yes. I don't know that yet and I want to penetrate there too, and with my usual force. They say it offers more resistance, it's smooth but it offers more resistance than emptiness does' (pp. 3–4).[50] An essay by Duras whose thesis is the potential for homosexuality within all men, and which is constructed around some rather crude generalizations, neither confirms nor denies the 'explanation' of the text homosexuality would provide:

Other people, from Peter Handke to Maurice Blanchot, have seen *The Malady of Death* as being against men in their relationship with women. If you like. But I say that if men have taken such an interest in the book it's because they've sensed there's something more to it than that – something of particular concern to them. It's extraordinary that they should have seen it.[51]

In his reading of the text, Maurice Blanchot in fact confirms the relevance of homosexuality whilst refuting the idea that it is the determining cause of the failure of the man's desire: 'Homosexuality, to come to that name which is never pronounced, is not "the malady of death," it only makes it appear, in a slightly artificial way.'[52] A similarly unbinding association of the two types of masculine sexuality is suggested by Duras in an allusion to her own relationship with a homosexual which confirms that the text is to some extent autobiographical: 'When I wrote *The Malady of Death*, I didn't know I was writing about Yann.'[53] But the negative form of her inference deters any attempt to set homosexuality up as a theme, a resistance of desiring writing to any determined mode which seems to increase with time, since after the publication of *Les yeux bleus cheveux noirs* Duras comments that homosexuality 'has become a false word . . . It says what it means badly and I believe above all that what it means doesn't exist, at least not in the form I would have believed it existed three years ago.'[54]

Homosexuality is insufficient explanation for the failure of desire (the text has something to say to all men), but remains the possible motivating factor *La Maladie de la mort* and its imperious narrating voice most obviously point to. The second-person voice which addresses the man is descriptive rather than judgemental, increasing curiosity as to why the man undertakes the 'experiment' at all, why he feels the obligation to try to love women. Behind or beyond the fleetingly implied desire for his own sex there seems to be a responsibility to otherness, of which (like his disease) he may not be aware, but which initially impels him to set up the encounter. What Duras, in one of her more objectionable politically polarized comparisons, has called 'the fabulous richness of heterosexuality', resists suppression by 'the incommensurable poverty of homosexuality'.[55] According to this view, homosexual desire, like the (male) 'hommosexualité' Irigaray identifies as governing Western metaphysical conceptions of femininity, is confined within a specular relation which constructs the other in its own image, rather than attempting any relation with the other *qua* other: homosexuals 'in loving the other, are really loving themselves'.[56] Heterosexuality, on the other hand, consists of a confrontation with alterity which is ethically more demanding, and therefore a more worthwhile negotiation:

> But this desire which binds us, I see it as a sort of result of the initial antagonism between them and us, men and women. We are irreconcilable, we're always trying – or have been for thousands of years – to be reconciled. Every time we fall in love.[57]

The trace of homosexuality alluded to in *La Maladie de la mort*, however, maintains the encounter in an undecidable space between the two types of relation. The pairing of a homosexual man and a heterosexual woman seems to suggest that each lover is trying to reach an other more, or more differently, different than just the other sex; this sexual difference can no longer be described as binary, since normative heterosexual desire with its promises of wholeness, completeness and exchange is nowhere held out as a possibility.

One commentator to pursue the difficult questions about the ethics of desire raised by Duras in *La Maladie de la mort* is Maurice Blanchot, who asks whether the apparently irresolvable aloofness of the sexes it stages is the same as that proposed by Levinas in his asymmetrical, non-reciprocal ethical relation between 'moi' and 'autrui', concluding 'This is not certain, and neither is it clear'.[58] What are the implications of Duras's starkly figured confrontation of man and woman for the ethical and erotic relations as conceived of by Levinas, and the relationship between them? Since the responsibility to the Other Levinas insists upon precedes any absolute or determined moral law, this relationship cannot simply be the opposition of rule-dominated morality to transgressive, ungovernable passion. It is far from certain that the relation with the Beloved (*l'Aimée*) or the feminine that Levinas describes is not to some extent one of responsibility. *La Maladie de la mort* obscures the borderlines between these two types of relation, suggesting they are in some way implicated in each other.

A reading of *La Maladie de la mort* which would emphasize the element of obligation in erotic relationships, understanding them to be guided by the kind of ethics of love Duras envisages as the necessary response to the irreparable breach in all relations of sexual difference, is considered by Blanchot: 'One could say that of the two protagonists it is he who in his attempt to love, in his ceaseless search, is the worthier, the one closer to that absolute he finds in not finding it.'[59] Repeating the masculine bias of Levinas's Eros, this view fails to take account of the fact that both man and woman consent willingly to the terms of the contract, and that which of them was more instrumental in setting it up is never revealed. Blanchot's criticism of the woman, who 'herself only offers herself to be loved (under contract) without ever giving any sign of her ability to go from passivity to limitless passion',[60] fails to appreciate the essential part played by passivity in any love-relationship, the activity within passivity, what Duras has elsewhere called 'an erotically functional role'.[61] And by valorizing activity, Blanchot could also be said (if Freud's notion of the libido is adhered to) to be attributing to the man exactly the love he is never capable of.

If the woman's patience, suspended between passivity and passion, is what sustains the encounter of *La Maladie de la mort*, a similar feminine endurance is equally crucial to the languorous temporality of *Les yeux bleus cheveux noirs*: 'She says any woman would have accepted, without knowing why, this blank and desperate union' (p. 19).[62] The scene, which is framed as such by an intradiegetic 'acteur' who opens and closes its action, stages a seemingly interminable wait for desire.[63] As in *La Maladie de la mort*, the lovers' mutual confinement is agreed upon in order to give desire a chance, against impossible odds, since love can never be willed, but only arise 'through a mistake, for instance . . . Never through an act of will' (p. 50).[64] Physical contact in sleep is fruitless, wasted: 'As soon as they've touched, the bodies go still' (p. 45), 'their hands touch, but only to draw away at once' (p. 44).[65] Desire exists only in the abstract, 'our desire for each other, which we don't do anything about' (p. 57).[66] Separation, one mark of death, is frequently envisaged (p. 74, p. 98), and as in *Agatha*, parting will mark not a radical change, but a continuity of the lovers' peculiar form of disunited eroticism; 'even when it's the last night it won't be worth making a point of, because it will only be the beginning of another story, the story of their parting' (p. 75).[67]

Death is at work on time, its drag can be felt on desire as it is on narrative, as when the man concedes, much later, that he may in fact never have wanted anything. Love is not an aim which can be projected in linear time, and this, the woman says, is the key to their love: 'You're my lover because of what you just said – that there's nothing you want' (p. 81).[68] The temporality of desire in *Les yeux bleus cheveux noirs* is thus practically immobile, produced by silence rather than speech: 'perhaps it's not the talking about it that creates the time she's trying to get hold of' (p. 50).[69] Their love is behind the rest of the world (p. 102, p. 133); their isolation from natural time is such that twilight is mistaken for daybreak (p. 115, p. 148).

As in *La Maladie de la mort*, the 'action' of this moribund narrative takes place against a blank, neutral backdrop, a white void of sheets spread out as its non-centre. The location seems a cell of desperation and solitude, 'a place that has just been deserted. Funereal' (p. 11). And yet this is not the space of intimacy, but public space, 'a kind of reception room' (ibid.[70]) which overlooks the desolate beach. Although the setting is less unequivocally public than the places and occasions where erotic encounters are attempted or occur in other of Duras's texts (*India Song, L'homme assis dans le couloir*), the house in which the contract is endured is no prison, opening onto the beach and the sea as in *La Maladie de la mort*. Eros is not defined negatively to the social order, but – an aspect of *Les yeux bleus cheveux noirs* doubled in allusions to sexual activity taking place on the beach – ambivalently situated in the public realm.[71] The difference between man and woman is repeated in their relationship to the world outside, a reminder of the structural similarity of social and erotic relations. In place of the model of community based on a fusion of identities or the formation of a totality, another type can be glimpsed, according to which love (like sociality) divides even as it unites, exposing the differences that subsist between lovers as being like those between any two related yet singular terms. 'Society' shares the intimacy of lovers and they share its *désoeuvrement*. Neither contained within an enveloping social circle nor situated outside it or on its margins, the community of lovers marks an internal limit which traverses the intermingled realms of 'private' and 'public', and divides and folds back on itself, invading the 'space' of the social realm.[72] The key to the common disappropriating structuration of the erotic and the social is death; 'la mort des amants, en effet, les expose entre eux aussi bien que hors d'eux à la communauté'.[73]

A further way in which *Les yeux bleus cheveux noirs* echoes *La Maladie de la mort* and recalls the fragility of the feminine Levinas stresses in his account of the erotic relation is in the foreignness to aggression figured by the woman's body. Unspeakable violence hovers around it, channelling into a fear the woman has, 'not the fear of death but the fear of being hurt as by an animal, of being clawed, disfigured' (p. 34).[74] But its usually inert form in fact offers up an infinitely resistant fragility, 'the strength behind the slimness' (p. 29).[75] A weighty unsignifying mass, the woman's body incarnates animal-like life and materiality (p. 13, p. 24). Her desire, however, is as deathly as the man's:

> As soon as you entered the café in the state you were in, that quiet grief – you remember, you wanted to die – I wanted to die too, in the same external, theatrical manner. I wanted to die with you. I thought, Let me put my body close to his and wait for death. (p. 60)[76]

The sexual difference staged in *Les yeux bleus cheveux noirs* tends towards the absolute, less perturbed by disseminating textuality than in *La Maladie de la mort*. The woman tells the man he is 'very close to a general idea of what man is' (p. 99),[77] almost a universal. One description of the woman sleeping opens with a bald statement of the ontological weight of sexuality: 'She is a woman' (p. 13).[78] And yet the difference at stake is not between woman and man, but between woman and homosexual; the man has never felt desire for a woman except at the moment the female protagonist described her passion for 'the' young stranger with blue eyes and black hair.[79] Homosexuality is unambiguously presented as the cause of the man's inability to love women, an infirmity as terrible as not believing in God (p. 31), a forgotten scourge of sterility.[80]

Against the background of this quasi-absolute sexual difference of the feminine from the homosexual, *Les yeux bleus cheveux noirs* tells of the genesis of an impossible desire. This does not develop according to any recognizable chronology; its hesitations and deferrals make it an ambiguous response to the woman's desire for the man, the birth of which she declares quite early on (p. 35, p. 51). Unrecoiling feeling for the woman is first expressed in the future tense, in the face of the impossibility of intending desire: 'he'll touch her lips with his fingers, the lips of her sex too; he'll kiss her closed eyes, the blue that flees the fingers' (p. 50).[81] Belief in an impossible future imperceptibly transmutes itself into a wish; the woman's late return to the house one day preoccupies the man because of the significance it could assume later, 'when he thinks he's started to love her' (p. 86).[82] An interval ensues in which intimacy is attempted, projected and implored by the woman, to no avail. Random moments of contact in which the man kisses her eyes, or they laugh together before reassuming their ritually patterned weeping, do not join up into any traceable linear progression of feeling. But it is out of this solitary yet shared mourning and despair that love seems to emerge; weeping together, which only their cohabitation has enabled to an extent which brings the man relief, produces a previously unknown intoxicating happiness. 'They weep as they would make love' (p. 86).[83]

That love has unaccountably become possible for the man is indicated by his sighting of a yacht which sails off course towards the beach, 'like an infinite caress' (p. 87).[84] This marks the end of his mourning for the young man with blue eyes and black hair; the woman becomes 'the one who doesn't know about the boat' (p. 91).[85] Where in *La Maladie de la mort* difference was equated with death, the woman now tells him 'that this difference, this inhibition you feel about me, is there to hide something to do with life' (p. 99).[86] After waiting for her to fall asleep, the man lies with her for the first time. 'The warmth becomes shared, like the skin, the inner life' (p. 101).[87] Covering the woman's body with his own and penetrating 'the hot slime of the centre' (p. 101),[88] the man lies immobile, awaiting his impossible and inevitable destiny, 'his body's will' (ibid.).[89]

Love is no sooner born than it is thwarted. The woman rejects the man, declaring that the God of wars and concentration camps has stolen her desire. Their first kiss, which the man initiates, effects an immediate separation and renders all contact impossible. *Après-coup*, it becomes their whole story: 'The kiss has turned into pleasure itself. It actually happened . . . There was no other kiss after. It alone occupies the place of all desire, is at once its emptiness and its immensity, its body and its soul' (p. 104).[90] With the kiss, the man enters a new realm of love and the sacred. Symbolically, he walks away from the area of the beach where strangers meet furtively to indulge perverse impulses. The woman makes the opposite complaint to her counterpart in *La Maladie de la mort*, identifying the cause of the man's weeping as his powerlessness to 'make people accept God' (p. 106).[91] But the kiss is of course also one of death: 'it's the thought of the kiss that leads him to the thought of his death' (p. 105).[92] The lovers sleep hand in hand, but their first night together is probably also their last (p. 111, p. 144). 'Around them, the room, destroyed' (p. 110).[93]

The text of *Les yeux bleus cheveux noirs* thus ends in an almost perfect, static oscillation between love and death. The idea of killing has been transformed into that of loving (p. 104, p. 135); in contradiction to the events of the narrative and the woman's own previous assertions, she does 'know' about the boat (she knows the man's desire). The couple experience unprecedented happiness ('so profound it frightens them' (p. 115)[94]), but their isolation from social time means that the new dawn they think is glimmering outside, which would symbolize a harmony of desire and temporality, is in fact returning twilight. It is left to the actor closing the scene to confirm, twice, that this is their last night together (p. 115 and p. 116, p. 149 and p. 150).

By (re)writing the dynamic of death and love as endlessly undecidable, *Les yeux bleus cheveux noirs* adds complexity to the unrelieved bleakness of *La Maladie de la mort*. Hopelessness and an apparently final non-conclusion in which love can only be lived '[by] losing it before it happened' (p. 55)[95] give way to a seemingly interminable but not sterile wait, from which intense desire and *jouissance* emerge and flicker unforgettably before once again receding into blackness. Although it constantly exposes love to difference and division, and emphasizes the precariousness of any communion of erotic love, Duras's writing never underestimates the incalculable value of such moments when they occur, living up to Georges Bataille's demand that the measure of the greatness of any erotics be its 'affirmation of life even into death'.[96] Neither *La Maladie de la mort* nor *Les yeux bleus cheveux noirs* pretends to offer a 'truth' of eroticism; rather, it is by repeating and developing the stark, minimal elements of the first text in the later novel that Duras articulates eroticism as 'between' – between life and death, between man and woman, between homosexual and heterosexual, between hope and despair.

Notes

1. *Marguerite Duras à Montréal*, Les éditions Spirale (Montréal), 1981, pp. 48–9.
2. On Duras's 'art de la pauvreté', see the comments by Hélène Cixous in 'A propos de Marguerite Duras', by Michel Foucault and Hélène Cixous, *Cahiers Renaud-Barrault* 89, 1975, pp. 8–22 (pp. 9–10).
3. Susan Rubin Suleiman, '(Re)writing the Body: The Politics and Poetics of Female Eroticism', *Poetics Today*, vol. 6, nos 1–2, 1985, pp. 43–65 (pp. 59–60). Jacques Derrida, 'Choreographies' (interview with Christie McDonald), *Diacritics*, 12, Summer 1982, pp. 66–76.
4. *L'homme assis dans le couloir*, Paris, Minuit, 1980, p. 29. This and subsequent translations are taken from Mary Lydon's 'Translating Duras: "The Seated Man in the Passage"', *Contemporary Literature*, vol. 24, no. 1, 1983, pp. 259–75, this reference p. 273. In subsequent translated quotations the page reference to the English is given in the text, and to the French original in the note.
5. The first is, obviously, the woman's body. This aspect of *L'homme assis dans le couloir*, according to which the sadistic man is both tormentor and erotic object, both adds to the conventional portrayal of male–female sadomasochistic relationships and is unusual in erotic fiction by women; see Lucienne Frappier-Mazur's 'Marginal Canons: Rewriting the Erotic', *Yale French Studies*, vol. 75, 1988, pp. 112–28, pp. 126–7. It also recalls the sexually ambiguous phallus Derrida weaves into his teasing reading of Nietzsche's fragment 'I have forgotten my umbrella' ('J'ai oublié mon parapluie'): 'the hermaphroditic spur of a phallus which is modestly enfolded in its veils, an organ which is at once aggressive and apotropaic, threatening and/or threatened. One doesn't just happen onto an unwonted object of this sort in a sewing-up machine on a castration table' ('l'éperon hermaphrodite d'un

phallus pudiquement replié dans ses voiles, organe à la fois agressif et apotropaïque, menaçant et/ou menacé, objet insolite qu'on ne trouve pas toujours par simple rencontre avec une machine à recoudre sur une table de castration'), *Spurs: Nietzsche's Styles/ Éperons: Les Styles de Nietzsche*, Chicago and London, 1979, pp. 129–31/128–30.

6. 'forme des premiers âges, indifferenciée des pierres, des lichens, immémoriale', p. 23.

7. 'Elle est arrivée près de lui, s'accroupit entre ses jambes et la regarde elle, et seulement elle', p. 24.

8. 'Elle est pleine de jouissance, remplie de jouissance plus qu'elle ne peut contenir et tant à l'étroit d'elle-même elle est devenue qu'on hésite à y porter la main', p. 25. This discomfited and divided phallocentrism closely resembles what Derrida, in *Glas*, calls 'the logic of the antherection'. As Sarah Kofman's reading of *Glas* explains, 'even more powerful when cut, divided, the erection has an oblique aspect, what Derrida calls the *antherection*, which makes it spill out, fall, reverse itself' ('D'autant plus puissant que divisé, coupé. D'où l'aspect oblique de l'érection, ce que Derrida appelle l'anthérection qui accompagne toute érection et qui la fait s'épancher, tomber, s'inverser'), 'Ça cloche', trans. by Caren Kaplan, in *Derrida and Deconstruction* (Continental Philosophy II) ed. by Hugh J. Silverman, London and New York, 1989, pp. 108–38 (p. 128) (*Lectures de Derrida*, Paris, 1984, pp. 115–51 (p. 145)).

9. Translation modified. 'Je le vois tout entier dans une proximité violente. Il ruisselle de sueur, il est dans un éclairement solaire d'une blancheur effrayante', p. 13.

10. 'Elle serait restée pendant un instant adossée au cadre de la porte avant de pénétrer dans la fraîcheur du couloir', p. 22.

11. 'La bouche ouverte, les yeux clos, elle est dans la caverne de l'homme, elle est retirée en lui, loin de lui, seule, dans l'obscurité du corps de l'homme', p. 30.

12. 'la mise à mort de toute parole érotique au féminin', 'La mort d'une érotique', *Cahiers Renaud-Barrault*, vol. 106, 1983, pp. 37–57 (p. 41).

13. E.g. Andrea Dworkin, *Pornography: Men Possessing Women*, London, 1981; Suzanne Kappeler, *The Pornography of Representation*, Cambridge, 1986.

14. See *Les Parleuses*, Paris, 1974, pp. 59–60. What Duras acknowledges is the link between her own experience and the erotic murder of *Moderato Cantabile*, published in 1958. The textual echoes between the desiring violence of the novel and the

two versions of *L'homme assis dans le couloir* are commented on by Yvonne Guers-Villate in 'De l'implicite à l'explicite: de *Moderato cantabile* à *L'homme assis dans le couloir*', French Review, vol. 58, no. 3, February 1985, pp. 377–81, and by Leslie Hill in *Marguerite Duras: Apocalyptic Desires*, London, 1993, pp. 57–8.

15. On male–female sadomasochistic relationships and the tendency of some feminist criticism to make an *a priori* judgement of their unacceptability, see Jessica Benjamin's *The Bonds of Love: Psychoanalysis, Feminism and the Problem of Domination*, London, 1988.

16. 'La mort d'une érotique', p. 39, pp. 40–1.

17. What finally detaches Duras's text from the pornographic genre, for Marini, is the painful path of experimentation and formal complexity the author had to pursue in order eventually to lay to rest the violence of her own experience, and the fact that *L'homme assis dans le couloir* does not retain the detached, clinical and triumphalist tone of pornography composed for effect ('La mort d'une érotique', pp. 47–8).

18. 'L'homme assis dans le couloir', *Les Yeux verts*, Cahiers du cinéma, 1980 and 1987, pp. 60–1.

19. 'Je t'aime. Toi', p. 18.

20. – Je t'aime
J'entends qu'il lui répond qu'il dit:
– Oui
(p. 23)

21. 'J'ai d'abord trouvé l'immensité indéfinie du paysage. Puis l'amour. L'amour était absent du premier texte', *Les Yeux verts*, p. 60.

22. *Le Vice-Consul*, Paris, 1966, p. 203. Here Charles Rossett entertains a retrospective fantasy of beating Anne-Marie Stretter, a description whose language directly prefigures that of *L'homme assis dans le couloir*.

23. The final sentence of the text insists on the unknowability of this identification: 'I haven't a clue; I don't know a thing; I don't know whether she is sleeping', p. 275 ('Je l'ignore, je ne sais rien, je ne sais pas si elle dort', p. 36). Leslie Hill's reading of *L'homme assis dans le couloir* in *Marguerite Duras: Apocalyptic Desires* brings out how the instability of sexual identity also functions at the level of the narrative discourse.

24. 'exténué d'amour et de désir', p. 21.

25. Tom Conley, 'A Malady of More', in *Remains to be Seen: Essays on Marguerite Duras*, ed. by S. S. Ames, New York, 1988, pp. 137–50 (p. 150).

26. 'Un jour je n'aimerai plus Tiène. A bien réfléchir, est-ce que je l'aime encore? Un jour, je vivrai sans le souvenir de Tiène . . . Un jour, je mourrai', *La Vie tranquille*, Paris, 1944 and 1972, p. 161.

27. *La Vie matérielle*, Paris, 1987, pp. 139–40, *Practicalities*, trans. by Barbara Bray, 1990, pp. 125–6.

28. *Practicalities*, p. 33; *La Vie matérielle*, p. 38.

29. 'cette fadeur . . . cette immobilité de sentiment', p. 46. This is a modification of the published translation, *The Malady of Death*, trans. by Barbara Bray, New York, Grove Weidenfeld, 1986, which is the version used in the text for all subsequent quotations. Here Bray opts to avoid Duras's impersonally nominal style by rendering this clause as 'because your feelings are so dull and sluggish', *The Malady of Death*, p. 44.

30. 'Elle ne saurait pas vous le dire, vous ne pourriez rien en apprendre d'elle . . . Elle, elle ne sait pas le savoir', pp. 19–20.

31. See Jean-Luc Nancy, *La Communauté désoeuvrée*, Paris, 1986, p. 91. This text is available in English as *The Inoperative Community*, ed. by Peter Connor, trans. by Peter Connor, Lisa Garbus, Michael Holland and Simona Sawhney, foreword by Christopher Fynsk, Minneapolis, 1991, but subsequent quotations from it are in my translation.

32. The 'fusion' model of community, based on unproblematic (spoken) communication between equal terms constellated around an ideal, applies equally to Plato's conception of social formations.

33. In 'Au-delà du visage', the final section of *Totalité et Infini: essai sur l'extériorité*, The Hague, 1961, and in *Le Temps et l'autre*, Paris, 1979, Levinas poses a direct challenge to Plato's model of erotic fusion. 'Neither is the difference between the sexes the duality of two complementary terms, for two complementary terms presuppose a preexisting whole. To say that sexual duality presupposes a whole is to posit love beforehand as fusion. The pathos of love, however, consists in an insurmountable duality of beings', 'Time and the Other', trans. by Richard A. Cohen in *The Levinas Reader*, ed. by Seán Hand, Oxford, 1989, pp. 37–58 (p. 49) ('La différence de sexes n'est pas non plus la dualité de deux termes complémentaires, car deux termes complémentaires supposent un tout préexistant. Or, dire que la dualité sexuelle suppose un tout, c'est d'avance poser l'amour comme fusion. Le pathétique de l'amour consiste dans une dualité insurmontable des êtres', *Le Temps et l'autre*, p. 78).

34. 'C'est curieux un mort', p. 35, p. 45.

35. 'une faille soudaine dans la logique de l'univers', p. 52.
36. 'Elle dit: Le jour est venu, tout va commencer, sauf vous. Vous, vous ne commencez jamais', pp. 50–1.
37. *Ce sexe qui n'en est pas un*, Paris, 1977.
38. 'Vous voyez d'abord les légers frémissements s'inscrire sur la peau, comme ceux justement de la souffrance. Et puis ensuite les paupières trembler tout comme si les yeux voulaient voir. Et puis ensuite la bouche s'ouvrir comme si la bouche voulait dire. Et puis ensuite vous percevez que sous vos caresses les lèvres du sexe se gonflent et que de leur velours sort une eau gluante et chaude comme serait le sang', pp. 39–40.
39. 'Vous avez tout regardé', p. 41.
40. 'l'intelligence de l'amour', *Marguerite Duras à Montréal*, p. 49. The word 'intelligence' also carries connotations of secrecy and complicity which seem significant in the way Duras uses it in this expression.
41. 'Vous regardez la maladie de votre vie, la maladie de la mort. C'est sur elle, sur son corps endormi, que vous la regardez', p. 36.
42. 'fait dans une seule coulée . . . comme par Dieu lui-même', p. 20.
43. 'Vous fermez les yeux pour vous retrouver dans votre différence, dans votre mort', p. 36.
44. 'vidée de vie . . . sans vous', p. 34.
45. 'Vous découvrez que c'est là, en elle, que se fomente la maladie de la mort, que c'est cette forme devant vous déployée qui décrète la maladie de la mort', p. 38.
46. 'Elle dit: Prenez-moi pour que cela ait été fait', p. 53. On the recurrence of the phrase 'C'est fait' and variations on it in Duras's writing, see Leslie Hill's *Marguerite Duras: Apocalyptic Desires*, pp. 56–7.
47. 'différence intégrale', p. 42.
48. On the way in which *La Maladie de la mort* stymies phallocentric plot structures, such as what Peter Brooks, in *Reading for the Plot* (Oxford, 1984), describes as Freud's 'masterplot', see George Moskos's 'Odd Coupling: Duras Reflects on Balzac', *Contemporary Literature*, vol. 32, no. 4, Winter 1991, pp. 520–33. Moskos shows how Duras's text conforms to some extent to the progression from metonymy (in this case a relation of contiguity between the woman and the sea) to metaphor (woman and sea become terms which may be substituted for each other), the shift Brooks identifies as the fundamental desire of plot. However, the woman's sudden departure deprives *La Maladie de la mort* of the 'proper end' the 'masterplot' requires to become narratable, an

ending which, if reached, would suppress feminine difference in a return to a masculine Same; in other words, Duras's text enacts Irigarayan *mimésis* in partly repeating a phallocentric narrative structure only to subvert and undo it. The reader, like the male protagonist, is left without a story to tell. However, in using a plot model which assumes narrative tension to be erotic in nature to read *La Maladie de la mort*, Moskos attributes to the male protagonist a desire *for* the woman and an intention to kill her which he never actually acquires, reflecting what is at least a partial desire on the part of a male reader to master Duras's text by (re)claiming it *as* narrative.

49. 'l'admirable impossibilité de la rejoindre à travers la différence qui vous sépare', p. 56.

50. 'Vous dites: Oui. Je ne connais pas encore, je voudrais pénétrer là aussi. Et aussi violemment que j'ai l'habitude. On dit que ça résiste plus encore, que c'est un velours qui résiste plus encore que le vide', pp. 9–10.

51. 'Les gens, de Peter Handke à Maurice Blanchot, ont cru que c'était contre les hommes face aux femmes, *La Maladie de la mort*. Si on veut. Mais je dis que si les hommes se sont intéressés à ce point à *La Maladie de la mort*, c'est qu'ils ont pressenti qu'il y avait là quelque chose en plus, et qui les concernait. Extraordinaire qu'ils aient vu', 'Les hommes', in *La Vie matérielle*, p. 38, *Practicalities*, p. 33. Duras comments further on the heterosexual matrix governing male writers' readings of her text in 'Dans les jardins d'Israel il ne faisait jamais nuit', first published in *Les Cahiers du Cinéma*, vol. 374, July–August 1985, and reprinted in the 1987 edition of *Les Yeux verts*, pp. 228–49. Reviews of Peter Handke's film version of *La Maladie de la mort*, which attempted a double translation into images and a German text read by Handke and incorporating material additional to that translated (including a poem by René Char and passages from Blanchot's *La Communauté inavouable*), bear out Duras's observation of men's blindness to the equivocality of male sexuality in her text. In an interview given to *Le Matin* on 20 May 1985 after the broadcast of his film on French television, Handke admitted to having 'had his masculinity attacked' (having felt 'agressé en tant qu'homme') by Duras's text, and to wanting to modify the available German translation because he found it 'too woolly, too feminine' ('trop floue, trop féminine'). And although Duras indicates in the Minuit edition of *La Maladie de la mort* that in a theatrical staging of the text the male protagonist should never be represented, the chief effect achieved by Handke's exclusion of him from the

frame seems to have been a fetishization of the woman's body: a masculinity of both text and image which was clinical where Duras's conception had been sensual. See also Olivier Séguret in *Libération* of 20 May 1985.

52. *The Unavowable Community*, trans. by Pierre Joris, Barrytown, New York, 1988, p. 51; *La Communauté inavouable*, Paris, 1983, p. 84. 'L'homosexualité, pour en venir à ce nom qui n'est jamais prononcée, n'est pas "la maladie de la mort", elle la fait seulement apparaître, d'une manière un peu factice.'

53. 'Quand j'ai écrit *La Maladie de la mort*, je ne savais pas écrire sur Yann', *La Pute de la côte normande*, Paris, 1986, p. 20.

54. 'est devenu un mot faux . . . Il dit mal ce qu'il veut dire et je crois surtout que ce qu'il veut dire n'existe pas, comme je l'aurais cru que cela existait il y a seulement trois ans', Interview in *Le Matin*, 14 November 1986, p. 24.

55. *Marguerite Duras à Montréal*, p. 69.

56. Ibid.

57. 'Mais ce désir qui nous lie, je le vois comme une sorte de résultante de l'antagonisme initial entre eux et nous, l'homme et la femme. Nous sommes irréconciliables, nous essayons toujours, depuis des millénaires de nous réconcilier. Cela à chaque amour', ibid.

58. *The Unavowable Community*, p. 40. 'Ce n'est pas si sûr et ce n'est pas si clair', *La Communauté inavouable*, pp. 67–8.

59. Ibid., p. 39. 'On pourrait affirmer que, des deux protagonistes, c'est lui qui dans sa tentative d'aimer, dans sa recherche sans relâche, est le plus digne, le plus proche, de cet absolu qu'il trouve en ne le trouvant pas', p. 66.

60. Ibid., p. 40, 'de son côté s'offre seulement à être aimée (sous contrat), sans donner jamais des signes de sa propre aptitude à aller de la passivité jusqu'à la passion sans limites', p. 67.

61. *Hiroshima mon amour*, Paris, 1960, p. 68.

62. 'Elle dit que toutes les femmes auraient accepté sans savoir pourquoi cette union blanche et désespérée', p. 31.

63. On the theatrical conception of narrative in both *La Maladie de la mort* and *Les yeux bleus cheveux noirs*, see Sharon Willis, 'Staging Sexual Difference: Reading, Recitation and Repetition in Duras's *Malady of Death*', in Enoch Brater (ed.), *Feminine Focus: The New Women Playwrights*, New York, 1989, pp. 109–25. Willis's analysis charts with admirable patience the slippage between reading as interpretation and reading as performance – the unstable splitting of a position available to both spectator/reader and character, and the reliance on exteriority and absence this implies – in both texts.

She also examines how the activity of reading in *L'homme assis dans le couloir* repeats the circulation of gender through the pronouns of the text in a structure of fantasy like that described by Freud in 'A Child is Being Beaten'. Gender positions are rendered permanently unstable by the lure and subsequent splitting of an identificatory reading position.

64. 'par exemple d'une erreur . . . jamais d'un vouloir', *La Maladie de la mort*, p. 52.

65. 'Dès lors qu'ils se sont touchés, les corps ne bougent plus', p. 62; 'leurs mains se touchent mais pour aussitôt se fuir', p. 61.

66. 'notre désir l'un de l'autre dont nous ne faisons rien', p. 76.

67. 'même lorsque ce sera la dernière nuit, ce ne sera pas la peine de la signaler, parce que ce sera le commencement d'une autre histoire, celle de leur séparation', p. 98.

68. 'Vous êtes mon amant pour cette raison que vous avez dite, que vous ne voulez rien', p. 106.

69. 'c'est peut-être de ne pas en parler qui fait se produire ce temps-là qu'elle, elle cherche à gagner', p. 75.

70. 'un lieu laissé mais à l'instant, funèbre', p. 21; 'une manière de salle de réception', ibid.

71. The lovers are 'neither apart from or above society, but exposed, as they are, as the lovers that they are, within the community' ('ni à l'écart, ni au-dessus de la société, mais en tant qu'ils sont, comme ces amants qu'il sont, exposés dans la communauté', *La Communauté désoeuvrée*, p. 93). This mutual interference of private and public can also be traced in Levinas's description of the erotic relation as both 'solitude à deux' and 'société à deux' in *Le Temps et l'autre* (p. 15).

72. On the internal limit and the 'partage' (dividing up *and* sharing) of the community, see Nancy, pp. 94–9, and also the first half of Blanchot's *The Unavowable Community*.

73. *La Communauté désoeuvrée*, p. 94. On the relationship between love, death, communication and the private/public opposition, see also the 'Envois', the love letters which make up the first part of Derrida's *La Carte postale: de Socrate à Freud et au-delà*, Paris, 1980, *The Post Card: From Socrates to Freud and Beyond*, trans. with an introduction by Alan Bass, Chicago and London, 1987.

74. 'pas la peur de mourir . . . celle d'être mise à mal, comme par une bête, d'être griffée, défigurée', p. 49.

75. 'la force à travers la minceur', p. 43.

76. 'Dès que vous êtes entré dans ce café dans l'état où vous étiez, dans cette douleur paisible, vous vous souvenez, vous aviez envie de mourir, j'ai voulu mourir à mon tour de cette façon théâtrale

et extérieure. Je voulais mourir avec vous. Je me suis dit: Mettre mon corps contre son corps et attendre la mort', p. 80.

77. 'très près d'une idée générale de l'homme', p. 129.

78. 'Elle est une femme', p. 23.

79. This may be the same man mourned by the male protagonist. But despite gradually converging, their respective histories never form the neat erotic triangle the reader is seduced into expecting. Memory fails under the traumatic weight of the novel's opening scene, in which the man saw a woman accompanying the young stranger with blue eyes and black hair he instantaneously and hopelessly loved. The recognition which would identify the female protagonist as this woman is missing; they are, she says, 'like witnesses of crimes who forgot to look at what was happening', p. 114 ('comme dans les crimes les témoins qui avaient oublié de regarder', p. 147).

80. 'But that must be the best, the easiest place for learning what despair is – among men without descendants who don't even know they are desperate', pp. 119–20 ('Ce doit être là qu'on est le mieux, le plus à l'aise pour vivre le désespoir, avec les hommes sans descendance qui ignorent être désespérés', p. 31).

81. 'Il touchera ses lèvres avec ses doigts, celles de son sexe aussi, il embrassera les yeux fermés, le bleu qui fuit sous les doigts', p. 68.

82. 'lorsqu'il lui arrivera de croire qu'il s'est mis à l'aimer', p. 72.

83. 'Ils pleurent comme ils s'aimeraient', p. 112.

84. 'comme une caresse infinie', p. 115.

85. 'celle qui ne sait pas pour le bateau', p. 119.

86. 'que cette différence, cet empêchement que vous éprouvez pour moi, il est là pour cacher une chose qui a trait à la vie', pp. 128–9.

87. 'La tiédeur devient commune, la peau, la vie intérieure', p. 131.

88. 'la vase chaude du centre', p. 132.

89. 'le vouloir de son corps', ibid.

90. 'Le baiser est devenu la jouissance. Il a eu lieu . . . Il n'a été suivi d'aucun autre baiser. Il occupe le désir tout entier, il est à lui seul son désert et son immensité, son esprit et son corps', p. 135.

91. 'imposer Dieu', p. 137.

92. 'c'est l'idée de ce baiser qui le conduit à celle de sa mort', pp. 136–7.

93. 'Autour d'eux, la chambre détruite', p. 143.

94. 'si profond, ils en sont effrayés', p. 148.

95. 'en le perdant avant qu'il ne soit advenu', *La Maladie de la mort*, p. 57.

96. 'approbation de la vie jusque dans la mort', *L'Erotisme, Oeuvres Complètes* X, Paris, 1987, pp. 7–270 (p. 17).

Bibliography

Selected Critical Studies of Authors

Texts included here have been selected by virtue of the insights they offer
into the various modes of 'desiring writing' created by the authors covered
in this study.

Rachilde

Besnard-Coursodon, Micheline, 'Monsieur Vénus, Madame Adonis: Sexe et
    discours', *Littérature*, 54, May 1984, pp. 121–7.
Birkett, Jennifer, *The Sins of the Fathers: Decadence in France 1870–1914*,
    London, Quartet, 1986.
Dauphiné, Claude, *Rachilde*, Paris, Mercure de France, 1991.
Dauphiné, Claude, Introduction to *La Jongleuse*, Paris, des femmes, 1982.
Dauphiné, Claude, 'Sade, Rachilde et Freud: lecture de *La marquise de Sade*',
    Bulletin de l'Association des Professeurs de lettres', 17, 1981, pp. 55–9.
Hawthorne, Melanie, '*Monsieur Vénus*: A Critique of Gender Roles',
    Nineteenth-Century French Studies, 16, 1987/8, pp. 162–79.
Hawthorne, Melanie, 'The Social Construction of Sexuality in Three Novels
    by Rachilde', *Michigan Romance Studies*, 9, 1989, pp. 49–59.
Waelti-Walters, Jennifer, *Feminist Novelists of the Belle Epoque*, Bloomington
    and Indianapolis, Indiana University Press, 1990, pp. 156–73.

Colette

Angelfors, Christina, *La Double Conscience: la prise de conscience féminine chez
    Colette, Simone de Beauvoir et Marie Cardinal*, Lund, Lund University Press,
    1989.
Biolley-Godino, Marcelle, *L'Homme-objet chez Colette*, Paris, Klincksieck,
    1972.
Dranch, Sherry, 'Reading through the Veiled Text: Colette's *The Pure and
    the Impure*', *Contemporary Literature*, 24, 1983, pp. 176–89.
Eisinger, Erica and McCarty, Mari (eds), *Colette: The Woman, the Writer*,

Bibliography

University Park: Pennsylvania State University Press, 1981.
Holmes, Diana, *Colette*, London, Macmillan, 1991.
Resch, Yannick, *Corps féminin, corps textuel*, Paris, Klincksieck, 1973.
Stewart, Joan, *Colette*, Boston, Twayne, 1983.
Waelti-Walters, Jennifer, *Feminist Novelists of the Belle Epoque*, Bloomington and Indianapolis, Indiana University Press, 1990, pp. 139–55.
Ward Jouve, Nicole, *Colette*, Brighton, Harvester, 1987.

Leduc

De Courtivron, Isabelle, *Violette Leduc*, Boston, Twayne, 1985.
Evans, Martha Noel, 'Violette Leduc: The Bastard', in *Masks of Tradition: Women and the Politics of Writing in Twentieth-Century France*, Ithaca, Cornell University Press, 1987, pp. 102–22.
Girard, Pièr, 'Thérèse et Isabelle: du pathétique à trois miroirs', *Homosexualité*, 7, 1989, pp. 171–88.
Hughes, Alex, *Violette Leduc: Mothers, Lovers and Language*, London, MHRA, 1994.
Neuman, Shirley, 'Autobiography and the Construction of the Feminine Body', *Signature*, 2, 1989, pp. 1–26.
Rule, Jane, 'Violette Leduc', in *Lesbian Images*, Garden City, NY, Doubleday, 1975, pp. 140–6.

Wittig

Crowder, Diane, 'Amazones de . . . demain?: la fiction utopique féministe et lesbienne', *Amazones d'hier, lesbiennes d'aujourd'hui*, 2, 1984, pp. 19–27.
Crowder, Diane, 'Amazons or Mothers? Monique Wittig, Hélène Cixous and Theories of Women's Writing', *Contemporary Literature*, 24, 1983, pp. 117–44.
Crowder, Diane, 'Une Armée d'amantes: l'image de l'Amazone dans l'oeuvre de Monique Wittig', *Vlasta*, 4, 1985, pp. 79–87.
Evans, Martha Noel, 'Monique Wittig: The Lesbian', in *Masks of Tradition: Women and the Politics of Writing in Twentieth-Century France*, Ithaca, Cornell University Press, 1987, pp. 185–219.
Hokeson, Jan, 'The Pronouns of Gomorrha: A Lesbian Prose Tradition', *Frontiers*, 10, 1988, pp. 62–9.
Lindsay, Cecile, 'Body/Language: French Feminist Utopias', *French Review*, 60, 1986, pp. 46–55.
Louppa, Laurence, Interview with Monique Wittig, *L'Art vivant*, 45, 1973/4, pp. 24–5.
Shaktini, Namascar, 'Displacing the Phallic Subject: Monique Wittig's Lesbian Writing', *Signs*, 8, 1982, pp. 29–44.
Vlasta, 4, 1985. Special issue devoted to Wittig.

Bibliography

Cixous

Boundary, 2, 1984. Special issue on Cixous, edited by Verena Andermatt Conley.

Conley, Verena Andermatt, *Hélène Cixous: Writing the Feminine*, Lincoln and London, University of Nebraska Press, 1984 and 1990.

Conley, Verena Andermatt, *Hélène Cixous*, London, Harvester Wheatsheaf, 1992.

Cornell, Sarah, 'Hélène Cixous's *Le Livre de Promethea*: Paradise Refound', in Sellers, Susan (ed.), *Writing Differences: Readings from the Seminar of Hélène Cixous*, Milton Keynes, Open University Press, 1988.

Crowder, Diane, 'Amazons or Mothers?', *Contemporary Literature*, 24, 1983, pp. 117–44.

Motard-Noar, Martine, *Les Fictions d'Hélène Cixous: Une autre langue de femme*, Kentucky, French Forum Publishers, 1991.

Shiach, Morag, *Hélène Cixous: A Politics of Writing*, London, Routledge, 1991.

Slama, Béatrice, 'Entre amour et écriture: *Le Livre de Promethea*', in van Rossum-Guyon, Françoise and Diaz-Diocaretz, Myriam (eds), *Hélène Cixous: chemins d'une écriture*, Amsterdam, Rodopi, 1990.

Duras

Ames, S. S. (ed.), *Remains to be Seen: Essays on Marguerite Duras*, New York, Peter Lang Publishing, Inc., 1988.

Ecrire, dit-elle: imaginaires de Marguerite Duras, textes réunis par Danielle Bajomée & Ralph Heyndels, Brussels, Editions de l'Université de Bruxelles, 1985.

Esprit Créateur, vol. XXX, no. 1, Spring 1990. Special issue on Duras.

Glassman, Deborah, *Marguerite Duras: Fascinating Vision and Narrative Cure*, Cranbury, NJ, Missisauga and London, Associated University Presses, 1991.

Guers-Villate, Yvonne, *Continuité/discontinuité de l'oeuvre durassienne*, Brussels, Editions de l'Université de Bruxelles, 1985.

Hill, Leslie, *Marguerite Duras: Apocalyptic Desires*, London, Routledge, 1993.

Kristeva, Julia, 'The Malady of Grief: Duras', in *Black Sun: Depression and Melancholia*, trans. by Leon S. Roudiez, New York, Columbia University Press, 1989. 'La Maladie de la douleur: Duras', in *Soleil noir*, Paris, Gallimard/Folio, 1987.

Marini, Marcelle, 'La mort d'une érotique', *Cahiers Renaud-Barrault*, 106, 1983, pp. 37–57.

Moskos, George, 'Odd Coupling: Duras Reflects on Balzac', *Contemporary Literature*, vol. 32, no. 4, Winter 1991, pp. 520–33.

Revue des sciences humaines, vol. 202, 1986. Special issue on Duras.

Willis, Sharon, 'Staging Sexual Difference: Reading, Recitation and Repetition in Duras's *Malady of Death*', in Enoch Brater (ed.), *Feminine*

Focus: The New Women Playwrights, New York, Oxford University Press, 1989, pp. 109–25.

Eroticism

In the following selection of texts, those marked * focus particularly on female-authored erotic discourse.

Alexandrian, *Histoire de la littérature érotique*, Paris, Seghers, 1989.

Bataille, Georges, *L'Erotisme, Oeuvres Complètes* X, Paris, Gallimard, 1987.

Brécourt-Villars, Claudine, *Ecrire d'amour: Anthologie des textes érotiques féminins 1799–1984*, Paris, Ramsay, 1985. *

Dardigna, Anne-Marie, *Les Châteaux d'Eros ou l'infortune du sexe des femmes*, Paris, Maspero, 1981.

Ducout, Françoise, *Plaisirs d'amour: L'Almanach érotique des femmes*, Paris, Lieu commun, 1982. *

Ducout, Françoise, *Plaisirs d'amour 2*, Paris, Calmann-Lévy, 1994. *

Dworkin, Andrea, *Pornography: Men Possessing Women*, New York, Perigee, 1981; London, the Women's Press, 1981.

Frappier-Mazur, Lucienne, 'Marginal Canons: Rewriting the Erotic', *Yale French Studies*, 75, 1988, pp. 112–28. *

Guiraud, Pierre, *Dictionnaire historique, stylistique, rhétorique, étymologique de la littérature érotique*, Paris, Payot, 1978.

Huston, Nancy, *Mosaïque de la pornographie*, Paris, Denoël/Gonthier, 1982.

Kappeler, Suzanne, *The Pornography of Representation*, Cambridge, Polity Press, 1986.

Marks, Elaine, 'Lesbian Intertextuality', in Stambolian, George and Marks, Elaine (eds), *Homosexualities and French Literature*, Ithaca, Cornell University Press, 1979, pp. 353–77. *

Miège, Denise, *Littérature érotique féminine*, Paris, Editions Civilisation nouvelle, 1970 (tome I), 1973 (tome II). *

Mills, Jane, *The Bloomsbury Guide to Erotic Literature*, London, Bloomsbury, 1994.

Pauvert, Jean-Jacques, *Anthologie historique des lectures érotiques*, Paris, Simoën, Ramsay, Garnier, 1979, 1980, 1982.

Sontag, Susan, 'The Pornographic Imagination', in Bataille, Georges, *Story of the Eye* (trans.), Harmondsworth, Penguin, 1982, pp. 83–118.

Suleiman, Susan, 'Pornography and the Avant-Garde', in Miller, Nancy K. (ed.), *The Poetics of Gender*, New York, Columbia University Press, 1986.

Suleiman, Susan Rubin, '(Re)Writing the Body: The Politics and Poetics of Female Eroticism', in Suleiman (ed.), *The Female Body in Western Culture*, Cambridge, Mass., Harvard University Press, 1986, pp. 7–29. *

Sullerot, Evelyne, *Histoire et mythologie de l'amour*, Paris, Hachette, 1974. Translated as *Women on Love*, London, Norman, 1980. *

Bibliography

Sexuality/Gender Theory

de Beauvoir, Simone, *The Second Sex*, trans. H. M. Parshley, London, Jonathan Cape, 1953.

Benjamin, Jessica, *The Bonds of Love: Psychoanalysis, Feminism and the Problem of Domination*, London, Virago, 1990.

Butler, Judith, *Gender Trouble: Feminism and the Subversion of Identity*, New York and London, Routledge, 1990.

Butler, Judith, *Bodies that Matter*, New York and London, Routledge, 1993.

Foucault, Michel, *The History of Sexuality: An Introduction*, Harmondsworth, Penguin, 1978, trans. of *La Volonté de savoir*, Paris, Editions Gallimard, 1976.

Fraisse, Geneviève, *Muse de la Raison*, Paris, Alinéa, 1989.

Fuss, Diana, *Inside/Out: Lesbian Theories, Gay Theories*, New York and London, Routledge, 1991.

Grosz, Elizabeth, *Jacques Lacan: A Feminist Introduction*, London and New York, Routledge, 1992.

Hirsch, Marianne, *The Mother/Daughter Plot: Narrative, Psychoanalysis, Feminism*, Bloomington and Indianapolis, Indiana University Press, 1989.

Jouir, special issue of *Les Cahiers du Grif*, no. 26, March 1983.

Kosofsky Sedgwick, Eve, *Epistemology of the Closet*, London, Harvester, 1991.

Kosofsky Sedgwick, Eve, *Between Men: English Literature and Male Homosocial Desire*, New York, Columbia University Press, 1985.

de Lauretis, Teresa, 'Film and the Visible', in Bad Object-Choices (ed.), *How Do I Look: Queer Film and Video*, Seattle, Bay Press, 1991.

Linden, Robin Ruth, Pagano, Darlene R., Russell, Diana E. H. and Starr, Susan L. (eds), *Against Sado-Masochism: A Radical Feminist Analysis*, East Palo Alto, California, Frog in the Well, 1982.

Mitchell, Juliet and Rose, Jacqueline (eds), *Feminine Sexuality: Jacques Lacan and the 'école freudienne'*, Basingstoke and London, Macmillan, 1982.

Ramazanoglu, Caroline (ed.), *Up Against Foucault: Explorations of Some Tensions between Foucault and Feminism*, London and New York, Routledge, 1993.

Snitow, Ann et al. (eds), *Desire: The Politics of Sexuality*, London, Virago, 1984.

Stambolian, George and Marks, Elaine (eds), *Homosexualities and French Literature: Cultural Contexts, Critical Texts*, Ithaca and London, Cornell University Press, 1979.

Wittig, Monique, 'The Mark of Gender', *Feminist Issues*, 5, 1985, pp. 3–12; also in Miller, Nancy K. (ed.), *The Poetics of Gender*, New York, Columbia University Press, 1986, pp. 63–73.

Wittig, Monique, 'On ne naît pas femme', *Questions féministes*, no. 8, mai 1980, pp. 75–84.

Bibliography

Other Writings

Albistur, Maïté and Armogathe, Daniel, *Histoire du féminisme français*, Paris, des femmes, 1977.

Barthes, Roland, *Roland Barthes by Roland Barthes*, trans. by Richard Howard, London, Macmillan, 1977; *Roland Barthes par Roland Barthes*, Paris, Seuil, 1975.

Blanchot, Maurice, *The Unavowable Community*, trans. by Pierre Joris, Barrytown, New York, Station Hill Press Inc., 1988.

Bouchardeau, Huguette, *Pas d'histoire, les femmes*, Paris, Syros, 1977.

Derrida, Jacques, *Spurs: Nietzsche's Styles/Eperons: Les Styles de Nietzsche*, Chicago and London, University of Chicago Press, 1979.

Derrida, Jacques, *The Post Card: From Socrates to Freud and Beyond*, trans. with an introduction by Alan Bass, Chicago and London, University of Chicago Press, 1987.

Duby, Georges and Perrot, Michelle (eds), *Histoire des femmes* IV and V, Paris, Plon, 1991/2.

Garcia, Irma, *Promenade femmillière*, Paris, des femmes, 1981.

Irigaray, Luce, *Ce Sexe qui n'en est pas un*, Paris, Minuit, 1977.

Jayle, Félix, *La Gynécologie: l'Anatomie morphologique de la femme*, Paris, Masson, 1918.

deJean, Joan and Miller, Nancy K. (eds), *The Politics of Tradition: Placing Women in French Literature*, Yale French Studies vol. 75, New Haven, Yale University Press, 1988.

Kelly, Dorothy, *Fictional Genders: Role and Representation in Nineteenth-Century French Literature*, Lincoln, University of Nebraska Press, 1989.

Kojève, Alexandre, *Introduction to the Reading of Hegel*, trans. James Nichols, New York and London, Basic Books, 1969.

Kristeva, Julia, *La Révolution du langage poétique*, Paris, Seuil, 1974.

Levinas, Emmanuel, *Totalité et Infini: essai sur l'extériorité*, The Hague, Martinus Nijhoff, 1961.

Levinas, Emmanuel, 'Time and the Other', trans. Richard Cohen, in Hand, Seán (ed.), *The Levinas Reader*, Oxford, Blackwell, 1989.

Marcuse, Herbert, *One-Dimensional Man: Studies in the Ideology of Advanced Industrial Society*, Boston, Beacon Press, 1964.

Marcuse, Herbert, *Eros and Civilisation: A Philosophical Inquiry into Freud*, Boston, Beacon Press, 1955.

Mossuz-Lavau, Janine, *Les Lois de l'amour: les politiques de la sexualité en France 1950–1990*, Paris, Payot, 1991.

Nancy, Jean-Luc, *La Communauté désoeuvrée*, Paris, Christian Bourgois, 1986.

Pierrot, Jean, *The Decadent Imagination 1800–1900*, trans. by D. Coltman, Chicago and London, University of Chicago Press, 1981.

Roudinesco, Elisabeth, *Jacques Lacan and Co. A History of Psychoanalysis in*

France 1925–1985, trans. by Jeffrey Mehlman, London, Free Association Books, 1990.

Sarup, Madan, *An Introductory Guide to Poststructuralism and Postmodernism*, New York and London, Harvester Wheatsheaf, 1993.

Sherzer, Dina, *Representation in Contemporary French Fiction*, Lincoln and London, University of Nebraska Press, 1986.

Slater, Phil, *Origin and Significance of the Frankfurt School: A Marxist Perspective*, London, Routledge & Kegan Paul, 1977.

Wyatt, Jean, *Reconstructing Desire: The Role of the Unconscious in Women's Reading and Writing*, Chapel Hill and London, University of North Carolina Press, 1990.

Zeldin, Theodor, *France 1848–1945, vol. I, Ambition, Love, Politics*, Oxford, Oxford University Press, 1973.

Zwang, Gérard, *Le Sexe de la femme*, Paris, La Jeune Parque, 1967, revised edition 1974.

Chronology

	Political and historical events concerning French women	Key moments marking the emergence of French women's desiring writing
1880–1900	Divorce is re-established, but the law precludes the possibility of divorce by mutual consent (1884).	Rachilde publishes *Monsieur Vénus* (1884).
	Marguerite Durand creates *La Fronde*, France's first feminist daily paper (1897).	Rachilde publishes *Les Hors nature* (1897) and *L'Heure sexuelle* (1898).
1900–1910		Rachilde publishes *La Jongleuse* (1900).
	Married women gain control over their earnings (1907).	Colette publishes *Claudine à L'école* (1900), followed by *Claudine à Paris* (1901), *La Retraite sentimentale* (1907) and *Les Vrilles de la vigne* (1908).
1910–1920		Colette publishes *La Vagabonde* (1910); *L'Entrave* (1913).
	The right to vote is a key concern of French	

feminists. However, the
Senate rejects suffrage
for women (1919).

/

The sale of
contraceptives is
banned (1920).

Women are allowed to
join unions (1920).

1920–1930	Abortion is outlawed (1923).	Colette publishes *Le Blé en herbe* (1923) and *La Seconde* (1929)
1930–1940		Colette publishes *Le Pur et l'impur* (1932) and *La Chatte* (1933).

The *Assemblée nationale*
sanctions votes for
women; the Senate
refuses to concede
(1936).

Married women cease
to be legal minors
(1938).

Anti-abortion measures
are intensified (1939).

1940–1950	Abortion becomes an offence punishable by the death penalty (1942).	
	Women get the vote (1944).	
	Women attain legal equality in most areas (1946).	The intellectual journal *Les Temps modernes*

	decides to publish extracts from the autobiographical *Vie d'une prostituée*, by Marie-Thérèse (1947).
	Violette Leduc publishes *L'Affamée* (1948).
Simone de Beauvoir publishes *Le Deuxième Sexe* (1949).	

1950–1960	'Pauline Réage' publishes the pornographic *Histoire d'O* (1954). The text is banned, and becomes the subject of legal wrangling.
	Gallimard remove the opening, highly (homo)erotic section of Leduc's *Ravages* before accepting the text for publication (1955).
The French family planning movement is founded (1956).	Erotico-literary censorship becomes more repressive. Duras publishes *Moderato Cantabile* (1958).

1960–1970	Leduc publishes *La Bâtarde*, Monique Wittig publishes *L'Opoponax* and Duras publishes *Le Ravissement de Lol V. Stein* (1964).

Married women acquire the right to control their own property, to exercise a profession without their husband's consent and to open a bank account (1965).

The excised section of Leduc's *Ravages*, focusing on adolescent lesbian love, is published in novella form, entitled *Thérèse et Isabelle* (1966).

The Loi Neuwirth legalizes the sale of contraceptives (1967).

In the wake of the events of May 1968, the French Women's Movement (MLF) takes shape.

Wittig publishes *Les Guérillères* (1969).

1970–1980

Feminist activism is intense in the early years of this decade.

Leduc publishes *Le Taxi* (1971).

343 women sign a manifesto declaring that they have had illegal abortions, and women march to call for free abortion and contraception (1971).

The *des femmes* publishing house is established (1973), to promote 'la parole de la femme'.

Wittig publishes *Le Corps lesbien* (1973).

The law banning abortion is annulled (1974).

	A Secretariat of State for women is set up (1974).	
	Divorce by mutual consent becomes legal (1975).	Hélène Cixous publishes *La Jeune Née* (1975).
1980–1990	A Ministry of Women's Rights is established by the new Socialist government (1981)	Duras publishes *L'homme assis dans le couloir* (1980); *La Maladie de la mort* (1982); *L'Amant* (1984); *Les yeux bleus cheveux noirs* (1986).
		Cixous publishes *Le Livre de Promethea* (1983) and *La Bataille d'Arcachon* (1986).

Index

Index